An American Pursuit Pilot in France

Roland W. Richardson's
Diaries and Letters
1917 - 1919

Lt. Richardson in front of Spad VII. Cazaux Gunnery School. France. 1918.

An American Pursuit Pilot in France

*Roland W. Richardson's
Diaries and Letters
1917 - 1919*

Edited by
Ritchie Thomas
and
Carl M. Becker

 White Mane Publishing Company, Inc.

Copyright © 1994 by Ritchie Thomas and Carl M. Becker

All of the photographs in this book are courtesy of Elizabeth Kurlin
and the Roland W. Richardson family.

This White Mane Publishing Company, Inc. publication
was printed by
Beidel Printing House, Inc.
63 West Burd Street
Shippensburg, PA 17257 USA

The acid-free paper used in this book meets the guidelines for
permanence and durability of the Committee on Production Guidelines
for Book Longevity of the Council on Library Resources.

For a complete list of available publications
please write
White Mane Publishing Company, Inc.
P.O. Box 152
Shippensburg, PA 17257 USA

Library of Congress Cataloging-in-Publication Data

Richardson, Roland W. (Roland Withenbury), 1897-1991.
    An American pursuit pilot in France, 1917-1919 : Roland W.
Richardson's diaries and letters, 1917-1919 / edited by Ritchie
Thomas and Carl M. Becker.
        p.   cm.
    Includes index.
    ISBN 0-942597-64-8 (alk. paper) : $24.95
    1. Richardson, Roland W. (Roland Withenbury), 1897-1991. 2. World
War, 1914-1918--Aerial operation, American. 3. World War,
1914-1918--Personal narratives, American. 4. World War, 1914-1918-
-Campaigns--France. 5. United States. Army Air Forces--Biography.
6. Fighter pilots--United States--Biography.   I. Thomas, Ritchie.
II. Becker. Carl M.   III. Title.
D790.R496R53   1994
940.4'4973--dc20   94-14178
                                                                    CIP

PRINTED IN THE UNITED STATES OF AMERICA

To the Memory of

Roland W. Richardson,

Pursuit Pilot

Reconnaissance

I journeyed to the east,
  Rolled on the surgent airs of autumn days:
Below, the earth lay creased
  With myriad meadows in the morning haze.
Far off, where lay the sea,
  A silvered mirror beckoned to my bent,
And, moving orderly,
  The high cloud-armies marched magnificent.

Some menace in the sky,
  Some quick alarm did wake me as I sped:
At once, unwarningly
  Streamed out repeated death, from one that fled
Headlong before my turn — —
  But, unavoiding of the answering blast,
Checked sudden, fell astern — —
  And unmolested fared I to the last.

Gordon Alchin

Contents

Maps and Photographs

Maps

Photographs

Preface

World War I stripped war of romantic notions of images of individuals controlling the outcome of battle. By its massive character, its intensive use of improved weapons, the machine gun, for example, and its employment of new motorized weaponry, most notably the armored tank and the airplane, the Great War often reduced soldiers to automatons who could not realistically believe that they fought in personalized combat, who saw survival as a matter of the rankest chance.

Ironically, the airplane served as a link to romantic and incorrect perceptions of the past. So memory had it, war had once been chivalric and individuated: knights of old had engaged one another in combat governed by a code of noble conduct, and common soldiers at Agincourt and Gettysburg had not drawn their bows or fired their muskets until they had seen the whites of their enemies' eyes.

For many aviators of World War I, no matter what nation they flew for, the airplane was a reversionary or residual mechanism, one allowing them to fight as a warrior class. They could see in the sky an open field of battle for their aerial steeds and fought there with an élan few weary infantrymen in the trenches could muster. Though combat in the air was less direct and tactile than the battle of knights, there men entered the lists as charismatic figures making the clouds their demesne. Contemporary accounts of their deeds, not surprisingly, bore such titles as *The Red Knight of Germany*, *Cavalry of the Clouds*, and *High Adventure*. In the popular mind, the pilots were a breed apart in their derring-do, their seeming defiance of routine. A collective biography of the Lafayette Escadrille — of men like James McConnell, Kiffin Rockwell, and others — would surely have used such words as "daring," "brave," "loyal," "commitment," "brash," and "zeal."

War and airplanes might evoke images of knights *a cheval* in battle, but modernity staked its claims, too; and aviators necessarily brought to their peculiar combat attitudes of their own century. As Henry Adams saw it, the dynamo, the machine, had become the emblem of the age, the source of energy for great civil and military deeds, as the Virgin Mary had been in medieval Europe. Men had once taken vows of valor to Her; centuries later they found mystery and power in all manner of machines in transport, manufacturing, and battle. For men in aviation, their mission became mastery of the machine in the air, with a consequent but almost secondary purpose the destruction of enemies. For all the motive power at their command, pilots flew with a shadow over their shoulder; the motor, unlike the Virgin, was a fragile thing, subject to chronic mechanical failure and impairments by weather, uncertain to the point of disaster for even the ablest aviator.

The machine in aerial combat, of course, embodied a logic appropriate to the day. Requiring as it did a vigil of care and repair, it called for the devotion of men who were rational in their approach to battle and who were matter-of-fact, not ritualists governed by outmoded tradition. Such men were on hand in American society, with its increasing industrial tenor, its mechanical environment, and its emphasis on order and efficiency.

In his letters and diaries, First Lieutenant Roland Richardson, pursuit pilot of the 213th Squadron of the American Air Service, often exemplified the attitudes and behavior of young men who saw flying as essentially a struggle against the frailties of the machine and the elements of nature. What he wrote was not the dramatic fare one may read in aviators' reminiscenses and biographies appearing during and just after World War I, but it constitutes a continuing record of the regimen demanded in training and combat, of the labor to keep airplanes in the air. His is history writ small of the first American effort to create a flying force for battle.

Richardson wrote his letters to his mother from July of 1917, shortly after he had enlisted in the United States Army, into January of 1919, just before he received his discharge. He kept his diary from January of 1918 into February of 1919. He brought his diaries home from France and later retrieved his letters from his mother. We first learned of them from Howard Blanning of Miami University, who had interviewed Richardson for making a video. They are now in the possession of his daughter, Elizabeth Kurlin, who lives in the family home in Glendale. She granted us access to them and other relevant materials.

In organizing the letters and entries in the diaries, we have arranged them chronologically, with each letter bearing the same date as that of the entry immediately preceding it, or one day thereafter. What Richardson confided to his diary, often he incorporated in an amplified way in his letters; at times, though, what he wrote in the diary, especially comments on accidents in training, he withheld from the letters. In editing the letters and diaries, we have noted but not corrected orthographic errors; and we have left intact grammatical slips, asking that readers understand that we recognized them but wished to preserve the original syntax. Similarly, we did not provide accent marks for the French place names that Richardson did not accent. Rather than identifying persons, aviation terms, and types of airplanes within the text, we have provided appropriate appendices. We edited out about ten names of persons whom Richardson mentioned but once and by last name only; they defied our search for identification. For the many events and incidents noted by Richardson, we have supplied, for the most part, clarifying notes; in two or three instances, Richardson was so allusive that we had to excise a few sentences.

As we pursued out labor, we learned again that research in editing is an interdependent endeavor — that we had to enlist the support of many individuals and institutions. Elizabeth Kurlin gave us vital personal information about her father. We have received assistance from numerous archivists and librarians at the Archives and Special Collections of Wright State University, the University Library at Wright State, the Cincinnati Historical Society, and the Archives and Rare Book Room at the University of Cincinnati. Wesley Henry, Museum Specialist at the United States Air Force Museum, gave us invaluable help for our understanding of airplanes used in World War I. For learning more about things Gallic, we looked to our colleague, Pierre Horn, a member of the Department of Modern Languages at Wright State. And for locating Roland Richardson in France, we are indebted to Karl M. Schab, our cartographer who created the maps accompanying the letters.

We leave our venture with the vivid impression particularly of one person: First Lieutenant Roland W. Richardson. When we began our work on his letters and diaries, he was still living. He was infirm and had lost some of his mental acuity. But at many moments, he had a clear vision of Caudrons, Nieuports, and Spads, of the days when he flew over the Western Front in the Great War; and he still remembered "with advantages what feats" he did in the skies of France. He died in 1991.

Ritchie Thomas

August, 1993   Carl M. Becker

Roland W. Richardson, His Life and Letters as an Air Service Pilot:

An Introduction

"... probably the dumbest officer...."

As the armistice of November 11, 1918, brought the Great War to an end, 767 pilots were in the Air Service, a division of the United States Army.[1] Many had fought the Germans in the air over the Western Front, especially during the Allies' assaults on the German lines in the fall of 1918. Among them was First Lieutenant Roland Withenbury Richardson. What he did and what he felt he recorded at times in letters to his mother and in a diary; his words, though hardly eloquent, paint a clear portrait of American aviators at war and of his own quest for a place in the war.

i

Born in 1897 in Glendale, Ohio, a community of about 1,500 people just north of Cincinnati, Richardson was the first child and only son of James Clement Richardson and Annis Withenbury Richardson.[2] His father along with four brothers, was the co-owner of the Richardson Paper Company, which operated a mill in the nearby town of Lockland producing boxboard and paperboard for housebuilders. The small family lived quite comfortably in a large non-descript frame house built in 1854 in a fashionable section of Glendale, a few blocks from the railroad station where businessmen boarded cars for their offices in Cincinnati. The rambling house afforded ample space for the three babies, Adelaide, Annis, and Emily born in 1898, 1899, and 1900. The Richardsons had no child in 1901 — and indeed no more. In 1902 James Richardson died, the victim of diptheria.

Fortunately, he left his family in a reasonably sound financial state, and his four brothers all gave assistance to the young family in the years immediately following his death. The Richardsons continued living in their large house. The children attended the public schools in Glendale, forming there and in other settings friendships with other children that would last a lifetime. Despite his father's death, Roland Richardson remembered his childhood as one of happiness. Very early he seemed to place his dead father in the far recesses of memory. Nowhere in his letters or diaries did he ever allude to him, as though he had never had a father. But he owed to him at least a legacy of material goods and an aptitude for understanding mechanical things.

Apparently life was placid enough for the Richardsons despite the absence of the father. Then the mother decided to take a dramatic step. Believing that her children should receive a broad, a cosmopolitan education, she resolved to take the family to Europe.[3] Her brothers-in-law providing some support, the family boarded an ocean liner sometime early in 1912 and began a journey to Neuchâtel in the French-speaking part of Switzerland. Here Roland attended the École Secondaire, a boy's public school; and his sisters went to a girls' school. They lived frugally in a pension and in so far as they could participated in the everyday life of the community.

Through all of 1913 Roland kept a diary, much in the same style as he did during the war.[4] In it, in his boyish language, he commented briefly on his school work, his social and recreational life, his travels in France, and many other subjects. He developed, as his mother wished, an ability to use the French language. Perhaps presaging his interest in aviation, often he spoke of working with two small motors that he purchased in Neuchâtel. Of both, at their purchase, he noted that he had "long longed" for them.[5] Often he was working on their armatures and coils, anticipating, as it were, his later repair of airplane engines. He "monkied" around with his motor; he worked "all morning on my motor."[6] On more than one occasion, he discussed electrical problems with teachers at his school and at the local university and with men in the town. Perhaps here he first thought of flying. Though he told an interviewer in 1978 that he first saw an airplane at the Panama-Pacific Exposition in San Francisco in 1915, he may have forgotten what he had learned and seen of airplanes in Europe in 1913.[7] At the university he attended a Séance of the Society Antoinette dealing with "aeroplanes."[8] In July, while visiting Paris, he saw "a lot of aeroplanes flying & on the ground & I got some photos of them."[9] In any event, certainly he knew something about aviation at the entry of the United States into the war.

The Richardsons continued their sojourn in Switzerland into 1914. Then, evidently seeking to broaden her family's experience, the mother decided to move on to Germany. She had even sent some luggage on to Germany when the war began in August.[10] Changing her plans, she returned the family to Glendale, where the son and daughters picked up threads of their old lives. In 1915 Roland enrolled at the University of Cincinnati, intending to study for a degree in mechanical engineering. He was a sophomore in 1917 when Congress declared war on Germany. Immediately, he joined a local unit of the National Guard, Battery E of the 136th Field Artillery Battalion. But frightened by the horses that he had to manage in the movement of artillery pieces, he cast around for other patriotic, less equestrian-like duty. His uncle, Colonel Theodore Lyster, had it ready for him. Lyster was a medical officer with the Aviation Section of the Signal Corps, which was then undertaking the task of organizing an American air force for service in France; it had, at one point, a goal of training over six thousand pilots and procurement of twenty-two thousand aircraft.[11] Though the army expected to train pilots primarily in the United States, it was also building training centers for them in France. The Corps particularly had plans for construction of a large center — twelve fields in all — at Issoudun in central France and had organized the Twenty-Ninth Provisional Squadron to preside over the project.

Richardson still had a good command of the French language, and so his uncle recommended him for an officer's commission, with an assignment as an interpreter for the squadron. The uncle's influence at work, he received a first lieutenancy. At the time, he noted years later, he gave the rank little notice, but "later on I thought why in the devil didn't they commission me a second lieutenant, [which] would have been more like it, because I was probably the dumbest officer that was ever commissioned in the service."[12]

ii

Surely Richardson, like his nation, was in the midst of rapid change. He received his commission on July 15 and his active orders on July 16 and sailed for Europe on July 17. "So in three days," he recalled later in selfdeprecation, "I converted from a dumb civilian to a dumber officer en route to France." Stopping in England en route to France, Richardson and the other men of the Twenty-Ninth arrived in Issoudun early in August. About seven miles from this "nice little town of about 10,000," they moved into a makeshift camp. They could do little at first because of delays in the shipment of building materials.[13] Rain turning the camp into a sea of mud added discomfort to boredom.

Not until late in August did construction really begin. Then Richardson became a kind of scavenger, scouring the countryside by motorcycle in search of building supplies, his ability to speak French supposedly easing his task. On one occasion he spent nearly three days hunting posts for fencing; on another he purchased a locomotive for pulling cars from Paris laden with supplies.

The lieutenant had little opportunity for social or recreational activity. Seldom did he go into Issoudun. Neither the American Red Cross nor the Young Men's Christian Association had yet opened canteens in the area. On Saturday evenings he did attend movies shown at the camp. No doubt he enjoyed acquaintanceships and friendships formed at the camp. Several times he met Eddie Rickenbacker, who was then an engineering officer but who would become the leading American "ace" of the war. A former race car driver, he was often driving officers from Paris, the "top brass," to Issoudun to check on progress there.[14] Richardson usually joined the party as an interpreter, sitting in the front seat of a "luxurious" automobile with Rickenbacker. He liked Rickenbacker, characterizing him as a "good man and a hell of a nice guy." He became a friend of Quentin Roosevelt, who came to Issoudun soon after a few barracks had been built. A Frenchman at Romorantin, a community near Issoudun, invited Richardson to his house for dinner and suggested that he in turn invite any other French-speaking officers to join them. Richardson asked Roosevelt to come along, and the Americans spent a pleasant evening at the Frenchman's home.[15] Richardson thought that Roosevelt was a "peach" and admired him for declaring that he would not be "sticking around here [Issoudun] anymore than necessary" and that he would fly and go to the front to fight. He did and died in combat in 1918.

Like Roosevelt, Richardson wanted to shake the mud of Issoudun off his feet. He came to realize that he was not indispensible to the mission there, for the French with whom the Americans worked often spoke English. He believed, too, that as the army let out contracts to the French for construction, he would be reduced to "sitting around and doing nothing." He had reached, he feared, the limits of his opportunities at Issoudun; and his only chance for achievement would come, he believed, as a flier. "I am crazy" about flying, he asserted. He applied for a transfer into pilot training and late in September went off to the Second Aviation Training Center at Tours for primary training.

iii

Located about 220 miles southwest of Paris on the Loire in the château country, Tours had once known the sound of battle. Near it, in 732 A.D., Charles Martel had led the French in repelling invading Saracens. But as a site for a new heroic stand, it was not promising. Richardson arrived there only a few days before the Air Service took over a French aviation school intended originally to train observers, but now was an American school for preliminary or basic training. Facilities and equipment were inadequate, and the school could not accommodate more than one hundred students a month, a number that would force cadets to wait for training.[16]

Almost at the moment of his arrival, Richardson had his first training flight in a Caudron G-III, with a French monitor, or instructor, giving him double control lessons. The Caudron in training used a seventy-horsepower radial Anzani motor. As Richardson remembered the airplane, it looked like a box kite. It had "no ailerons on the wings: you warped the wings to get lateral control."[17] Nonetheless, he found it to be a "pretty stable, substantial airplane."

After effecting a number of take-offs and landings and logging nearly six hours on the Caudron, Richardson took his first solo flight late in November. To his surprise, he learned that his training did not prepare him well for the flight. He had been flying a Caudron with an Anzani engine, but now he had to fly a Caudron with an eighty-horsepower Le Rhone rotary motor. The motor had more torque than the Anzani and thus tended to swerve the airplane off course during take-off. Fortunately, the empennage — the tail assembly — was heavy enough to reduce the swerving. Though finding his initial flight to be "quite an experience," Richardson survived it and went on to training at Tours in stunt, altitude, and cross-country flying. He fell behind in his schedule for graduation by two weeks, though, when he suffered a broken collar bone in a motorcycle accident. In his final month of training in January of 1918, he also had to serve as the assistant transportation officer for the school.

After receiving his brevet license in January, Richardson returned to Issoudun, now organized as a secondary flying school with all of its fields in operation. Though Issoudun was a center primarily for the training of pursuit pilots — chasse pilots — Richardson was not certain as to what branch of the Air Service he wished to enter.[18] He could choose to become a pilot in bombardment. Bombardment squadrons carried bombs for attacks on rail heads, transport trains, and troop concentrations. Or he could have entered an observation squadron; such a squadron made aerial photographs enabling artillery units and bombardment aircraft to attack vulnerable targets. If he became a pursuit pilot, his squadron, employing mostly machine guns, would seek to control air space by attacks on enemy pursuit aircraft and might also attack ground troops and observation balloons. Men in the Air Service tended to believe that pursuit was a "higher and more desirable form of aviation duty" than bombardment and observation.[19] With its prospect for individuated combat, certainly it seemed more exciting. Richardson leaned in various directions but gradually gravitated to pursuit, notwithstanding the advice of his Uncle Ted, who urged him to become a bombardment pilot.

At Issoudun simulation was essential to training. With an instructor at his side, a pilot first flew a Nieuport 12, a double-control airplane fitted with an eighty-horsepower Le Rhone motor. But because it could easily swerve off course during take-off, a trainee prepared himself for that experience in a Penguin — a so-called Roulleur.[20] The Penguin was nearly identical with the Nieuport, except for its clipped wings preventing flight. Sometimes pilots came off the runway in it and ran into bushes or trees; but they knew more then about what to expect in the Nieuport.

Richardson used the Penguin eight times, always staying on the runway, and then advanced to the Nieuport. Still he had problems with it, particularly in stunt flying. Underpowered, it inhibited that kind of flying because it easily stalled. Soon, though, Richardson soloed on the Nieuport 12 and then turned to the Nieuport 10, which could also test a pilot's mettle owing to problems in controlling it. One of Richardson's friends spun into the ground in one and was killed. Accidents in the Nieuports, whatever the type, were not uncommon at Issoudun. Later in 1918, according to one pilot's reminiscenses, German prisoners there were digging on average six graves a day for men killed in smash-ups.[21] Undoubtedly, that figure was quite inaccurate, for altogether at all training fields 218 pilots were killed during the war.[22] Nonetheless, men who trained at Issoudun had to know that theirs was a dangerous business.

On completion of training in the Nieuport 10, Richardson moved to Field 5 at Issoudun, there to fly the Nieuport 21 in acrobatics. A single-seated plane equipped with an eighty-horsepower Le Rhone, this Nieuport, Richardson wrote, was a "very delightful little plane to fly."[23] The training for acrobatics required, literally, a flight in imagination. Casey Jones, a colorful instructor all remembered, had the student sit in a fuselage of an airplane that did not fly and showed him how to manipulate the control stick and rudder for a prescribed stunt. And then the student went up and performed the stunt, which could be a spin, renversement, vertical turn, vrille, or wing slip. Even before he got into the air, Richardson had an accident. Performing a "Cheval de Bois," or ground loop, he broke the tail skid and wing tip of his machine. Nonetheless, he successfully finished the course in acrobatics.

From Field 5 Richardson went to Field 7 for training in formation flying in a Nieuport 24. A popular airplane among the students, this Nieuport, equipped with a 120 horsepower motor, was more powerful than the Nieuport 10 and 21 and was, said Richardson, "very nice to fly."[24] Taking off in Nieuports 24s, five or seven pilots rendezvoused at an appointed altitude and practiced flying in formation. The pilots could not stay too close together because they needed latitude to look around and to maneuver.

Formation training over, Richardson moved to Field 8 for combat practice. Now he flew a Nieuport 27, a rather streamlined version of the Nieuport 24. Attached to it was a camera permitting a pilot to simulate a dog-fight. Pulling a trigger on the control stick, he actuated the shutter of the camera that in turn took a picture of whatever he had in his sights — not necessarily what he was aiming at. Thus a pilot in practice could shoot another pilot down. The film often embarrassed the man who had badly missed his target. For Richardson such training was a "lot of fun."

All the while Richardson and other pilots at Issoudun were honing their skills in gunnery in other ways. Frequently, they were trap shooting or firing pistols and Vickers machine guns. The use of pistols implied a romantic side of combat, with men acting as though they were cavalry charging the enemy or knights engaged in close personal combat with an identifiable enemy.

If the use of camera guns or machine guns and pistols on the ground was a far step from reality in battle, Richardson and his fellow pilots came closer to it when, in April of 1918, they went to the French aerial gunnery school at Cazaux. On the Bay of Biscay in a relatively uninhabited area — the French had been worried about aerial gunnery in well-populated areas — Cazaux was at once a source of pain and pleasure. The barracks there, the Corneau barracks, once occupied by Russian soldiers, had no occupants but a large pack of rats.[25] The runway at Cazaux, though, was excellent, a very sandy expanse of ground. After a downpour of rain, within a few minutes, a pilot could take off or land without fear that the wheels of his airplane would throw mud into the propeller and seriously damage it, as had happened too often at Issoudun.

The airplanes assigned to Richardson and many of his friends — Nieuport 27s — were in deplorable condition: among other problems, control wire and struts were loose, and the wings wobbled in flight. So the pilots resolved not to "fly the damned things anymore until they fixed them up."[26] French mechanics bristled at their complaints; and the American officer commanding the aviators, an infantryman, dressed them down in a small crowded room. Out of fright or the closeness of the room, one pilot fainted. The pilots escaped punishment but heard no promise of improvements in the Nieuports. Perhaps their commanding officer did hear them: at least the Nieuports were in better condition thereafter.

Flying the Nieuport with Lewis guns mounted on the top wing that fired over the propeller, a cadet worked at his calling. Initially, he practiced diving at a balloon at eight or nine thousand feet and then could actually shoot at one on condition that he direct his fire at a lake in the background. (In a tragic incident involving indiscriminate firing, a stray bullet had struck a French student sitting in a classroom.) A pilot also fired his guns at a sleeve target pulled by another airplane. On his first pass at a sleeve, Richardson knocked it down — but admitted later that perhaps he had struck the towing rope with his airplane. With a score of 13 percent, his group supposedly set the record for the school.

In May Richardson returned to Issoudun to complete his combat training, much of it in mock engagements. Along with other pilots, he had to face Lieutenant Jack Osgood, already a legendary figure there. Osgood was a taskmaster but also was a source of amusement: a tall man, he always wore a football-like helmet to protect his head, which because of his height would have surely hit the ground if his airplane turned over. Though the training went well enough for Richardson, it ended on a sour note.

To become a pursuit pilot, as he wished, he had, as a final test, to fly in mock combat against an instructor, who then decided whether he was qualified. For reasons he could not explain more than sixty years later, Richardson just "didn't feel like going into combat with the guy. [There was] nothing wrong with him, but I just didn't feel like I wanted to do it. So when he swooped down on me, I just kept on going in a straight line and paid no attention to him. I can't imagine why I did a thing like that, looking back on it."[27] The instructor washed him out as a pursuit pilot, declaring that he would have to fly a bomber.

Whether or not he was willing to fly a bomber, Richardson next had to go to Orly, just south of Paris, as did many pilots on completion of their training, to serve as a ferry pilot. Virtually a pasture with hangars around it, Orly was an "acceptance" center; personnel here received airplanes from factories, tested them, and ferried them to training fields around France and to the front.[28]

At first Richardson took some satisfaction as a test pilot for the Sopwith, an English airplane; he saw to its testing, repair, and ferrying. Occasionally, he flew an army photographer over Paris and the surrounding area to take photographs. He had the time and freedom to fly mock combat with other pilots at Orly, particularly Warren Eaton. Eaton usually flew a Spad, Richardson a Nieuport 28 with a monosoupape (single valve) 150 horsepower motor. As he recalled the Nieuport, "it was a beautiful airplane, very maneuverable . . . . It was a hell of a nice airplane." Below about ten thousand feet, the Nieuport outmaneuvered the Spad; above that altitude, the Spad ordinarily won the day. Richardson also had time on earth for frequent visits to Paris — though clearly his was not the way of the rake there. But he became increasingly unhappy at Orly, his mind fixed on going to the front before the war ended.

Finally, in what he viewed as a piece of good luck, he was on his way to fight the Boche. Jack Ogden, one of Richardson's friends, was at headquarters at Orly. Ogden, also thirsting for combat, somehow received the assignment of selecting additional pilots for the 213th Aero Squadron, which had recently arrived in France from England and which was preparing for the battle at the front.[29] Ignoring or ignorant of Richardson's washout as a pursuit pilot, he chose him as one of the new pilots for the 213th. And early in August of 1918, the Squadron received orders taking it into the maelstrom of the war.

iv

The squadron, in the Third Pursuit Group and under the command of Captain John A. Hambelton, went first to Vaucouleurs, a small town near Toul at the end of the German salient at St. Mihiel.[30] Receiving Spad

XIIIs, a good airplane that everybody wanted "to go out to the Front on," the men of the squadron looked forward to success in the skies. But certainly Richardson did not find the Spad to be a receptive host of fortune. On his first flight, one of his many patrols over the lines, his aircraft developed an oil leak welling up a pool of oil on the floor of the cockpit. Then as he was about to land, one of the magnetos fell apart, causing the engine to lose about four hundred revolutions. But Richardson was able to maintain a speed sufficient to land safely.

It was but the beginning of a train of mechanical problems. Ordinarily, so Richardson believed, the Spad was an excellent airplane; but the French kept the best Spads and sold Americans ones that had "probably been in wrecks and banged up and rebuilt and patched up. We didn't know the difference. They looked good, but we didn't know their past history."[31] Moreover, the American mechanics had problems in servicing the motor on the Spads. They had been trained on rotary motors, but now they had to work on the Hispano-Suiza engine, a stationary motor. The motor proved to be a hazard. It would quit "at the drop of a hat," and the pilot had little chance of "catching" it. A rotary motor, on the other hand, kept windmilling after it stopped, giving a pilot the opportunity to manipulate the throttles to get it started again. Richardson repeatedly noted in his letters and diaries that he had faced the problem of catching his motor.

Richardson had chronic problems, too, with his gas tank located on the belly of the Spad. A small pump on the cam shaft housing pumped air through a tube into the tank forcing gasoline up to the carburetor. Occasionally, the tube broke; then the pilot heard a sputter as the motor stopped. If the motor rotated for a moment, he might be able to connect it with an emergency tank on the top wing. If he kept the motor going, he had to shut off the valve from the tank to the little tube and pump his way home by hand with an air pump. He had but one hand remaining to work the control stick and to work the throttle. Several times Richardson faced this crisis of ambidexterity; unlike some other pilots, he did not crack up his airplane in a forced landing.

Richardson did, of course, experience forced landings; indeed, he "panned" his airplane more than once. Losing oil pressure in one instance and abandoning his formation, he chose two open fields lying side-by-side as optional sites for landing, assuming from his view that both afforded safety. Keeping his motor idling to avoid a rapid descent — with its motor off, a Spad had the "gliding angle of a brick" — he panned in one field and then discovered that the other one was full of barbed wire. "So somebody was looking after me when I picked that field." Altogether, including forced landings and failure to join a patrol because of mechanical or electrical problems, his airplanes were out of commission at least thirty-five days out of eighty-three days from early in August into November.[32]

Despite those perpetual problems, Richardson did fly in combat. He was often over the lines in fairly routine patrols. But for a few days in

September he was at one of the crucial points of the great Allied drive near St. Mihiel that wiped out the German salient held for so many months. Early in the drive, on September 12, he was in a patrol attacking German troops retreating on the road between Chambley and Mars-le-Tours. Diving on the Germans, Richardson and other pilots of the squadron shot up the road, scattering horses, trucks, and soldiers along the way. They fired on a railway station and railroad cars loaded with German soldiers and on "everything we could." Richardson exclaimed "we sure did give the Boche h - - l!"[33] The Germans responded with anti-aircraft fire — "archies" as the pilots called it — from rifles and machine guns. Richardson escaped unscathed.

On September 14 after another day of combat in the air, Richardson earned a slice of aviation immortality. Encountering a Fokker monoplane, he, Lieutenant S. P. Gaillard, and Captain Charles Grey, the flight commander, dove and fired on it, sending it into a vrille. Later, they received confirmation of their kill, each receiving one-third credit for it.

During the offensive, Richardson lost his Spad in a bizarre incident. One day when he was not scheduled to fly, Ogden, whose plane was grounded, borrowed his Spad for a patrol. As usual, the engine did not run well, and Ogden dropped out of formation and lost his bearings. He saw a town with an airdrome near it and landed, expecting to obtain gas and directions for returning home. He looked again at the airplanes that he had seen from above: they bore black crosses. He had come down at a German airport! His captors gave him a tour of the facility, fed him, and bedded him down for the night as though he were a special guest —and then sent him of to a prison camp.

After the conclusion of the St. Mihiel campaign, Richardson's squadron followed the advancing Allied lines, moving toward the Meuse-Argonne sector. First it went to Lisle-en-Barrois. There Richardson and four other pilots lived for a while with the mayor. Against the passage of many decades, he retained a fond and pungent recollection of the mayor, his hospitality, and his accommodations: "He was a real nice guy. We used to have tea and cognac in his living room, which was just a room next to the stable where they kept the cow. We could drink the tea and taste the cognac and smell the manure from the cow, all at the same time."[34] The pilots repaid him for his generosity: "We used to liberate sugar and flour from our kitchen. We were very generous people in those days, and the French had trouble getting flour and sugar . . . . So we would bring him in a five pound sack of flour or sugar. We were very popular. We all liked him."

From Lisle-en-Barrois, Richardson flew many patrols and a few bombing missions, but none to equal those of September near St. Mihiel. On one patrol, though, he was "archied" rather badly, one shell damaging both the upper and lower wings of his Spad on the left-hand side. Wing-heavy on one side, he panned his machine near Clermont.

Early in November, the 213th moved again, this time to Foucacourt, about thirty miles north of Bar le Duc. On the way there from Lisle-en-Barrois, his patrol had a "scrap" with Germans resulting in losses on both sides. Flying from Foucacourt, Richardson participated in two bombing attacks on towns along the lines and then the war ended. Recently two of his friends had been killed, and he was ready for the end. Writing to his mother on armistice day, he told her that "I guess and hope I flew my last time with hostile intention yesterday PM when we went over to bomb a town and it doesn't make me a bit mad either. You see it took me and Foch about three months to end this war . : . ."[35]

Richardson remained at Foucacourt until early in December when he said goodbye to the squadron almost at the moment that a photographer took its official photograph. He went on to Paris, laid over there for a day, and traveled to Issoudun, his old training center. He "bummed around" there for about a month, leading a "very lazy life." He flew occasionally "just for the hell of it." Just after Christmas, he spent three days in Paris, then returned to Issoudun to continue his life of indolence. Early in January, along with a large contingent of soldiers from every branch of the army, he went to Brest to await sailing to the United States. He "bummed around" for nearly three weeks before he boarded a troop ship, the *Adriatic*, for the homeward passage. The voyage, taking eight days, ended at Hoboken. There aviators, infantrymen, and artillerymen all disembarked. What should have been a joyous occasion took an embarrassing turn: all the officers had to remove their Sam Browne belts as they disembarked, evidently because beltless officers at the port did not want to stand conspicuous as homefront soldiers.

Going through physical and psychological examinations, Richardson received his discharge. He took a train to Cincinnati and reached the city on February 6, 1919. He met his family and sweetheart at the station. It "sure made him feel good." Within a few days he was engaged to be married, and a month later he took a position in the sales department of the Richardson Paper Company. He continued to fly but never again with "hostile intention."

v

The young man who enlisted in the Air Service, endured training and duty in France, and then entered the lists of battle was hardly a complex or exciting person. To the extent that he revealed himself in his letters and diurnal notes, he appeared as an ordinary man in thought and deeds. True enough, he was adept, even innovative, in the mechanical realm, where he was at home working with magnetos, fuel pumps, and motors. But his interest and ability in mechanical things did not carry him into contemplation of the vast maw into which he had been drawn. Though he had lived abroad as a teen-ager and had attended a large university, he remained a small-town boy who lacked the experience and intellect to define the whirl of great events. But like millions of other young men, his duty was not to think, but to fight and, if necessary, die.

At a rather abstract level, as he looked at national purposes, Lieutenant Richardson was not especially articulate. Never in his letters and diaries did he speak as one engaged in a mighty crusade for the nation, as one playing a role in making the world safe for democracy. Certainly he approved of Woodrow Wilson as a national leader and diplomat, but never did he second the president's eloquent motions for war and peace. At most he saw himself enlisting as a patriot, as what he had to do. Like many men entering the army, whether by enlistment or conscription, he had only an indistinct perception of why he was in France. Though occasionally speaking of Germans and the Kaiser Wilhelm in sarcastic or derisive language, he did not personalize them, even as he called them "Huns," as barbarians threatening the fabric of western civilization. Surely he was no Kiffin Rockwell of the Lafayette Escadrille, who was "imbued with the spirit of the cause" and who declared that he intended to "pay my part for Lafayette and Rochambeau."[36] He was, of course, yet a very young man.

Richardson might have portrayed himself acting on behalf of his religion, race, region, or relatives. But again nowhere in his words did he give expression to such motivation. Indeed, rarely did he even allude to religion; and he seemed quite unaware of any ethnic implications in the war. In an army in which men still felt regional or local loyalties, a vestige of the Civil War and earlier when men enlisted in regiments named by their states, Richardson had no identification with his state or local community. He was interested in learning about men from Glendale who were in France, but he did not call on them to sustain the honor of the community. Nor did he see himself as one defending his family or protecting its good name.

Like soldiers of most wars, Richardson developed loyalties after he entered the lists — to his "outfit" and his comrades. His attachment to his training groups had been tenuous, but he was developing a real kinship with the men of the 213th as the war was ending. At the death or disappearance in combat of one of these men, he expressed continuing concern and more sorrow than he had when a pilot in training had died in an accident. Probably, though, his loyalty was more personal than institutional. His squadron never exhibited a distinct, a coherent character. The men composing it were not the stuff of post-war movies such as *Dawn Patrol*. They were not dashing men, picaresque adventurers, irresponsible but always brave, always ready to meet death with a smile.

Soldiers cannot escape examining their fear of combat or speculating on the way in which they will face battle. In the Civil War often men had internalized a societal view calling for them never to admit fear and to undertake heroic acts without thought of flinching. Especially in a war when men still believed that an individual could influence the outcome of battle — rather than the machine — such a belief had a semblance of reality. In the twentieth century, though, American soldiers were more likely to argue that only a fool would not acknowledge fear as a comrade in battle — that what was truly heroic was to fight despite one's fears. Again, though, Richardson seldom spoke to such concerns, never shared with his family his understanding of what men should feel or do in the face of death. In a rare instance, he admitted that "something" could happen to him or that "somebody" had taken care of him at a moment of great danger. Often he looked at combat in the air as a kind of game. Perhaps he was one of a residual breed that personalized battle; aviators were cavalrymen of the skies dashing here and there relatively oblivious to massed assaults of anonymous soldiers who lived in agony.

Surely flying in training and combat was dangerous. Yet Richardson seldom commented on the accidents that were commonplace. Indeed, often he assured his mother that flying was quite safe, especially after a pilot had completed his training in acrobatics. Yet he did not readily reveal to her — in fact concealed from her — that students in his group had died in accidents. Perhaps as a kind of defensive mechanism, he seemed to view such deaths as a matter of course, as what one had to expect and endure.

In consonance with his indifference to the overarching meaning of the war, Richardson did not view it in close personal terms. He never confided to his diary or his mother a view of the world that he might live in at the close of battle. And seemingly he had no great concern about the kind of life awaiting him at home. Despite ever facing death, seldom if ever did he take emotional or psychological refuge in religion — in contemplating his fate, in reading the Bible, in prayer, in attending religious services. As a boy, apparently he had occasionally attended service at the Episcopal church near his home; in France, though, he kept his distance from worship. One Sunday, he "thought" about going to church at camp, then thought better of it and did not go.

Outside of the cockpit and camp apparently Richardson was fairly straight-laced. Essentially he was a small-town boy who did not permit the times and place to govern his behavior. When he left camp on pass to visit Paris or to go "downtown" in a small French community, he did not become a rake kicking over the traces. He might attend a movie or vaudeville show or dine at a good restaurant; but if he dallied in flesh or got into his cups, he gave no hint to his diary of such behavior. His was antiseptic conduct. At one point he told his mother that he had no interest in strong drink; chewing gum was enough. He seemed to be developing at least a strong friendship with Mary Johnston, a young woman from Glendale, as he showed her the sights of Paris; but one would have to read his diaries with the eye of an imaginative voyeur to discover a relationship that was anything but platonic.

If Richardson had any idiosyncratic manner, it came in his attire, or his consciousness of what he could wear with good effect. More than men in other military branches, aviators affected, de rigueur, a jaunty look, in keeping with what they saw as their distinctive duty, as though they were knights whose armor set them apart from other soldiers. In any event, Richardson often wrote to his mother about his clothing. He wished that she could see his "cute" little cap giving him the "cockie" look of the English. Obviously he took pleasure in sporting his Sam Browne belt. Momentarily, he was happy with his "nice" olive drab uniform; then soon complaining that he was the only officer who had to wear olive drab, he purchased a "dandy" suit in which he could look "decent." Repeatedly he let his family know of his need for gold and black hat cord. Though taking pride in a new leather trench coat, he made an icon out of his high lace boots, his expensive boots costing four hundred francs: "They are fine boots"; they "sure are great"; "they are some boots"; "Everybody" was "envious of them." He was certain that "it pays to get the best." He was, moreover, meticulous in describing the way in which he donned his clothing — a squire ritualistically preparing for his vows of knighthood.

Richardson was rather pedestrian in his prose. His letters were grammatical enough, and his diaries strung together phrases compressed into limited space. He punctuated his language with cliches and colloquialisms of the day — — "Gee," "Gosh," "She's a peach," "Believe me," and so on. He employed one verb in particular to denote his pursuit of the ordinary: he was ever "bumming around" in camp or town. What he did when he "bummed around" he never detailed, as would be in keeping with the common routines of life.

Better than many of his friends, Richardson could use language as a means of meeting with and talking to the French. But apparently he did not go out of his way to cultivate friendships with French civilians. On one occasion, as noted earlier, he visited a French family in the company of Quentin Roosevelt. He did not repeat such visits. At one point he expressed admiration of the French. Yet by the time that he left France, he had come to view the country in a harsh light. He believed the nation to be backward and dirty. Other American soldiers, especially after seeing the cleanliness and order of German communities, also found France wanting.

As the only male in the Richardson family, Roland Richardson could have assumed the role of a father-figure, even at a far remove from Glendale, and brought to his letters all kinds of counsel. But only occasionally did he write words clearly advising or lecturing the family. His mother, after all, was beyond him in more than miles. She had long directed affairs of the family and had shown a remarkable determination and independence in taking her children to Europe. On one occasion, the son did scold her for proposing to come to France. Ironically, he had opened the door to such a prospect when he facetiously wrote to her that "if you could only come over, we would have a blow out . . . ." Ordinarily, he merely commented on his sisters' activities with words of approbation. But when he learned that the oldest sister, Bobby, had become engaged to a man who would be entering military service, he urged her not to hasten into a marriage under the chancy circumstances of war. Evidently neither woman responded directly to his counsel; but neither did what he advised against.

The aviator in the letters, though hardly a complex man, was ambivalent and uncertain about war. He had a foot in a past that romanticized war and a foot in an age that recognized war as a material contest. He could grouse about the army, but he also knew his duty and did it as well as he could. He was a good soldier.

PART ONE
Training for the Front

In July of 1917, about three months after the United States entered the Great War, Roland Richardson, who had enlisted in the National Guard early in April before the American declaration of war, received a commission as a first lieutenant in the Air Service of the United States Army. Within a few days, he was sailing to France as a member of the Twenty-Ninth Provisional Squadron, which had the responsibility of constructing a large American aviation school at Issoudun in central France. There Richardson acted as an interpreter and procured building supplies in the countryside. Finding his work wearisome, he sought and received a transfer into the "flying corps."

Assigned to the Second Aviation Instruction Center at Tours in October, he took his preliminary training in a Caudron G-3. His training completed in January, he returned to Issoudun for advanced combat training, ostensibly to become a pursuit pilot. Here he flew various kinds of Nieuports in acrobatic maneuvers and learned the rudiments of aerial gunnery. For about two weeks he was at the French School of Aerial Fire at Cazaux, firing first at stationary targets and then at airborne sleeves. At his return to Issoudun, he failed the qualifying flight required of pursuit pilots, with the result that he expected to become a bombardment pilot. Instead, in May he was assigned to the First Army Aviation Acceptance Park at Orly, there to test airplanes and ferry them to training fields in France and to the front.

Chapter One

Working at Issoudun

"Flying is really the chief thing...."

AT SEA
July 25, 1917
U.S.M.S. "St. Paul"[1]

Dear Mother and Folks at Home:

Well, here we are all O.K. I really do not believe there are any submarines in the ocean at all. We have * * * on our boat and all of them ready * * * * * * practice, the second or third day out and they sure did shoot straight. This boat has made seventy three trips since war was declared and has not even seen a submarine.

We land Friday, the 27th, and it seems as though we won't see a submarine at all.

There is not much to tell you about the voyage, except that we have had no rough weather at all and a fine trip altogether.

I have a state-room all to myself and am fixed up in great style. We get fine eats and lots of them. It is hard to believe there is a war at all.

Captain [George] Goldtwaite and Captain [Thomas] Lyster are both fine — * who are all nice fellows. I had to scratch that out as it would not pass the censor.

I will cable you when I reach our destination, but I can't tell you where it will be, but, nevertheless, I can tell you that we will be in France soon after we land.

I have learned how to run a typewriter while en voyage, and can do it with two fingers now. Maybe after a while I can use three. I may want you to send me something if I need anything else. If I do I will ask you and you can just send it to my address which I will give you as soon as I know it.

Tell Bobby [Adelaide Richardson] I am sorry that I didn't say good bye to her . . . .

We are going to be awfully busy when we get to France, so I won't have time to write you much, but I will do my best. Give all my friends my best and keep lots of love for yourself.

Ever your son,
Roland.

P.S. We picked up two American destroyers yesterday morning, who convoyed us and swept the seas in front of us until some time last night, when the Admirality ordered us into [Liverpool] Harbor, where we stayed until morning. We are now on our way to [Southampton], where we will get off, then go straight to France. I will not cable you from there, but from our next port. I have already given the cablegram to the Steward. It will cost $1.25, but it is worth it. I have a $ or so now, so that when we land, I can do any business that I have to. They sunk a good many boats this week, it seems, although you never can believe everything, but we are perfectly safe here now and are still convoyed, but not by the same boats.[2]

I think the submarines are afraid of us. I am wearing the sweater now and it sure is fine.

Ever your son.
Roland.

*　　　　*　　　　*

Hotel de Castille   August 1, 1917
37 Rue Cambon
Paris

Dear Mother:

We arrived here in due time and have been here two days and two nights. We will probably leave for [Issoudun] this afternoon. I am sorry that I can't give you some definite information. We have reported, signed up, etc., and are now ready to go. By the way, I have not told you of another streak of luck that has come my way. At the last minute in New York, Capt. [F. Daniel] Huntington, one of our party, thought we needed another man along, so he brought his nephew, a boy of about 21 and a dandy fellow. We are already old pals.

Last night Capt. Lyster had some business to attend to, so we went off for a good time, this fellow, Walter Powers, Lieut. [G. S.] Frank and myself. Don't get worried now for we were all safely in bed by 11:15 PM. We had supper in a Cafe, and went to a show afterwards. It sure was some experience, and it took some work to keep unattached, get me? Between the acts everybody went out to get a drink, so we decided we would walk around the restaurant which was attached to the theater and see the sights. Well, three unattached boys, two in uniform and one "en civil" were a goal for all the unattached girls in the place, and they pestered the life out of us to buy them a drink. But not so as you could notice it. The poor men that did get worked had the girls laying all over them before they had finished, it sure was some sight, not for mine though, and I think the other two felt the same. And coming home it was the same, they were hanging around all the corners and would come up to you and try to take your arm and engage you in conversation, etc. But thank goodness we got out safely. Some of them were good looking, but they were all too anxious. Nevertheless, it was an interesting experience, and if one keeps his wits about him there is no danger. Paris is *some* city, take it from me.

We all bought a new attachment for our uniforms today, a belt to go on the outside with a strap going from one side, over the right shoulder and back down to the same side again.[3]

As yet I have seen no one that I know. I wrote to Jean Leon Ruetter yesterday and told him that I might see him some time soon. I just ran across three more Americans who are going in the Aviation Corps — all good fellows. So far they have had a fight every night in the cafes and theatres. Some place believe me. The sooner we get out the better. I have to eat dinner now so good bye for awhile. Give my love to the girls and Althea [Ford] and all my friends.

Your son,
Roland.

*   *   *

Hotel de Castille   Somewhere in France
37, Rue Cambon   August 5, 1917
Paris

Dear Mother:

It seems as though we have been here a year. We are now at the place where we are to stay, and, moreover, I can give you my address and expect a letter in a month or so.

Sites of Richardson's Training and Service in France, 1917-1918.

Lieutenant Roland W. Richardson, American Aviation School, 29th Provisional Squadron, c/o American Expeditionary Force, France.

All that is my address. We are situated in a nice little town of about 10,000 inhabitants, and are in a hotel at present, but we soon will go to Camp about 14 k.m. out of town [Issoudun]. About all I've done lately is act as an interpreter, and I guess I am holding down the job O.K. I sure am glad that I know French. I forgot to tell you that none of us were sea-sick coming over, and we had a fine trip. I hope you received my cable and letters. I wrote about four I think to you. I will keep sending my address in all my letters until I hear from you, so then I will know you know it. If you hear of any stray candy, fudge, chocolate, etc. floating around without anybody to look after it, why just ship it over to me. I would also appreciate an automobile or any little thing like that. Anything you send, be sure and address it to ME, at my address, otherwise I will never see it. You can send me over some more socks if you can. One-half dozen pairs of both wool and cotton #10½ Army Socks. Uncle Ted [Theodore Lyster] can get them I think. I bought a pair of great big shoes yesterday for 90 Fcs. the kind that come pretty near up to my knees. They will be fine for winter snows and mud. There is a lot of mud here.

Today is Sunday but you would never know it. All the stores are open and everything running. We are working just the same, although we really havn't had any real hard work yet. The Germans won't last much longer now and I think that we will be home in a year.

Outside of the socks and a shirt or two O. D. 14½, I have all that I need to get thru the winter, but there are lots of little things not absolutely necessary that would nevertheless be accepted with many thanks if you could send them. Don't go to any great expense please, but you know that I like chocolate, etc. Anyway it isn't cigarettes, etc. that I want thank goodness. Please give my love to all the relatives and friends and keep lots for yourselves.

Your son,
Roland.

*   *   *

Hotel de Castille   Aug. 13, 1917.

Dear Mother:

Just a word to let you know that I am all right and will stay so. I can't say much only that work is very interesting and I like it very much.

My address is —

Lieut. Roland W. Richardson, c/o 29th Provisional Aero Squadron, American Expeditionary Force, France.

I have written a number of letters and post cards but goodness knows if you and the rest of the family and friends ever got them. I'll do my best to write you once a week, but if I don't, don't worry. Give my address to anybody that wants it as I will be glad to hear from them.

There is not much doing around here, so we get to bed about 9:30 etc. every evening. They have a movie show every Sunday night and last night we saw Charlie Chaplin — he looked quite natural.[4] I won't write to many people yet for I am running a little short of funds and will have to wait until I am paid. This is sure some life. If you can send any candy or anything over don't hesitate, for I can use it very nicely. Tell Tanta [Lyster] and Uncle Ted that I am going to write them a letter soon and that I have already sent them a post card. Happy birthday to you and Emily [Richardson], this may do for Bobby too, but better late than never. Love to all the girls and Althea and keep lots for yourself.

> Your son,
> Roland.

*   *   *

> Somewhere in France,
> August 20, 1918 [1917]

Dear Mother:

We are now in Camp and the work is really beginning. It sure is fine out here. I have had a motor cycle and side car assigned to my own private use, it is all mine, only I don't pay for its up-keep. Pretty soft isn't it. I got paid for July the other day, and it sure did come in handy.

My address is —
Lieut. Roland W. Richardson, 29th Provisional Squadron, Aviation, American Expeditionary Force, France.

I have heard no word yet from the U.S.A. and I will sure be glad to hear from you all. If you can, I would like to have you send me my banjo and the extra strings that you will find in the little drawer, the low wide one on the left side of my desk. They are in a red box. If it takes too much trouble, do not do it, and any other little thing that you think would go nice over here, just send it along. There is really not much to say in these letters, and I can't say all that is going on, so naturally my letters will not be bulky . . . . I have been feeling fine ever since I have been here and everything is going along O.K. We see so many aeroplanes now that we don't pay more attention to them. Well I guess there is nothing more to say. Give my love to the girls and Althea.

> Your son,
> Roland.

(over)

P.S. Just ran out of ink. Got some more in my trunk though. Took a bath in a small creek today, about four feet wide and one foot deep, much mud, frogs, etc. Cold too, but it sure did feel good after getting all dirty on the motorcycle. I wore the same pair of pajamas for a month, when I took them off for a clean pair, they stood up by themselves.

Tell Althea that I am going to write her next. This is one of the envelopes she gave me, so you can tell her that the housewife and comfort bag combined is sure fine.[5]

We sure see some funny things over here. Just now an Engineer from an Engineer's camp about three miles away, came up and asked me how to get back to his camp. He said that he had been snipe hunting and held the bag while the others cleaned up the snipe.[6] Poor kid, same old story. I am sorry I didn't send you and Emily anything for a birthday present, but it was nearly impossible.

Well it is ten o'clock and I think I'll go to bed. I'll have to catch a perchman around our railroad in our Marmon tomorrow and get some dope on his work.[7]

Love to all,
Roland.

Remember me to Uncle Russ [Withenbury] and Aunt Virginia [Withenbury].

* * *

Somewhere in France
August 29, 1917.

Dear Mother:

I received your first letter, and believe me, I sure was glad to get it. It was written on the 31st of July. The address is O.K. There is not very much I can say to you in my letters, except that I am O.K. The work is going along as well as can be expected. Here is a little daily routine stuff.

I am sleeping and living in a tent about 10 x 8 feet with another officer, a dandy fellow. We have in the tent, two cots, a table, a box, a wooden floor below the cots and our luggage (the tent nearly blew over today). I wake up in the morning and look over at F. and yell — Get up you _____, and hear only a grunt, then all of a sudden he jumps up and out of bed like a shot and tries to pull me up. Sometimes we take a cold bath out in front of the tent (about 20 feet from the main road to [Issoudun]). Then we get dressed. Our clothes are usually very damp, but we soon warm them up. Then at 7 our breakfast comes in brought by our tent orderly. Right after breakfast work begins. I usually go down to the station and keep things moving down at that end. As it is, tomorrow I have to take a trip to another town about thirty miles away on my motorcycle after some pipe, etc. I usually don't get any dinner or am late for it, it is always cold if I do get it. Then go to it in the P.M. and get some, or come in about 6 for supper. After supper until time to go to bed I plan out the work for the next day, write letters, or go to town on my motor cycle and see a movie, then sleep. Its a great life. You can see why I can't write much. There are two fellows in my tent now who are talking etc. and of course I am listening and don't write at the same time. I got Coombsie's [Annis Richardson] and Althea's letters, which sure did hit the spot. I will answer them next. My French sure comes in fine and I can talk as well as I could in Switzerland.

I sure have learned a lot. I can take a bath in a cup of cold water. I do this once every two weeks or so and sew on buttons, well, you ought to see me, they never do come off when I once get them on.

Everything is fine. My money is coming in O.K. and I am going to get milage for the whole trip from Washington to here.

Well I guess I will go to bed as I have to get up early tomorrow and leave with "Joseph" thats my motorcycle.

Give all the family and my friends my love and especially to one young lady who lives just up the street, and also all the sisters, and keep lots for yourself.

> Your loving son,
> Roland.

*   *   *

> Somewhere in France
> Sept. 7, 1917.

Dear Mother:

Everything is all right except the weather and it is awful. It has rained steady for two days and one night. This morning there was water 2 inches deep in the bottom of our tent, a regular river running thru it. Thank goodness we had put our shoes on the board floor or goodness knows where they would have been when we got up. We put on our raincoats, already wet from the day before, and swiped a few spades and dug ditches around our tents, more fun? The only trouble was that these darn rain coats arn't worth a _____, I mean a darn, and when the ditches were dug I had to change suit of O.Ds. I do hate to put on wet pants, especially when I am wearing my B.V.Ds., that cold clammy feeling is all but comfortable. My 90Fcs. leather high shoes are fine, only they won't stand this as well as rubber boots. By the way, I have a good pair of rubber boots down in the shop hanging in the S.W. corner of it, would it be too much trouble, and could you afford it, for I wish you would send them over with a good really waterproof slicker. Don't send anything but a real oiled slicker with a sou-wester hat. Get it good and long and really waterproof. If you can't get just that don't bother. I hate to ask you for such things, but you can't get them over here and they are really necessary. Pay for them out of my salary when you get it. If it hadn't been for the rain we would sleep in barracks tonight, but we are out of luck. We havn't done a thing today but sit around, so our work isn't advancing much. I have only received three letters since I have been here, one from you, Coombsie, and Althea, and everybody else here gets letters every once in awhile, well maybe they have been delayed somewhere, or sunk, anyway don't think I have forgotten you if the same thing happens to my letters — it will all come out in the wash. That is another difficulty, washing, for things will get dirty, and it takes quite awhile to get them washed. Ha Ha. I took a real bath day before yesterday, I think I'll make it a habit to take one at the bath house here every month, whether I need it or not, it only costs Fc. 1.40. Give everybody my best and all the family, Althea and the girls my love and keep lots from your soldier boy,

Roland.

*   *   *

Somewhere in France,
Sept. 19, 1917.

Dearest Mother:

I received your letter of August 19th and sure was glad to get it. To begin with, now that Uncle Ted is coming over, I will tell you what I would like to have, I have already asked for it, but you might not get the letter.

My rubber boots hanging up in the S.W. corner of my shop and a *good* slicker about size 1 or 2. It rains a lot over here and my army rain coat is N.G. [no good] for real rain. Also you can send me over my kodak and a good supply of (3A) films. Then also I would like to have a new officer's hat cord (gold and black), 2 pair of (U.S. Rs.) and 2 pair of Signal Corps ensignia and 4 Lieutenant [bars?]. These things are impossible to get over here and I have sold, lent or lost all my extra ones and am in dire need of them. Pay for all these things out of my pay. You will receive my pay for September and October. I am well fixed over here, 1600 francs in the bank to the good, 4 pair of shoes, 6 uniforms and 5 shirts, 2 pair of putties, etc. So I won't need any clothes for quite awhile. Please send to Uncle Ted for any pay vouchers that I left with him and send them to:

The Depot Quartermaster
U.S. Army,
Washington, D.C.

at the end of the month. They are made out for you and you will receive $183.34 per month. By the way I got commutation last month for my stay at the hotel, my pay and all amounting to $204.80, pretty good "n'est ce pas". Have my slicker plenty long enough and I can wear it riding my motorcycle and still have my knees covered. My French has sure come in fine and didn't fail me at all. That is one reason I get to go round the country buying gas engines, pumps, railroad switches and renting locomotives, etc, so you can understand how pleased I am to be able to "parlen". I give you a kind of itinery [sic] of my daily work in one of my other letters, but I'll do it again, so if you didn't get it you might get this. It is this way:

About 6:30 AM we have reveille, then we, or rather I get up about 6:45, get dressed, wash and clean my teeth and go to breakfast, which usually consists of flap-jacks, karo syrup, bacon, toast, butter and coffee, sometimes oatmeal (what could be better?). Then we come back to our barracks, for we are not in tents any more, and go into our office and start work. I make the rounds of all the gas engines in operation and do various other jobs, then maybe a trip in the afternoon and write in my progress diary after 5:30 PM, and clean up for supper. In the meantime of course we have a good dinner, meat, potatoes, chocolate, bread and a desert [sic], then supper is about the same thing. After supper we go in the reading and writing room. We have one all right and listen to Poor Butterfly on the victrola, or write letters, or anything, then to bed and sleep, O my![8] Not such a bad life is it? I have a German striker, i.e. a Batman, who shines my shoes, my Sam Browne belt, my pullies and does everything for me, even sews up my underclothes, etc., all for 9¢ a day, pretty soft isn't? He is one of our prisoners, who has been wounded and can't do hard work. We can't give them money, so we give them tobacco, canned goods, sugar, etc. Mine has a family of nine children and consequently doesn't receive anything from home, so today I gave him a box of P.A. and 4 lbs. of sugar.[9] He is a good old scout and will do anything for me, he even washes my clothes, my hair brushes and comb. Salutes me everytime I come by and all that.

Here is a little diagram of my room that I have all to myself. It is 10'x 12'. How do you like this arrangement of my various articles of furniture. I am every bit as comfortable as though I was home. All of our officers are dandy fellows and we have a dandy time. We have with us Captain Lyster, who is now a Major, Capt. Huntington, Lieut. Quentin Roosevelt (who is a peach), Lieut. Alonzo Meyers, M. R. C. . . . then some civilians. . . .[10]

I am sending you a photo of myself taken in front of our tent in my working clothes. You can give it to Althea after you are thru with it, if she wants it. I got a letter from Mary Johnston, Gramps [Russell Withenbury, Sr.], Angeline [Faran] and Bobby, and one from Althea and Joe [Hark], all at the same time and am having difficulty in answering them. This is the first long letter I have written. "Marque de temps et place".

We have electric lights. In your last letter, i.e. August 19th, you evidently know where we are. Near here there is an American Hospital being established and M.C. and nurses have already arrived.[11]

It sure is fine about Jim Moss, you tell him if he don't beat those old Eastern boys he hadn't better speak to me again. What is Jim Carruthers doing? Is he still mashing hearts, or has he kind of lost his place in the Glendale girls affections. I don't hear you speak of him. What are the girls doing about school, Althea tells me she is going to Miss Kendricks, that's fine.[12] I can feel for Bobby entering the University, and I hope she makes the Tri Delts.[13] Tell her to give all the Tri Delts my best. What has happened in Glendale? Anybody dead? Anybody born, etc? Well I have about exhausted my supply of news, etc. I think I'll take a bath tomorrow if I can get off long enough. I will enclose a little note for Aunt Virginia and Uncle Russ, please give it to them.

Well give everybody my best and remember I am well, happy and all that as you can see after reading this. We didn't go to London, only stayed in England two and a half days and traveled all the time. Glad you are keeping Grace [?] and paying her out of my salary. Give her my best and tell her there are no colored people over here. Congratulate Elizabeth Brown for me please. There were passengers and troops on our boat. There is no Church to go to here. We are nine miles out of town. There will be a Y.M.C.A. here soon. I just went thru your letter and answered your questions as well as I could considering. I will also enclose a letter for the fellows in "Battery E", if you will send it to them I will be much obliged.

Hoping to hear from you soon again, I am always,

Your loving son,
Roland.

＊   ＊   ＊

Somewhere in France,
Sept. 22, 1917.

Dearest Mother:

Just to prove that I can work a typewriter I am typing this letter, anyway I have something very important to tell you. This construction job is going to peter out in a bunch of contracts, that is the heads of the construction department have found that it is impossible for us to do the work with what little men we have and we can't be spared any more for this kind of work. That means that we either loose [sic] our jobs or be inspectors, which naturally does not appeal to me, as it would mean more or less sitting around and doing nothing. So, now that everything is explained I will tell you what I am going to do, for I don't want to get left in the learch [*sic*] when I really could be supporting the cause to much better advantage. In short I am going to fly. I put in an application today to be transferred into the flying corps and believe me I can't wait until I start. To tell the truth I havn't been doing any real good here, simply because I havn't had any experience in construction itself and the electrical end of the job is contracted for. Don't think that I have been wasting time here, but I have just about reached my limit on this job, and my only chance to rise is to be a real flier. I have seen so much flying that I am crazy about it, and want to do some myself. I have talked it all over with our commanding officer, Major [Lawrence] Churchill, who by the way is a peach, and also with Capt. Huntington, and the application will have to go thru Capt. Lyster's office, which is at _____, not here, (by the way Capt. Lyster is a Major now). I will also see him tomorrow and have a talk with him.

For goodness sake don't get scared now and think all kind of things, for flying is really the chief thing in this war, and I want to be in it, it is too good a chance to let slip by. Just talk to Lt. Col. Lyster in Washington, D.C. and see what he says.

All our officers are practically going to do the same thing, really they are all getting tired of the job and all want to fly some. My application is probably a starter and I will wager that the rest do the same thing as soon as they can. It is not the job that is at fault, but the fact that the job isn't going to amount to anything for us for which we are all disappointed, but "c'est la guerre, qu'est que vous voulez." It is going to be fine I tell you and I will be one very disappointed guy if I get stuck in this undertaking as I nearly did in this construction business. You will understand I know that I want to be really in it and doing something with the rest of them, you won't find Lt. Roosevelt sticking around here any more than necessary. He made Col. Somebody in Paris promise to send him to the front as soon as anybody, and I don't want to stick here either.

Well I guess that covers everything I wanted to tell you and there isn't any news as I just wrote you the other night.

Please give my love to the girls and the family at large (for it is quite large when you think about it) and my best to my friends. Don't forget that Althea is included in "girls". Think of me as probably flying when you get this letter. Gosh it seems too good to be true.

Much love to you dear Mother and please consider my change as one to the good.

Ever your loving son,
Roland.

P.S. I rode a motorcycle without a side car today for the first time, and it went fine, tres facile n'est ce pas oui, oui, oui.

*   *   *

October 6, 1918

Dearest Mother:

It seems like a long time since I wrote you last. As yet my plans havn't been changed, and I have not started to fly, but expect to receive orders any day to that effect. Things are going along pretty smoothly, only last night it started to rain and get cold, and it hasn't let up since, and don't seem to want to, e'en then we worry not, for, as it were, we are in barracks with stones, yea a multitude of stones surround us.[14] You don't like that kind of talk do you? Well, I'll stop, being as it is you. I feel fine this evening, had a bath, shave and hair cut. Cost me 1.40 Fcs. but it was worth it. They have a bath house here and they sure give you a royal bath for the money. About two feet of hot water, and believe me, soaking in that removes the scales from 1904. I received three of your letters in a bunch the other day, and nine others besides. That is the way they come — all in a bunch.

I'll tell you again what I'd like when Uncle Ted comes over. My other letters might have gotten lost. My rubber boots, a good oiled slicker with Sou-wester hat, my kodak and film and ensignia, bars, crossed flags and U.S. R.s. I havn't received the jam as yet, but hope to any day. I did receive Althea's cookies, and they sure did hit the spot. Much encouragement along those lines. Don't send any shirts, send socks, if it don't bother you much to knit them. Never mind other kinds as I have plenty. You will get my pay for September and October. If you don't get it [in] due time, write to the Depot Quartermaster at Washington and remind him of it. Please pay all my debts and do what you think best with the rest, i.e. pay for things I am asking for. I bought a new very nice O.D. suit that I can use for a Sunday suit for $6.36, what do you think of that. I had it fitted and ribbon sewed on the sleeves for 7 fcs., and now have a perfectly good dress suit. I have opened an account with a branch of the Guaranty Trust Co. at Paris and have about 1400 Fcs. deposited to my credit. I have a folding check book and am right up to date. If you could only come over tomorrow, we would have a blow out and I'd treat you to a good feed. We have received some planes and things are beginning to look pretty good. We have a number of barracks up, and expect more troops soon. Well I can't tell you any more about that, or I may be Court Marshaled [sic]. We sure have a dandy bunch of men over here. The Assistant in charge of construction, namely, Lieut. G. S. Frank is a dandy and all the rest are the same, so, altogether we have a good time out here, miles out of any town. If you get any pictures that would interest me, send them — of you, the girls or some others; one of myself in uniform to put in my identification book. Merci. Give everybody my best and Althea and the girls my love, and keep lots for yourself. I think of you all often and wish I could show you around our little American town. Remember me to all the family, etc. Hope Bobby enjoys U.C. and the girls Miss Kendricks.

Much love from your son,
Roland.

*   *   *

October 13, 1917

Dearest Mother:

I have two letters of yours to answer and I want to thank you muchly for them. Well, I received the peanut brittle, the jam and name plates to sew on my clothes, and it sure was good of you to send it all. The candy is entirely too popular, and I am afraid won't last long, any way it certainly is good. I havn't tried the jam yet but will very soon. No word yet from my application, but am pulling all the necessary strings to have it go thru. I sure do want to fly.

I've had the best time these last three days and I want to tell you about it.

Thursday morning, right after breakfast, Capt. Huntington called me into the office and said he had a job for me. Here is just exactly all he told me.

"I want 1000 posts from 4-8 feet long and from 6-8 inches in diameter. There are some piled up along the road between _____ and _____." That was all. Well, _____ and _____ are about 75 miles from here.[15] It was a rush job and it was raining all kinds of things. Well, I put on my little brown sweater (my life saver) and my old rain coat and old leather gloves Q. M. gloves and found my goggles, borrowed 100 Fcs. for I was broke at the time, and went out to the motor cycle shed and told Lt. Roosevelt that I wanted a single motorcycle fixed up right away with tools, oil, gas, etc. Mud, you ought to have seen our camp that morning, and it is just the same now and ever will be. It was cold too any my heavy O.D. [olive drab] suit, sweater and raincoat were none too much. About 9 AM, after I had inspected the motorcycle myself (safety first), we all pronounced it O.K. and about four of us pushed it out onto the main highway and, I went off in a cloud of dust, or rather mud and rain. It was about 20 miles to the first town, and I thought I would freeze en route, but of course didn't. Then as I am not entirely wed to a single motorcycle, having heretofore driven a side car, it made it all the harder driving with wet numb hands. Sounds awful, doesn't it, but it sure was great. Being pretty well acquainted with the foreman, etc. at the factory at this first town, I stopped and got warmed up and dried off a bit. I left there about 10:30 AM and went on towards "la ville de Joan D'Arc."[16] Well by then it had stopped raining, and I took my hat off and it went much easier. It rained off and on until I arrived at a little town at 11:30 where I stopped to eat. I left there at 1 PM, after first making sure that I could get gas and oil from the military authorities when I came back. Well, it didn't rain any more and I arrived at said "ville" at 3, taking note of all the wood on the road. Then I turned around and came back and stopped by the first wood pile and saw mill on the road. I found the wood we needed and found I'd have to stay all night in the town, because the manufacturer would not be back until the morning.

Well, so I put up in the best hotel, no night clothes, tooth brush or anything. Had a fine supper and slept like a log. Next morning I saw the manufacturer, got his price and terms and got him to hold the wood for a week, which he promised to do. Then telephoned Capt. H. and told him. He told me to get his terms in black and white, and then come home when I could. More rain and mud. Well, I bummed around the town all morning, had my face shaved and hair brushed by the town barber, who by the way was a woman of about 35, and just before dinner located another wood merchant. After dinner, I went to see him and got his prices, terms, etc. then decided to come back, rain or shine, as it happened it rained. Well, I had to buy some gasoline and pay my bill, which money I will never see again and left about 2:30 PM. I asked once more about wood en route, but got no satisfaction, so went on. My motorcycle was a great curiosity to the peasants and they all came out to gaze upon me, and of course I went as fast as I dared when they did, went slow on the country roads and fast through the towns, the temptation was too great I'm afraid. Well, I couldn't wear my hat of course for the wind and rain were too strong, so I had to stick it inside my raincoat, which I had tied around my legs. The rain hitting my face felt like so many pins sticking me, fine stuff. I then arrived at the town where I had arranged to get gasoline, so after making two round trips from the station to the military headquarters, this by the way is a distinct French method of giving you directions. Well, to make a long story short, I finally was very formally presented to the French Colonel, and I bet he sure thought I was crazy. Muddy from head to foot and wet all over. No hat on and goggles locked upon my forehead, my rain coat tied around my legs looked like bloomers. Well, he identified me, etc., and sent a man with me to get gas and oil. I signed up for it about four times, and everything being O.K., we went to look for the gasoline. The garage was empty and the Colonel's chauffeur had the key to the gasoline shed, and he was out riding. We hunted around and finally trailed the Chauffeur as he was going by and eventually got my gasoline and oil. Altogether it took me about one hour and 15 minutes to get about two gallons of gas and one pint of oil. Still it was raining. Well, I got on my old bike and left there about 6 AM. Out of the first town I hit coming, where I had warmed up, the old engine started to act up and only hit on one cylinder. Well, I knew what that was. The water had at last short circuited the ignition and one plug, nothing to do but go on into town on one cylinder. Still raining, I got to town about 4 PM, and went into the shop, where I went before and tried to fix my engine. Well, it wouldn't run, so I decided to stay all night, and let them fix it the next morning. So I did and had another night's sleep away from home. Next morning I got up and went up to the shop where I found my motorcycle running O.K. It had dried out. Well, it was still raining, so I tried to telephone Camp, and tell them if I wasn't there by noon today to come after me in a truck, but I couldn't get them and had to leave a message and let the engineers, who have a camp there, do it. I found out afterwards that they did all right. Well, it had stopped raining by then so I set out. She wouldn't go slow, so I let her out to about 50 or 55 miles per hour and had some ride. The wind at times nearly blew the machine and all off the road, but finally I arrived in sight of the old camp, running on two cylinders too, and believe me, I was glad to see it.

Well, to make a long story short again, I handed my report to Capt. H. and he gave me orders to order wood from both people, which I promptly did, and fixed everything up. I arrived about 11:30 AM I forgot to tell you.

Well, I guess I'll clean my teeth now. Thanks again for sending the candy and jam.

As ever your loving son,
Roland.

P.S. Wrote to Gramps.

*   *   *

October 21, 1917.

Dearest Mother:

Just a word to tell you that I have at last received my orders to train to fly. I am reporting to headquarters tomorrow, and will probably stay a few days here in Paris until I get my orders telling me where I will go to start training. I just arrived here this evening at 7 PM, and hope to leave soon, for naturally I am anxious to start my new work. I hated to leave down there, for I sure have some good friends there, but I will see them all again soon.

Give my love to all. I will write more later when I know where I am going.

As ever your son,
Roland.

Chapter Two

Flight Training at Tours

"...it is easier to keep straight than a motorcycle..."

October 26, 1917.

Dearest Mother:

Just a word to tell you where I am stationed. Same address for you as before though. Arrived here this noon, everything fine. Will start flying tomorrow. Fine N'est ce pas? Also I want to tell you that my pay will be increased now, so that my vouchers that I left at the Q.M. in Washington are no good, and I will write and tell them to destroy them. Anyway I'll deposit all my pay in the Guaranty Trust Company here in Paris and send you some off and on. You are entitled to my pay of September and October, so if you don't get it let me know about it. I had a good time in Paris and didn't spend much either. I was there four days and only took a taxi twice, when I arrived and left. I know the subways by heart, and I saw lots of the city at very little expense. My hotel bill only came to 51 Fcs. not bad eh?

Love to all,
Ever your loving son.

*   *   *

October 28, 1917.

Dearest Mother and Family:

Having a great time have been up in the air three times and took the control myself the second and third time. Of course my pilot was there, ready to correct me when anything went wrong. Here is the system: As I had never been up before, I was taken up by my pilot as a passenger the first time. We have a class of about seven officers and we all take turns going up with the same pilot. Well, of course the first time the pilot did all kinds of fancy stunts, standing on one ear, etc., and it was great. Then the next time my turn came, I got in and was told to take the control and start her off. Well, you can imagine that I was a little startled, it being my second trip. Well, we went up and of course I did a lot of things I shouldn't have done and my pilot of course corrected me. You have no idea how safe and stable you feel up there, it sure did surprise me, it is easier to keep straight than a motorcycle. I felt as if I would never make a flier the first time I steered, but got lots of encouragement the second time, not from my pilot so much as the way I felt myself, that was this morning. I would have gone up again, but the motor went on the bum, and our class had to stop. We have a lecture every evening at five and then go to bed early and get up early. It sure is fine. Hope we will go up this PM. If you havn't already sent my boots, don't do it, as I have a pair I got on a memo receipt from the Q.M.

I'll have to stop now and go to dinner. Give my love to the girls and Althea and all the family any my best wishes to all my friends. Will write soon again.

Your loving son,
Roland.

*   *   *

November 4, 1917.

Dearest Mother:

I just want to write and tell you that I am sending some money to you, $25.00 in all by draft on the Guaranty Trust Company of New York, via their Paris bank. The draft will be duplicates and sent by different mails, so you can be on the lookout for it. The money is to be spent for Christmas presents, as follows:

$5.00 for yourself and don't by [sic] goods to make dresses for the girls with it or anything else like that. I won't like it a bit if you don't spend it for and on yourself. $2.50 for each of the three girls. $5.00 for Althea and the rest $7.50 for the relations and friends as you see fit. I'll leave it to you to do the shopping, or giving the money around, just as you see fit. Don't think it is too extravagant, etc., just do it and forget about the expenses, etc. I'm a rich man you see I get flying pay now. I get about $224 a month, see. I am getting along fine and like flying very much. I got the banjo, it arrived in fine shape, and I am sure much obliged to you for sending it, I only wish that I really knew how to play it. We havn't flown for a day or two on account of the rain, but hope to fly soon again. That book "Flying for France" is fine and explains things right.[1] We have one of the Esquadrille [sic] men here with us as a teacher.

Well, I'll have to stop now. Please give my love to everybody, the girls, Althea and all my friends and keep lots and lots for yourself.

Your loving son,
Roland.

*   *   *

November 8, 1917.

Dearest Mother:

I have received two letters from you lately, the boots, Althea's' socks, i.e. two pairs, the book "Flying for France" and the box of candied orange peel, which sure is good and is quite popular. As you know I am not at [Issoudun] any more, but at [Tours] and am learning to fly. I like it immensely and am getting along as well as possible. The weather delays us a lot for it is pretty bad, either too rainy, cloudy, foggy or windy. Regarding our comfort here, we live very well and have all we want to eat and could wish for nothing better under the circumstances. I couldn't tell you the contrary, even if it were so, for it is against censor regulations, but nevertheless, it is true we eat very well, but additions from home are very much to be desired even so, but don't under any circumstances stint yourselves to give me something. Remember I can afford to live even better than you, and officers as a rule always do live well. I have sent you a draft on the Guaranty Trust Company of New York for $25.00 for Christmas presents. Comme la $5.00 for yourself and really and truly something for your own self, $5.00 for Althea, and get something nice, or give her the money, just as you choose, $2.50 for each of the three girls, and $7.50 for the rest of the relations and friends, do as you think best about that. So far I think I have gotten everything you sent, except papers and they will be here soon. Don't be discouraged just send right along and U.S. will take care of it, there has been very little mail lost. I will send you some snap shots soon. You ought to see the cute little aviation cap I have, it is pointed at both ends, and has a kind of rounded edge on top, you kind of sit it on the side of your head, it looks quite "cockie", like the English aviators. I also got the banjo, but can't do very much with it sorry to say.

It is too bad about the Cincinnati B.H.U. not being called this winter, and I can imagine how they feel.[2] I wrote to Gramps quite awhile ago but will do it again, to make sure.

As to recreation, there is no Y.M.C.A. here, and even if there were one it would be for the men and not for the officers. We go down town to see movies in the evening or write letters in the Officer's Club, or sit and talk. Anyway don't worry about that, as I can get along on very little amusements in the evening after a day's flying, which, believe me, gives you enough amusement to last a week. It sure is great sport, and I shall never regret my change as yet. I don't know what you think about my getting transferred, but don't worry whatever you do. Good news about M. V A C K all right n'est ce pas?[3] Another thing you will have to get over and that is this notion about coming over seas.[4] Mother dear you have your hands full and running over at home, and take my word for it, you can do a thousand times more good at home than here. . . . I think it is all right to talk about, but just think it over *once*, and you will see how foolish and useless it is. Really that's so, I've been to Y.M.C.A. Camp, etc. and it is no place for women, about the best they could do with you is to have you cook or serve quick lunches for the soldiers, now how would you like that? And you have a family of three girls to take care of. If you come over I'll send you right back, so don't think about it, just take my advice for once, I havn't been here nearly four months for nothing, and I have a little sense. Don't think I am trying to be cross with you but really Mother the idea is so absurd that I could hardly believe my eyes when you expressed yourself. You tell Althea for me that she sure is a peach, just think of all she has done for me and then tell her what you think best. If I was home I'd tell her all right and surprise you all. You don't know your little boy since he is an officer in the U.S. Army. He thinks he is some cheese all right. We have some awfully nice officers here, and we are all Lieutenants, nothing more nor less, even the C.O. is a Lieutenant U.S.R. too. So we all tell each other where to get off, and don't give a hoot for anybody. I sure will be glad to hear from Uncle Ted and then to see him. Gee, he ought to be over in a week or so now. Well it is 8 or 9 PM, so I guess I'll go to bed (and eat some orange peel). Please give my love to the family and Althea, and my best to all my friends and keep lots and lots of love for your self.

Your devoted son,
Roland.

*　　　*　　　*

November 15, 1917

Dearest Mother:

I have no more news to tell you, it is all in Coombsie's letter. I just wrote to tell you that I took out $10,000 worth of life insurance the other day under the new law, War Risk Insurance. You probably already know that $10,000 is the limit, or I would have taken out $20,000. The premiums are ridiculously low, $6.50 per month, too good a claim to let go by. I am worth more dead than alive now, but I'll *try* and live a little longer. Asern! Anyway I just wanted to tell you for it is written out in your name. Nuf ced on that subject.

We are going along as best we can now. Am feeling fine, never felt better in my life. Coombsie has my new address. Much love to you

Your devoted son,
Roland.

*　　　*　　　*

November 18, 1917.

Dearest Mother:

I sure was glad to get your letter of October 22nd. I also received two bundles of papers, in one was that S.E.P. comes "for decoration", which is now up on my wall.[5] Thanks much for the same. Am glad to hear you are all well and happy. There is not much news to tell from this side. We just go along as usual and fly whenever the weather permits, which is none too often. I went up this morning for a short trip, but it grew foggy, and we came down. I may go up after dinner. When we don't fly here there is absolutely nothing to do, but read, write and eat. We are situated just outside the town where the Resors spent the winter . . . .

I would like very much to give something to the Red Cross, but I am at rock bottom just now, and will be until I get my next pay, you see I have been living three months on one month's pay, and living is higher than at [Issoudun], but soon I'll get more pay, I hope, then I'll give whatever I can. Now that I have annulled my pay vouchers left in Washington, I'll have it all over here, but will send you some whenever possible. I hope you got the $25, I've had word that the draft has been sent you and 144 Fcs has been deducted from my account. I would have sent more, but just now havn't it.

Please don't give all you have Mother and make it uncomfortable to any great extent for yourselves, for remember we must give in proportion

Lt. R. W. Richardson just before leaving home for active duty in France, July 1917.

(Richardson had light brown hair, stood about 5 feet-8 inches, and weighed around 140 pounds.)

Althea Ford and Annis W. Richardson, ca. 1918.

Richardson and Sisters Adelaide and Annis, July 1917.

Richardson and Sister Emily, July 1917.

Richardson visiting the Normants (Quentin Roosevelt in center), 1917.

French Instructor (Monitor) at Tours, 1917.

Richardson prepared for Altitude Test, Tours, 1917.

Richardson by Caudron G-3, Tours, 1917.

*Richardson in Caudron G-3,
Tours, 1917.*

Richardson on "Crash
Wagon," Tours, 1917.

Richardson at Pilots'
Barracks, Issoudun,
1918.

Hangars at Issoudun, 1918.

Richardson (at fuselage) by Nieuport 27, Issoudun, 1918.

Richardson in Nieuport 24, Issoudun, 1918.

Richardson in Nieuport 24, Issoudun, 1918.

Lineup of Nieuport 27s, Cazaux, 1918.

to what we have, and you are somewhat inclined to let your emotions get the best of you and give too much to Charitable Organizations. Let me tell you right here the Red Cross is doing things over here that is not at all in its scope. Serving quick lunches, running canteens, etc. are not to my mind or to many officers' minds Red Cross work. They are at swords points with the Y.M.C.A. all the time. It seems that they have so much money that they are trying to overrun the Y.M.C.A. Regimental Canteen and everything.[6] The trouble is you only hear one side of the question, whereas, we over here, get the whole thing, and it is clearly evident that the Red Cross is trying to do things entirely out of its scope. Its all right to give, but don't give too freely and suffer for it afterwards. I am not trying to bawl you out Mother, but think it over. The Red Cross has by now over $100,000,000 and the Y.M.C.A. about as much. Now if they would keep on their own side of the fence and not step all over each other's toes every chance they get, they could both do wonders. Get me? . . . Please don't try and come over here, as I said in my last letter your place to do the most good is HOME, and not here.

I havn't met a soul that I knew in the States yet but expect to any day. Uncle Ted ought to be due soon. I sure will be glad to see him. Thanks for giving him my kodak and some films.

My new address is —

U.S. Air Service
Via New York. A.E.F. Paris, France.

I sure hope Bobby makes Tri Delta, she probably has by now. Please give my love to the family, Althea and my very best to all my friends and keep lots and lots of love for yourself.

Your ever devoted son,
Roland.

*   *   *

November 23, 1917.

My very dearest Mother:

I have just received some very good news. Yesterday after making about six landings and doing about 30 minutes flying, my instructor told me that one more day's flying and I would be "loched" — get that? That means that I'll begin to fly myself. I only hope that I won't break up any machines, as some of the "hoppers" have done. A "hopper" is a student that is just taking his first flight. I feel very confident and always sure. You have no idea how safe you feel in one of these machines it really is remarkable. I made all six landings yesterday by myself, and the fifth one was a peach; the others were good, in fact none of them were dangerous at all. Now I'll stop talking about myself.

Uncle Ted is here, at least so several people have told me. Naturally he is very busy and hasn't gotten around to give us any of his time yet, but I expect to hear from him most any time now. I do hope I shall see him, but I am afraid he will have to come to see me, as I can't get an order to go to Paris until I have finished my training here. The weather is rotten here today and we were doing no flying at all. Yesterday I drove the machine home from the flying field to the school field, and we went "hunting" as they call it; this consists of flying along then swooping down on a field that has grass and weeds on it and running down any quail that fly up, oftentimes you get a whole covey that way. We didn't get any souvenirs, but just missed a flock of them. This is pretty dangerous sport, as you fly only a few feet off the ground. Don't get scared now Ma, as the instructor had the stick, ready to correct any mistake I might make, and he was the one that wanted to go hunting, not I, nor will I very soon. On the trip just before me they landed out in a field and while landing a flock quail flew right up into the machine and they stopped and recovered about 1 and three quarters birds. The propellor must have hit one and cut him in three and one fourth parts. This sounds horribly cruel, doesn't it, but it is all in the game.

I was officer of the day the other day and had a grand time. The only man that ranked me that day was . . . the Commanding Officer. I mounted the guard and gave them all h_____ excuse my language please, but that is the best way to express it.

Enclosed find a photograph of yours truly all dressed up in flying costume, that union suit effect is a "Combination" and is made of fur lined raincoat material, and believe me it is sure warm. You can just see the rudders and elevators of a machine to one side. I received two letters from Gramps and answered three yesterday. Am so glad he has heard from me. Please send the other photo to him, as I didn't get them until this morning. Have not received the slicker as yet, but hope to soon, in fact I havn't received any mail to speak of for a few days. Never mind sending any sugar, it really isn't worth while, as we have all we want at mess and don't need it. Send anything else you want though that won't bother you too much. Have just ordered a suit. I am the only Officer here that has to wear O.D. and I'm going to look decent from now on. Love to all the family, the girls and Althea and best wishes to all my friends. Merry Christmas to you all and a Happy New Year. Lots of love to yourself Mother from your devoted son,

> Roland.
> November 24, 1917.

PS. Just received the package from you with my kodak films, insignia, hat cord and chocolate for which I thank you more than I can tell. The insignia especially is much to be desired. I had expected Uncle Ted to give them to me as I remember you said he was to bring them over with him. As yet I have not heard from him. I wrote him about two days ago, telling him where I am, so expect to hear from him soon. Am not "loched" yet. Made four more good landings yesterday PM.

Everything is O.K. Thank you a 100,000,000 times for the package. Love to all.

PS No. 2.

Just came in from 1 PM flight in the air. About a 40 mile wind was blowing and believe me it was some job keeping the old buss steady. Made three good landings and my pilot told me that after one more flight I would be "loched" — great stuff eh! When I returned to quarters I found a letter from Uncle Ted telling me that you were all well and that he hoped to see me soon. If I keep on holding his letter, you will never get it, naturally, but something has happened just before mail time right along now.

Well, love to all the folks and best wishes to all.

R.

*　　　*　　　*

November 28, 1917.

Dearest Mother:

I know you will be glad to hear this good news and believe me, I am glad to be able to write it to you. I made my "hop" this morning and my first real solo flight this afternoon, all this alone, mind you, and it all went off to perfection, both good landings and no trouble at all whatsoever.

The "hop" was most exciting, you get into a strange machine with a strange motor and they set the throttle and tell you to cut off the motor and you come down as you "pique" (I suppose you understand all these terms). "Pique" means to nose the motor down. Well, they started the motor and gave the signal and off I went. I went up one hundred feet about and then cut and piqued and landed very well. Caught the motor and taxied back to the starting place for the next hopper. This PM I was the last one up and it was getting pretty dark, but they let me go anyway. The start was the same as the hop and instead of just keeping a straight line I went up over the [field] (as directed) and made a wide circle, coming down where I went up and in the same direction in all about five minutes in the air, came down and made a dandy landing, caught the motor before it stopped and taxied the machine up to the [hangar] all O.K. It sure is great stuff. The real fun and pleasure of flying is just beginning now for me and I am crazy about it. To be the one and only master of an airplane and sailing around thru space all by yourself is great. These machines work fine and are very sensitive, which makes handling them a dream. Well, there you are, I am a real aviator now and feel confident of becoming a good one. Havn't seen Uncle Ted yet but hope to soon. I think I'll loop the loop tomorrow or do something like that. It ought to be great sport, Ha, Ha. Don' t worry old top I won't do anything rash. Please give my love to the family and Althea and my best to all my friends.

Your loving son,
Roland.

*   *   *

December 3, 1917.

Dearest Mother:

Well, I've been waiting for something exciting to happen before I wrote you, but nothing unusual has happened. You know of course by now that I am flying alone, and have been for several days. Have made 15 landings and trips alone and havn't even broken a wire (knock wood). Well, this PM as I was going up for my sixteenth tour de porte, I had a funny thing happen to me. I got all set, goggles and gloves on and gave the signal to let her go. I cut the motor once to test the switch then off I went, and just as I was leaving the ground I heard an awful bang! The whole machine jarred so, I stopped the engine and taxied back to where I'd started, and found that my propellor had struck a rock or something and had the end knocked off of it. I sure am glad I stopped instead of going on as I might have done. Of course that little accident wasn't my fault and the propellor can be easily repaired. The other two officers in my class have both broken a machine; one of them turned turtle and then in another trip ran into a machine on the ground. The other climbed too fast, lost speed and came down in a wingslip. Well, I suppose my turn is next, but I'm not the least bit unconfident about my flying and feel that I have the machine always in perfect control. I'm not trying to boast, but it is simple enough, once you get the hang of it.

I received two letters from you and at last found out how you felt about my putting in an application about flying. Of course that is all ancient history now, but I sure was glad to hear that you felt the way you do about it. I shouldn't be surprised if I would be thru here by Christmas. We had a dandy Thanksgiving dinner, turkey and all, only they served the turkey as pie and didn't roast it. We didn't have any cranberry sauce, but the old bird tasted very good all the same.

Just to change the subject, I was as sick as four dogs last night, and got up about 3 AM and tore out to the _____ and wow! I lost my lunch in great style and incidentally nearly froze to death, as last night was the coldest night we have had so far. It sure was cold this AM when I took my two flights too. My face was nearly a block of ice when I came down, but don't worry because I was dressed plenty warm enough and enjoyed it immensely. Its a great life all right. I suppose I'll go down to the place where I was just stationed when I finish here and get my viewport training, acrobatics, etc.

Havn't seen Uncle Ted yet, but expect to anyday now. I havn't gotten my suit yet, but will soon and when I do, I will just about outshine them all around here.

I told you in another letter that I had taken out $10,000 worth of War Risk Insurance lately at $6.50 a month premium, ridiculously low when you come to think about it. By the way does my present $1000 worth of insurance become invalid when I enter the Service, or when I take my first flight in plane, see if it does, will you please? Jerry Barnes is here, he was assistant physical instructor at the U.C. last year, and went over in May and joined the American Ambulance Service, well, he is down here now and I sure was glad to see him. I guess that is about all the news there is. Please give my love to all the family and Althea and my very best to all my friends. These photos you can pass around to anybody that wants them, they are more of a curiosity than anything else, the clothes, etc. Received the jar of haw apple jam too, but havn't eaten it yet, am trying to get some bread to eat it on. Thanks very much for it Mother, you sure are a peach. The pajamas were very welcome and I wear them now.

Lots and lots of love from your devoted son,

Roland.

*　　　　*　　　　*

December 13, 1917.

My dearest Mother:

Lots of good things going on now. The latest is that Uncle Ted arrives here tomorrow, won't that be great though. Gee but I'll be glad to see him. I have just gotten out of quarters when I have been confined by the doctor on account of a sore throat that I contracted on the field. It was a humdinger too, but all's well now. Luckily I roomed then with a doctor, so I got all kinds of care etc. I flew again today for the first time in four days, and guess what happened? Well, I am now in the spiral class and the instructor told me, or rather asked me if I'd take the machine back to the school, the spiral field being about two miles away from the school. Well, after we were thru flying for the day, I jumped in and went off in a cloud of mud, for the wheels threw mud all over the machine. Well, all went well, in fact very well until I reached the school, sailing about 750 feet high then in order to land on the big field, one has to find in which direction the (T) points to get the wind direction and so as not to cross in front of other landing machines. Well, there were a bunch of students standing, sitting and lying on this (T), so I couldn't see it, so I circled around and tried to get a crack at it, but of no use, just then however, a double control machine glided in and landed. Well that gave me my direction, so I maneuvered into position, cut my motor and piqued, steered clear of all the machines in sight, made a perfect landing, but knocked a flag pole down. These flag poles, two in all, designate the line from which the double control machines start. I didn't see it as it was getting rather dark and I was looking out for other machines. I only hit it with the tip of my wing, but that was enough to break a rib and punch a hole in the wing. Nothing serious, in fact it is not even worth mentioning, but I havn't broken even a wire so far and I wanted to go through the course with a good reputation, but now I have to admit that I really broke part of a machine. The landing and all was great but "c'est la guerre", you have read that little expression no doubt. Well it has grown to be the national hymn over here, they use it for everything.

I am nearly thru my training here and am waiting to consult Uncle Ted to what branch of the Service I'd better go into. All I have to do now is make my spiral and hairpin turn, which is a cinch, then my altitude which is a bore and my voyages, or cross country trips which are very interesting. So you see you'll soon have a full fledged aviator in the family wearing two little silver wings on his breast and generally making himself a nuisance. I ate the haw apple jelley, and believe me it was sure good. Well Mother, I'm getting all your letters and sure do look forward to them, but there is a holdup somewhere in the packages. I've sent 30 Christmas cards to all in the family, relations, friends, etc. I hope they will all reach their destination. . . . They may be late but better late than jamais. Please give my love to the family and Althea and remember me to my friends. Hope you all have a dandy Christmas and Holidays.

Your loving son,
Roland.

* * *

December 22, 1917.

Dearest Mother:

I just received your letter of November 12th, which as usual arrived about a week later than the one dated November 25th. We are getting so used to such things now that we just casually mention them. The mail system is not the best, but I suppose it is as good as can be under the circumstances.

It certainly was a shock to me to hear about Mrs. [Reba] Carruthers, my that must have been awful. Please tell Jim that I truly sympathize with him, poor fellow, it must have been an awful jar to him and to Mr. [Thomas] Carruthers too.

I'm nearly thru my [Brevet] now. Finished my hairpin turn and spiral the same day and have had bad weather ever since until today. This morning after I relieved the old officer of the day (O.D.), me being the O.D. today, I asked the pilot if I could do my altitude, i.e. stay up 2500 meters for hr. 15 m. It was very windy and a little foggy and below zero, well I wanted to try it and so he said O.K. I went down and had the Sg't pick me out a good [machine] and time it up and I went up to quarters and dressed. I wore underclothes, a suit, two sweaters, a newspaper on chest and back, pants, leather coat, muffler, 3 pr. socks, slippers and a big pair of lined shoes, a fur lined Teddy bear suit, 3 helmets, two wool and one fur lined, goggles, wristlets, and two pair of gloves. Well, I went down and got it, tried the engine an 80 h.p. Le Rhone motor, installed the recording barometer and went off, got a good start, but the wind was awful. I don't suppose I traveled five miles an hour against the wind and about 150 mile an hour with it. Well, I went up to about 2000 meters in 30 minutes and then the fog got so thick that I had to come down. Of course I was way up above the clouds but I was afraid of getting lost, so I spiralled down and made a good landing, but stalled the engine. A mechanic came out and started me again and I taxied back to the hangar. One of the Monitors was the only one up besides me today and it sure was windy too. Well it didn't count so I'll have to do it over again, maybe tomorrow morning. We are going to shut up the school tomorrow noon and not open up until the 26th, so another Lieut. and myself have planned a walking trip to the _____ District down to _____ by way of Langais, maybe you remember _____. I'll write you about it when we get back. I've just spent about $125 for clothes lately and have a dandy suit, 2 pair of pants and had another pair of pants made for a coat I have, incidentally I grew out of the pants that belong to the coat.

I had a dandy visit with Uncle Ted and after getting his point of view, I think I'll go into the wireless and observation branch of the Service, it looks pretty good to me . . . I am going to answer Bobby and Althea very soon, but I owed you a letter for the longest time. I received a dandy letter from both Bobby and Althea.

I just received a package from Aunt Angie and the Dansons. I'm going to thank them soon. Everything is fine here, we keep warm and well. I feel fine now and my sore throat is gone.

We have a Y.M.C.A. here and the men are all crazy about it. Bishop [Charles H.] Brent spoke to us the other evening. Well good bye for the present and lots and lots of good luck. received my order for flying pay.

Ever
Roland.

*   *   *

December 29, 1917.

Dearest Mother:

Well, I just received your letter of November 19th about a week after the one dated December 3rd. How's that for speed, etc. I am glad you know I'm flying by now, and I hope you received my cablegram, telling you that I'd been flying alone for over a week. I wrote a letter to Althea telling of the experiences of a friend and myself during the two days leave we received for Christmas. We didn't want to go to Paris, so you get Althea to read that part to you. I asked her if she would. Well I'm still flying and in about 20 minutes I'm going to get on my togs and do the rest of my altitude test, which consists of climbing to over 2000 meters and staying there for over 10 minutes. I did the first half, i.e. the same thing about three days ago, and believe me it was some cold. I had a bum machine and she wouldn't climb at all, so it took me 20 minutes to get up to 1500 m. and clear up to 1200 m. It was so bumpy that it was all I could do to keep the old buss on an even keel. Well at 13-1500 m. I had to go thru a cloud, which was quite exciting, as I couldn't tell where I was, nor just what the machine was doing. Well, after that it was easy climbing up to 2400 meters and cold as the North Pole. I nearly froze my face, and had to wiggle my mouth, nose and cheeks to keep them from hardening. They still feel funny. Well, after staying at 2400 m. for about 15 minutes, my motor started to miss and act funny, and I found that the oil had frozen in the pipes, also it was getting so cloudy that I couldn't see where I was, and I started her off and nosed her down. Just before going thru the clouds I tried the motor, all O.K., so I plunged into them, a great big black one and in about 20 minutes (it seemed) I emerged on the earth side at about 1000 m. turned over the motor and nothing doing. Well from 1000 m. to 600 m. that motor wouldn't catch, and I was getting a little nervous and looking down for a landing place for I was about 4 k.m. from camp and at 600 m. she started and just did bring me around to Camp, in fact when I started to land I was only 50 m. high, pretty close, but my old motor stuck to it. Of course I could have hit camp from 2400 m. thru the clouds, in fact I am going to do that today, as it [is] clear as crystal, but cold as both the North and South Poles together.

That picture of Quentin Roosevelt, is not Q. Roosevelt, but somebody else, or else I am blind in one eye and can't see out of the other. I am sending it back to you, for the machine is exactly the kind I am going up in this P.M. and the kind which I have trained in.

I have had a friend take my picture in my altitude togs and in my machine just before I went up that day and I will send you some soon. They are the first pictures I've taken with my kodak. I just heard that

Uncle Ted wants me to come up over New Years i.e. to Paris where he is sick in bed with a cold. I hope I can get permission to go.

I'm glad to hear that Glendale is doing so well and showing so much spirit in voluntary service. I guess I am the youngest officer in camp and don't have any special aptitude for running a machine, except I havn't broken anything in landing, which isn't so bad either.

Well goodbye my twenty minutes are up and I'm going to leave the country. Take good care of Althea and the girls for me and give them my love. Remember me to all my friends and love to all the family. Lots and lots of love to yourself and thanks ever so much for your nice letter.

Your loving son,
Roland.

Jan. 1, 1918   Big Holliday. Otherwise not much doing, went out after Supper to M. Berger's and had eats, etc.

Wednesday 2   No flying, bad weather. Nothing doing.

Jan. 3, 1918   Flew to Pontlevoy today on Brevet test voyage. Arrived OK & landed in a snowstorm. Hell of a mess, left after dinner in good weather. Got home OK. Student [Frank Elmer] Starret was killed today. Tried for altitude, plug missed came down.

Friday 4   Flew triangle Chateaudun Pontlevoy Tours. Made it in 2 h. 50 m. Went up 2500 m. Made it OK, no trouble. Pretty cold at 2500 m. but was well dressed up & didn't mind, machine rather stiff but good engine, 2995.

January 4, 1918.

Dearest Mother and family:

Well, I received both the packages and believe me they were fine. I can't begin to thank you all for them, and really I don't deserve all of it either. I was ashamed to look at it all, there were so many good things. I sure think you are a good chooser, because there isn't an article amongst them that isn't useable to the last particle. I received a total of 17 bundles from nearly all the family and many more besides, and I am sure that I don't deserve it all. It is too much for one person. Everything arrived in fine shape, including Aunt Va's [Virginia Richardson] jar of pickle, which is the real stuff. I am thanking people by degrees and you and the Fords are all I can manage tonight, because I'm dead tired, made about a

150 miles flight today in 2 hrs. and 50 minutes in the air and it [was] very tiring. This was my triangle I will make another tomorrow if the good weather holds out. This makes my second voyage, as I made one yesterday and had a dickens of a time, but got back O.K. and same today only had beautiful weather all around. I flew most of the time at 2500 meters, not knowing it however for my altimeter was off and only registered 1400 m. but the recording boragraph registered 2500 m. Pretty high, but is great sport. I left at 9:45 A.M. and headed right with the wind, using the map and compass and arrived at the first station at 11:05 A.M. Left at 11:25 A.M. after filling up on gasoline and arrived at the second station, same system at 12:15 P.M. had lunch and left at 2:30 P.M. and arrived back here at 3:15 P.M. After one more triangle and another small trip and 10 min. above 2000 m. I'm a full fledged pilot and wear the silver wings which you have seen no doubt. Uncle Ted is up and around again. Was glad to hear it. Am going to send you all and Althea something by him if he will have room for it. Althea's gloves saved my life. Had everything but good gloves. I'm all O.K. Please give my love to everybody in the family and all my friends. Thank you all again for the boxes. Yours as ever Roland.

Jan. 5, 1918   Flew 2nd Triangle. Pontlevoy, Chateaudun, Tours, arrived P. ok. Changed plugs & made altitude flight. P & C 2800 m. Stayed above 2000 m. for 1.10 arrived home ok no trouble. Some boat 2995. Broke collar bone falling from motorcycle tonight. S. O. L.[7]

Sunday 6   Would have finished up today if it hadn't been for my - - - - collar bone which rather annoyed me today. Stayed in bed.

Jan. 7, 1918   Collarbone still be on the bum. Got up today, otherwise OK.

Tuesday 8   Collarbone still on bum.

Jan. 9, 1918   Had an x-ray of it taken today. All OK. Still hurts a little.

Thursday 10   Was O.D. & Censor today. Shoulder better.

Jan. 11, 1918   No flying. Shoulder better. Don't think I'll fly for awhile yet.

Saturday 12   Shoulder better, will fly Tuesday I think. Order out by C.O., no flying till further notice.

Jan. 13, 1918   Shoulder better, went down to M. Berger's tonight, had a good time. Came out in car 10:00 P.M.

January 13, 1918.

My dearest Mother:

I received your letter of December 9th and was very glad to get it. So the old parties still thrive on Sunday evening. Well that's fine, only I can imagine there aren't as many visitors as before "la guerre". It is too bad you all had another gas shortage, I should have thought that the Gas Company would have arranged for that after what happened last winter.

I also received your cablegrams — one from Annis W. Richardson and one from [?] Richardson, did you send them both? Also one from Mrs. [Jean] Procter, which was very thoughtful of her. In my letter to Althea yesterday, I told her to read the part about my cross country trip to you, so you can see her about it, also about me busting my collar bone. Now don't worry, for its all right now and only a little sore, but it made me sore to have to loose [sic] a week's flying when one more small trip would have finished me up. I am a little undecided as to what I'll do when I leave here. I wanted to take the wireless as well as the aerial gunnery course, but I hear that there is a demand for fliers on the front, so I don't think I ought to be a slacker behind the lines any more than necessary, anyway I'll have a talk with our Major in charge of the school and see what he thinks, also with Uncle Ted if I can ever get a hold of him again.

By the way, have you ever paid Aunt Gertrude [Richardson] the $150 I owed her. You said you paid Tanta and Uncle Ted before you bought the bonds and the French orphan, but you didn't say anything about Aunt G.[8] I hope you paid her before buying those other things. Please send me my orphan's address. I may have a chance to see him or her over here. Also I'm going to send you some more money this month. Would have done so sooner, but my pay voucher came back because I misplaced a comma somewhere. I fixed it up and sent it back yesterday, so my check is soon forthcoming. Use what you need and don't be stingy on yourselves. Do with it what you think best, only don't spend it all on Red Cross, for there are lots of other things more worthy of our money than it. That may sound funny to you but I know what the Red Cross is doing, and you only know what they are saying, and there are reasons why I think that our money can be spent to a better advantage elsewhere. Also some of the people the Red Cross send over here have foolishly invested money that you and the rest of us gave them to be spent wisely. It may turn out all right and I hope it does, but just now it does not look so good. However, I'll agree on Liberty Bonds, buy me some more if there is any money left. Another thing Mother, how about the people right at home. I know you have always looked after them, the unfortunate ones, well I would wager that some of them need more attention than the "Boys in France". How does Mrs. [Elizabeth] Ford get along, is she comfortably fixed? Please answer me these questions and give me an idea of what you need from my salary, which is entirely too much for me to use up.

It certainly is fine to hear how the Glendale people are going into army work, and you bet it helps a lot over here to hear how well we are being backed up at home. I hope to see George Thompson some day and also the rest of the Glendale crowd in service, but as yet have seen none of them. We are very well situated here and very comfortable, only we have nothing to do when the weather is bad and it makes us feel like slackers to have you people write us such nice letters and send us such nice packages and boxes. However, we content ourselves by saying that we risk our lives everytime we get off the ground in a machine, and that's as far as it goes. Its a funny world for the very day that I spilled up against a tree out of a motor cycle and broke my collar bone, I had been flying in the air for 3 hrs. and 25 minutes, going up as high as 2800 meters and didn't even have a mishap, and then to take a ride in a motorcycle, the same one that was assigned to me at [Issoudun], on which I had ridden over 2000 miles, and spill the way we did, c'est la guerre, n'est ce pas? Well, I'll have to stop now. Please give my love to the family and my best to all my friends. Take good care of Althea now, I'm depending on you all, get me?

> Ever your loving son,
> Roland.

Monday 14   No flying on account of CO's order. Didn't do much of anything. Helped censor mail. Went up as a passenger in G4 [Caudron].

Jan. 15, 1918   No flying, bad weather. Helped censor mail. Showed some officers how to run a G4. Went up to retreat. Talked to Major [A. R.] Christie and told him that I wanted to get up on the line as soon as possible. Am going to Issoudun to get Nieuport training OK.

Wednesday 16   No flying, bad weather. Cleared up at 4:00 P.M. Was assigned a barrack to take care of today. Went down town tonight. Will probably fly tomorrow.

Jan. 17, 1918   No flying — — too muddy. Nothing much happened today. Still slacking around. Was censor today, some job. A Nieuport landed this evening in the dark. Pilot was not hurt. Lucky.

Friday 18   No flying — — too windy. Was appointed Asst. Transportation Officer. Am in charge of all transportation as my Capt. has supply & has turned Tran. over to me. Busy all day. Getting things in order & installing new system.

Jan. 19, 1918   NO FLYING. Worked all day on Transportation and tried to keep things moving. Have a motorcycle assigned to me. Went to town this evening, had my overcoat tried on, but couldn't get a bath.

Sunday 20   NO FLYING. Getting the Transportation Dept in order. Things are running better today. Have about 33 machines in my dept, 12 motorcycles, 3 machines & 18 trucks. Went out calling this evening. Came back on the 10:00 PM car.

Jan. 21, 1918   Voyages class & altitude flew this P.M. not me. Transportation is coming around fine now, am getting bawled out by most everybody & bawling out everybody else myself so all runs smoothly. C'est la guerre.

Tuesday 22   Flew to Vendome this morning after giving orders to the Trans. Dept. Came back in the rain. Everything went all right and am finished as far as voyages are concerned but have 55 minutes to make up. I need a bath very bad.

January 22, 1918.

My dearest Mother:

I just receved your letter of December 16th acknowledging the cable I sent you. It didn't come much behind your cable either. Its hardly worth while sending cables either, but they help a little. Now I'll answer your questions. We really didn't have much in our lectures, just the fundamentals of the motor wings, tail and running of a plane, general hints, and how to travel with a map and compass, all was very simple and didn't amount to much. The system over here is to teach the students as little about the machine as possible, so they won't know how fragile they are, and consequently be more daring at the front. The man that lectured was an American in the French Army, detailed to aviation, and he is very good, only about 26 years old. Our pilots were Frenchmen when I was flying double control. I don't see Q. Roosevelt any more as, of course I am not at the same place he is and havn't been since I left back in October.

Now, please share this letter with Althea, so I won't need to repeat in her letter. I'll tell you what luck has come since I wrote you last. You know by now that I wanted to finish up all training right away and go to the front, as I was tired of laying around here. Well, I still do but as I havn't finished here, owing to bad weather here's what happened. The major gave me the job of assistant transportation officer under a Captain, who has another department and never bothers me at all, so I am practically free to run the department myself, and believe me it's running too. We have a bunch of trucks, motorcycles (of which I have one) this time its a Harley Davidson, and we have touring cars, busses, etc., quite a few in all, over thirty and its my job to keep them running and to keep everybody happy and satisfied and supplied with the necessary transportation. Its quite a job. I have a good sergeant, and corporal under me and one clerk, who is a stenographer, orderly and general office worker. Also I have an office, which I am getting all fixed up, typewriter and all. I'm just like a kid with a new toy. Can't you see me. Well, we are running along fine, sending trucks to Paris. Have one there now and three more tomorrow will leave for there. The man who had the job before me was a Captain, flying officer here and didn't evidently like the job and didn't have any system or anything, so I can start now from the bottom up. This is really a very important department as everything coming to and going from school is handled thru us, so you can see what we have on our hands.

By the way, my shoulder, collar bone, etc. are all O.K., it only bothers a little. My new motorcycle is a dandy brand new H. D. Its a little different from the Indian, so I took a few trips around camp with it first before I went out on the road.[9] Now to get away from my new job, and to something more exciting. I flew again today for the first time in three weeks, and believe me it was some little trip. I made my last cross country, and luckily made it without any trouble, was trouble enough in the air. To begin with I had my same old machines, and was therefore sure of getting a good motor, but before I had to use both hands on the stick to bank her up. Well, we turned the motor up and she registered 1100 R.P.M. on the tachometer. So I set out, but no sooner did I leave the ground than the tachometer stopped running, but as the motor ran O.K. I went on. Well it was pretty cloudy and I had about 30 miles to go so I climbed to about 1200 m. and sighted a storm ahead. I tried to go round it but it hit the compass and got rained on. Rain in an aeroplane is the most uncomfortable thing I know of, worse than snow, getting wet is the least of its discomfort, it is thrown back in your face by the propellor and feels like pins being stuck in you. Well, I finally passed it and landed at my stop in another storm (same kind). I had to taxi for quite a way, and as it was awfully muddy the wheels were throwing mud around and the propellor was picking it up and depositing it in my lap, face, etc. until I was plastered. Well, when I got out, I found that the propellor was broken, a big piece of mud had flown into it and split it open. I then managed to get a new one put on and went for some dinner. Before I left two serious accidents happened two machines collided in the air, killing both pilots and one machine fell killing both occupants.

Well, I left about 2 PM and got up about 1000 m. and hit another rain storm. This was on the way home. The wind was against me and it rained practically the whole time. Where it took me 30 min. to get there it took me one hour to get back and it [was] raining all the time. Gosh, but it was uncomfortable. When I finally arrived over our field, I wanted to kill time, I had some to make up before completing the 25 days necessary for the license. Well I spiralled around over camp banking way up and going this way — — — etc. which is quite a sensation, especially going up. Then it started to rain again, so I came down and landed finding I had about 1 hr to make up before I could get my license brevet or R.M. whatever you want to call it.[10] So there is where I now stand. Goodness knows when I'll ever get that behind me. The machine ran fine today and I didn't worry about anything, except the rain which was a little uncomfortable, but after all nothing to worry about. Well I'll have to stop now and go down to the garage and see if anybody has run off with any of the motorcycles. Enclosed find some pictures, these are the first I've taken. The ones of me all clothed up were taken just before I went up on an altitude, this was also my machine that day. Read labels on back of photos. My best to everybody and love to the family, the girls and Althea and lots of love to yourself.

> Your loving son,
> Roland.

Jan. 23, 1918   Flew this P.M. Made up my last 40 min. of time required in the Brevet Test. Finished with 25 hrs. 10 min. & 54 landings. It took 33 days of flying weather to do it. Transportation going fine. All OK. Uncle Ted came down today but didn't stay long.

Thursday 24   A new Squadron came in the 16th and I had to miss my breakfast to get trucks down town to meet them. Transportation went OK. Today we finished & sent out a Hudson car today. Put my wing on this evening. Went calling to our friends house this evening.

January 25, 1918   All OK. Transportation going along all right. Nothing new to say.

Saturday 26   Sent a truck to Nevers today. . . . All O.K. here.

Jan. 27, 1918   All O.K. Transportation dept. had a vacation this P.M. I took a motorcycle ride to Amboise this P.M. Got held up by a major for speeding.

Monday 28   Nothing new happened today. Trans. dept. went all right.

Jan. 29, 1918 . . . . . met our new CO today. A Maj. Green has me up on the carpet about our trucks etc. All OK.

Wednesday 30 All OK today. 2 of our trucks [and] . . . the Hudson came in this P.M. Went down town & had picture taken. Sent 1200 frc. to Paris Bank tonight.

Jan. 31, 1918 Did some D.L. [?] in G4 Caudron today. Made 5 trips all together. Everything went fine. . . .

Feb. 1 Nothing out of the ordinary happened today. All OK.

Feb. 2, 1918 All went OK today. Nothing happened out of the ordinary.

Sunday 3 Had truck inspection today. Watched fellow do stunts in a Nieuport at about 100 ft. off the field. Nothing much else happened today.

Feb. 4, 1918 Nothing much happened today. Took a bath. Everything is running OK in Transportation. Gt 2 trucks ready to go to Paris. Took my first ride in a car since being Asst. Trans. officer.

Tuesday 5 Went down town this AM. Trans. OK. Have a telephone in office. Went to Issoudun in Fiat. . . . Had 2 punctures & came in to camp on the rim. Sleeping in Hotel de France tonight & will leave tomorrow again.

Feb. 6, 1918 Met a lot of old friends also Walt Powers wife in Chateauroux Hospital. Had a fine time, left about 11:00 A.M. & arrived town 5:00 P.M. Had lunch en route & arrived without any mishaps. All went well. Altheas picture arrived certainly looks good too.

Chapter Three

Combat Training
at Issoudun and Cazaux

"... it is as easy as falling off a log..."

Feb. 8, 1918   Left for Paris this A.M. Arrived at noon. All O.K. Went out to the Hotel des Invalides & saw some war planes & trophies. Came home to Hotel. I bought a pair of leather boots went to a movie then came home & went to bed.

Saturday 9   Went down to station to go to Iss. but missed the train because of luggage difficulties. Went out & walked around the city, had dinner & caught the 2:35 train & arrived Iss. Ok. No rooms in town, went out to camp & slept with Dr. [E. Garnsey] Brownell.

Feb. 10, 1918   Reported & got all fixed up today. Have double bunk bed now. Some change from room at Tours. Went for a walk this P.M. Baggage arrived this evening.

Monday 11   Have not been assigned to a section yet but will be tomorrow. Did a little machine gun work this AM. Bummed around all P.M. Went to a boxing match at the Y.M.C.A. after supper.

Feb. 12, 1918   I have charge of my end of Barracks now & also am Section marcher of my section #38. My flying number is 449. Had motor & machine gun instruction this AM & Rouleurs this PM, was loched from Rouleurs.

On Active Service with the
AMERICAN EXPEDITIONARY FORCES
February 12, 1918.

Dearest Mother:

Am now back at [Issoudun] and have already started my training, it is very interesting work — machine gunnery and flying. I am the section leader of my section in all and also in charge of my end of our barracks, which are both regular thankless, rotten jobs, but they may give me some experience. I can't tell you how we are quartered but not as good as at [Tours] and the light is poor and writing conditions bad, so I can only write short letters. Received some more S. E. P's sent by you and other magazines. You needn't send me any more warm clothes as I have all I need. This letter will have to do for you and the girls as I have to cut down on my correspondence a lot. Its no job keeping up the correspondence I've started, especially under the present circumstances. Tell Bobby I am glad she had such a good time during the X'mas vacation and am glad she made the Tri Delta and likes U.C. Am also glad to hear that the girls like Miss Kendricks so well. Please give my love to all my friends. Explain to them that its very hard writing here so that they won't think I've forgotten them altogether. Went to Paris for day en route here. Am well and happy and feel really better than at [Tours].

Lots of love from your son,
Roland.

Wednesday 13   Had trap shooting and theorie [sic] of flight this PM, and nothing this morning, rained. Not much else going. We are treated like a lot of kids here, sure is hell.

February 14, 1918   Nothing doing this AM, rained. Had pistol instruction in PM & theorie [sic] of flight. Am not very good with pistol. Not much else going.

Friday 15   Cold today, other half of class finished Rouleurs today. Had pistol instruction and trap shooting this P.M. Some of us officers went over & shot 50 rounds at trap field this AM. I shot 8 of the 25 birds.

Feb. 16, 1918   Cold as Greenlands icy mts. all night & today. Had machine gun & trap shooting this morning and went out to do 23 D.C. [double-control] this P.M. but it was too bumpy for instruction.

Sunday 17   No flying or classes today, didn't do much. Reveille an hour later. Stayed home all evening.

Feb. 18, 1918   Had machine gun & trap shooting this morning. Got hell because I overslept & the whole barrack was late to reveille. This P.M. I had 6 tours de porte on [Nieuport] 23 [meter] DC it was fine & I sure do like it. Saw a boxing match this evening at Y.M.C.A.

Tuesday 19   Had trap shooting & machine gun this AM. I got 18 out of 25 birds & 9 out of 25. This PM had 3 trips on 23 DC, goes pretty good. Went to the Red Cross this evening after supper & saw the movies.

AMERICAN EXPEDITIONARY FORCES
February 19, 1918

Dearest Mother:

I just this minute finished reading your letter of January 12th, which arrived just now. I'm sorry to hear that you are having such cold weather home. Over here we are very comfortable and please don't worry. It really is a shame how we fellows are made heroes of over here by you people at home, when we really live like Kings, etc. We have good food, plenty of heat and clothes and everything we need, so you needn't worry about me at all. I'm fixed to stand the worst cold spell that could happen. We just had an issue of cigarettes, and as I am in charge of this barracks, I had to do the distributing. Believe me, it was a very exciting job. The fellows acted like a crowd of barbarians.

Have been flying here already and these machines are lots better and nicer to handle than the others. This PM in about 15 minutes, I will be out on the field waiting my turn again. I can't answer your questions, because the censor is getting stricter all the time. BUT for goodness sake don't worry about me. I'm as fat as a young pig. We get up and stand reveille at 5:30 AM now, how is that? Outside of that we have no right to be thought of as Martyrs by you people at home. Its getting to be a joke with us over here that "Our boys in France" stuff. Cables take nearly as long as letters here. My love to the family and Althea and all my friends. Think of me as tearing through the air this PM — great stuff.

> Your loving son,
> Roland.

Feb. 20, 1918   Had 2 trips 23 CC this morning, am loched to 23 Single. Had my picture taken for identification card. Sent pay voucher in. Had trap shooting & theorie [sic] of flight this P.M. Got 10 birds out of 25.

Thursday 21   Had armament, deflection & armament this morning. Didn't fly this P.M. because of wet weather. Rec'd mail and more socks today. Weather got better this evening, will probably fly tomorrow. Look out for the 23 DC.

Feb. 22, 1918   Had 2 classes in machine gun, Vickers and one class in deflection which isn't interesting at all. We didn't hop today because of bad weather. Went to a dance at the A.R.C. tonight and had a real good time.

Saturday 23   Went out to fly this morning but didn't because there were only 2 machines for 3 sections & they were smashed by 9:30 A.M. Had 2 machine gun classes & one deflection class this PM. Went to the movies at the Y.M.C.A. tonight.

Feb. 24, 1918   Had regular classes today all day, lots of machine gun, etc. but no flying. I nearly went to church today but finally didn't.

Monday 25   Still ground classes & no flying. This P.M. I went to the funeral of a student who was killed in a fall. I went to movie at A.R.C. tonight.

Feb. 26, 1918.   Still ground classes & no flying. We finally fired a Vickers and had stoppages [?] this morning. I'm still rotton [sic] in pistol practice.

Wednesday 27   Still ground classes, no flying, rotten weather. Had Vickers & pistol practice today.

Feb. 28, 1918   Had bombing and pistol practice today. This P.M. all classes were called off and we had regular monthly muster. After supper I went to the Y and saw the movies.

March 1, 1918 Had bombing, trap shooting and pistol practice to-day. This P.M. I was detailed as assistant O.D. rotton [*sic*] job, not much to do but I have to sleep at the guard house. Pas bon!

Saturday 2 Had ground classes all day but I was on guard, didn't go to town, it was a mean day, snowed & blew all day.

AMERICAN EXPEDITIONARY FORCE
March 2, 1918.

Dearest Mother:

I have just received three letters from you at a crack and believe me I sure was glad to hear from you. I received yours and Bobby's letter at the same time, telling me of, well you can guess what, and I was one of the most surprised people on the earth. I wrote to Bobby congratulating her an hour after I read her letter. Well, that's one of the biggest things that ever happened to our family. (Its nearly time for your famous dog face). I wrote a lot to Bobby and tried to give her some advice, but may-be I made a mess of it, I'm not much good on those things, but I know what a fellow is up against when he comes over here in the A.E.F. and it is no joke either. You know what I mean so try and patch up my little advice, and make her see just what her man is up against, then she can be better able to help him along. I would not advise marriage until after the war, or if the war lasts very long and they still feel the same, during some furlough home. Try and make them see that now is no time to get married. The fellows who are engaged or nearly so over here behave a lot better, as a rule, than the married ones.

I don't know Hugh [Garvin] very well, probably not as well even as you do, but all the time that I was in Battery E I never heard any one say anything that would mar his character in any way whatever, now that is all I can tell you, if I knew any more about him, I wouldn't hesitate to tell you all, but I don't. I hope Uncle Ted has arrived home and that you had a chance to see him. I don't believe he can tell you much about me, for I only saw him twice, and once for only about two minutes. That was the day I finished up all my flying at [Tours] and got my wings. I don't know where Uncle Ted got all those compliments you told me about in your last letter, I think he was trying to jolly you along, well don't take all that too much to heart, because I'm no different from anybody else, and you havn't any saintly wise guy for a son at all. I wish you people at home would stop making heroes, so to speak, of us over here. Remember what I told you in my last letter about us living like young millionaire's sons, considering everything, and so far we havn't done any good at all and are still training at the Government's expense. Wait until we get on the front a while, then if we are any good then don't spoil us. — get me? I don't mean to bawl you out but I don't feel that I deserve all that you think I ought to have. Well anyhow we won't waste any time over that.

There isn't any news of any importance to tell you. I'm getting the papers and magazines regularly. We havn't flown for over a week now, and we have machine gun and aerial gunnery classes all the time. It is very interesting work, but I sure would like to get into flying some more. The weather has been so bad that flying is out of the question. You know of course now that I'm not going into the wireless end of aviation, but am taking the straight course as all fliers do, and will keep on the lookout for the branch I like best as soon as I find out which one that is and more about it all I may go bombing maybe, _____ maybe artillery _____ or contact patrol. I like the first two best so far but I am going to wait before I make any more decisions. Maybe Uncle Ted won't think I'm doing the best thing but I'll take all the blame. Sorry to hear that you are having such bad weather. We are too now. Its pretty cold, but don't worry about me. I have plenty of warm clothes, thanks to you all.

Well, I guess I'll quit for today. I'm writing in the guardhouse, me being detailed to assist the Officer of the Day. Bum job and nothing to do, so I wrote to you, Althea and Gramps. Isn't that a dandy picture of Althea, you and Althea still reign, side by each in my portfolio. By the way my photographs have not come yet, but when they do I'll send them. I wrote a letter to you to give to the Glendale Canteen, thanking them for the plum pudding. Hope you got it. I've thanked everybody who sent me presents now. So if anybody didn't hear from me, I either didn't hear from them, or my letter was lost. Sent you $100 last month, will send more soon.

Please buy Althea a birthday present for me. I am sending Bobby $50 to get herself an engagement present and Althea's graduation present. Hope you got my box I sent home by Uncle Ted. You'll laugh over what I sent Althea. I don't know why I sent it. I am going to send Althea that hat cord and insignia just as soon as I can. Am holding it up for an overseas cap please tell her.

Give my love to all the family and Althea and my best to all my friends and lots of love to yourself.

> Your devoted son,
> Roland.

P.S. Some clipping you sent me about quail hunting by aeroplane, great stuff.[1]

Sunday 3   Had a holiday today. Bummed around all morning & went for a walk with Major Goldtwaite this P.M. Movies in the evening, took cadet retreat this evening.

March 4, 1918   Nearly everybody was sick this morning, dierea [*sic*]. Our classes were excused only 3 showed up out of 12. Didn't do anything all day. Sent photographs off. Went to movie evening. Had retreat.

Tuesday 5   All well today. Had ground classes all day today. Nothing much out of the ordinary happened.

March 6, 1918   Something very unordinary happened today. We flew DC 3 trips A.M. & solo 4 trips this P.M. Went in the machine, wasn't so hard to fly as I thought. All OK.

Thursday 7   Had aerial gunnery all day today, & finished up machine guns, etc. [The] Capt. . . talked to sect. leaders about combining our vrille with flying formation. Sounds very good. [Arthur] Perrault was killed today.

March 8, 1918   Flew again all day today, got 7 trips on 23 Singles today, went to Lt. Perrault's funeral. Certainly was too bad, he was a dandy fellow. We will probably be loched in 18s tomorrow. We fly tomorrow.

Saturday 9   Finished 23 Singles this A.M., had 4 trips making a total of 15 trips. Went to 18 meters this P.M., had 9 landings then ½ hr. in the air, then I did 2 spirals to the left & to the right, the left one went bad but the right one was better. Ordered to field 5 tonight.

March 10, 1918   Went or rather moved over to Field 5 this morning. Got straightened up over there, after dinner came back & to main camp for supper & bummed around. Stayed at Red Cross movies & went back to camp, field.

Monday 11   Started in landings on 15 [meter], had 18 this A.M. 7 broke two tires a tail skid and cheval de bois'ed on a wing. Otherwise O.K. Very briefly in the air. Shot 26 out of 50 traps this PM. Went over to the main field and back.

March 12, 1918   Did 4 spirals from 1200 m. this A.M. & also my altitude 12000 ft. for 15 min., pretty cold. After lunch I shot traps and went over to the main field. We may go to Paris to get some machines tomorrow.

Wednesday 13   Did some acrobatics this A.M. — 2 vrilles which was pretty exciting. After dinner I went to Vinets on a cross country. We don't go to Paris after all. Anyway they are bringing 23's down. Received a dandy letter from Althea today.

March 14, 1918   Went to Romorantin this morning and back on my last cross country. Had a good trip & flew pretty high. Pretty foggy this P.M. I didn't fly wrote some letters and that was all.

March 14, 1918.

Dearest Mother:

I've written to my French orphan and everything so we are square on that subject. I also sent Bobby $50 and you $100. Will send more later. I had a dandy letter from both you and Althea. I usually get your letters at the same time, you and Althea. Althea is a peach to write so often and such nice letters and so are you, both of you are all right to think of me so often. Glad you liked the pictures. Hope you get my personal photography all right, I sent them in three packages, one to Althea, and two to you, eleven pictures in all. They only made eleven. I am afraid I won't be able to send you any more photographs, unless the censor loosens up a little. Glad to hear the winter has lifted and you are enjoying good weather again. We have had a week of perfect weather and much flying. My leave will come some day I hope. I'm due to leave nearly now for its seven days every four months, but one can't let them accumulate, so I'm out of luck. You are right about my birthday being in the near vicinity, glad you reminded me of it. I think I'll celebrate and buy a dozen of oranges and a few packages of gum at the Y.M.C.A., won't that be just grand, lots better than getting drunk which is the only other thing one can do here, and as you know which doesn't in the least appeal to me, so I'll stick to oranges and gum. I don't think I'll smoke either for I get along very well without it and don't really like it, so why begin just because I'm 21. What say you? Thank you very much for the share of P. & G.² You are a peach to do that and I certainly appreciate it. Awfully glad Bobby's getting along so well at U.C. She is on down hill work now that the first semester is over and that she is a regular Tri Delt. I can't get over Bobby engaged yet, but I'm awfully glad she is so happy and I hope Hugh is the right kind of a fellow. I imagine Bobby knows what she is doing all right. I guess poor old Bob Richardson has his foot in it now if he is connected with the Supply Department, for I know what it is and he may stay home or way back of the line all during the war, but nevertheless somebody has to do it, but it is a thankless, unexciting job and not for me at all. Sorry you can't realize all I'm doing, the truth really is that I havn't until lately been doing much of anything. I suppose I could have stayed in the transportation at [Tours ?] until the end of the war, but I wouldn't have had the flying that I'm getting now. I'll sure cable you if I ever go to the front. I had my last lesson in double control again. I am flying the cutest little machine now that you ever saw, just room for one and only your head sticks out, no long flabby tail or wires like the old Caudrons but this is a real fighting machine with a place for a machine gun and everything. I have done all my cross countries, etc., and am waiting to finish acrobatics, which are quite interesting. I made a "vrille" the other day, that is going straight down and turning around, the nose acts as a pivot and the wings turn around. Then we do a vertical turn like this #2 and a flip over on your back and then nose out underneath. A trick known as a rennerse-ment [renversement]. Then a wing slip in which you lock her up on one wing and let her fall down and then come out in a spiral, etc. It all sounds terrible to you I suppose, I can just see you shiver and say "Oh how terrible" but really it is as easy as falling off a log and not at all dangerous, so you needn't worry.

Well, by the way I think that's a good idea about giving the girls an allowance out of my money. I'm sending it to you to do as you like and it's up to you to do as you like with it. I told you about it in my Easter card. I sent cards to all the family and lots of friends. Give my love to the family and Althea and my best to all my friends and lots of love to yourself.

Your devoted son,
Roland.

Friday 15   Went over to the main field today to bring a 15 back but found that there wasn't any so I didn't fly today. After awhile I went back to the field & shot traps etc.

March 16, 1918   Finished acrobatics today. 2 more vrilles 4 vertical virages 4 rennersements [renversements] and wing slips. Some excitement. Guess I was loched. Gen. [John] Pershing, Sect. [Newton] Baker & staff inspected the camp today & had us all toeing the mark.

Sunday 17   Got up late this morning and moved over to field 7 on St. Valentines field. Here we will fly 120's, went back to the main field after dinner & stayed until 9:00 P.M.[3]

March 18, 1918   Made 3 landings in a 120 this A.M. & only caught my motor once. Then we went up in a formation of 4 & flew around for about an hour it is interesting work & quite a job to keep in the right place. 120's are sure great.

March 18, 1918.

Dearest Mother and Sisters:

I'm sorry but I'll have to combine my letters to each of you into one, you are all so good about writing that I can't keep up the pace, so if you don't mind I'll answer your letters right here. Mother, please don't send any more pictures or letters of mine to any newspaper, or anything like that, for if a copy of said paper ever got over here I'd never hear the end of it and anyway I don't care for so much publication. Don't think I am offended, but I'd just rather you wouldn't do it any more. Thank you Coombsie for the pictures they were great. Gee you people sure did have some snow. That ought to have made good skiing. Thanks "E" for your letter, don't get too excited about what I sent to you all by Uncle Ted for it isn't much and there really wasn't much to choose from and everything is so hard to send. I hope you get it all right. They are just souvenirs of France. I sent you all pictures by mail which I hope you'll get. Now for the news:

I have finished all my acrobatics and believe me it was some exciting, in all we did four vrilles, four verticle [sic] "virages" four [renversements] and two wing slips, the latter are the most uncomfortable. We did it all at about 1200 meters altitude. I can't explain it all to you, for it would take ages but you can just imagine me flipping around up there, first on my back, then straight down, then side slipping, spinning, etc. After all though it really isn't very difficult. I will again Sunday and am now doing formation flying in a very fast and powerful machine. Same size as the one I did acrobatics in with a motor of 120 H.P. instead of 80 H.P. Well maybe you think these machines can't go, they fly past an old Caudron, just as if the latter were going backwards. I went up in a formation of four today and we covered about 70 or 80 miles. These machines will do 150 M.P.H. about. We get and will get a lot of flying over here and it is a good thing too for the more flying the better. I have had about 40 hours in the air now including everything. I can't tell you any more of my work here because it is prohibited by the censor, but I'll tell you about it when I get home. I hope you Mother have seen Uncle Ted by now, and he has told you that I am well and happy, etc. but don't let him "bull you" with a lot of slushy things, because that don't get anybody anywhere. Anyway I sure was glad to see him, even if I did only have a very short time with him. I am hoping to see some of my friends blow in here any time, but as yet, no luck. They will all pass thru here unless they are going to be bombers or observers. Mother, please buy Coombsie a nice birthday present for me out of my money and see that Bobby gets herself something nice with the money I sent her. I sent $50, $30 for her and $20 for Althea's graduation present and flowers. Will send you another $100 soon again. I don't know when I'll get my seven day's leave now whether it will be in Suisse or not, will tell you when I know. I wish I could send you a picture of one of these machines we are driving. You may see some big old heavy lumbering Curtiss at home, and think they are like that, but they can run circles around a Curtiss. They resemble a Curtiss somewhat in shape, but that is all.

Please give my love to the family and Althea and take good care of yourselves.

Your son and brother,
Roland.

Tuesday 19   Flew this A.M. in a formation of 3 me leading came down too early went up again. Didn't fly this P.M. because of bad weather, went over to the main camp & bummed around a little then came home & went to bed.

March 20, 1918   Didn't fly all day today because of bad weather. So I went over to the main camp and took a bath, had tea and bummed around in general. Came back on the returning truck. Had supper & went to bed.

Thursday 21   Flew all day in 4 formations of 3, went pretty much all over the country today. I led the last formation & went over to Vinets & dropped off my tobacco for the frenchman thereby creating quite a little excitement. Had about 6 hr. in the air today. Some tired tonight.

March 22, 1918   Flew all day today in 3 formations including one altitude formation up to 5000 m. So was cold & high up there, came down & was pretty tired so we shot traps for the rest of the afternoon. All O.K.

Saturday 23   Flew in two formations this A.M. lead the first & the second was a stunt formation. Had the good luck to go to Tours this P.M. So I got all dolled up & left in a machine & arrived there about 3:00 P.M. 35 min. en route. Saw all my friends & slept out at Camp.

March 24, 1918   Had a good sleep, bummed around till 10:00 A.M. got the old bus out & took a ride down & lost my motor & stayed out on the field till 2:00 from 10:30 & finally wheeled her in, took her apart & put her together again & at 5:00 p.m. she ran so I climbed aboard & came back, arrived a little after 6:00 p.m. Had a fine time.

March 24, 1918.

My dearest Mother and Sister Bob:

I am writing to you both at the same time, for I owe you both a letter and I'll combine them in one for twice told news ceases to be news. Well,

Bob I sure was glad to get your picture which just arrived, it is fine and looks like you. Now I have a good picture of everybody in the family and am proud of them all you can count on that. I'm having such a grand time that I'm usually too tired at night to do anything but sleep. It seems that luck and the powers that be are, and always have been with me since I arrived here. I'm flying the fastest machine in the school now and so far so good, it is great and I'm crazy about it.

Out of our old Section 38 that I was in at the start here, we are only two left that got this far, the others either had bad luck and broke up or got transferred to bombing or some other branch of aviation. Well, I have been very lucky and have arrived at the most enviable stage of the game in fine shape. They offered me a job as tester here the other day. Of course it was somewhat of a compliment, but when I investigated the regiments, I found that I'd have to sign up for six months, so I told them that I couldn't see myself staying around here six months. Anyway afterwards I found out that it wasn't such a compliment either for anybody can try out for it, so I don't think I am loosing [sic] anything. Then as far as I can see, its as dangerous as going to the front, and not near as interesting so all's well.

Now just to set you all straight about this dangerous business, why to read some of you peoples' letters, it makes me shudder to think of all the dangers and risks you think I'm taking. I even shudder with a laugh now and then for its all so ridiculous and funny. Why, if you only knew how safe you feel and really at home one feels in one of these machines you'd never speak of dangers again.

I tell you that the danger point is past. Nobody ever gets killed after they have had acrobatics, and I've had them and feel very confident now. Another thing about this going to the front business, just now that is hopelessly in the future, and I wonder at times if I'll ever get there, and if the war will be over when I do. And another thing, just about 90% (so we'av been told) of the aviators at the front who are killed, are killed doing stunts, etc. around the hangars and I don't do that nor ever will, so you can always rest easy when you are thinking of me in the air. Now *please* don't worry for these are facts and not fiction.

Well I've had a good time today. All last week I was a good boy and piled up my blankets every morning and was at hand at roll call, more or less awake, mostly less, and havn't (knock wood) broken any planes as yet, so Saturday PM I received the joyful news that I could take a machine and go to [Tours] (where I got my first training) and stay until Sunday P.M. and be back here Sunday evening. Well I got all dolled up boots, new suit, shaved and even washed my face and cleaned my fingernails, and went out and jumped aboard a nifty little plane, painted in a camouflage design and looking altogether pretty "chic", and hit it up for [Tours]. Well you can follow me on the map right down the river and

I left here at 2:15 P.M. and arrived at [Tours] at 2:50 P.M. and you can get a good idea of how speedy our little ships are. I had a breeze behind me though and that helped some. Nevertheless, 35 minutes is pretty good time. Well I saw all my old friends and bummed around found a bed and slept out at Camp all night. Next morning, that is this morning I had her up and I set out to do a little showing off etc. Well I "showed off" all right, ⸍ for I stayed up about one half hour and buzzed around, the old wagon running fine and pretty sporty, all camouflaged up. Well, I was feeling pretty big cheese, etc. so I came down to receive the glory etc. and in doing so nearly pushed a Caudron off the field, just missed it and lost my motor. Well, of all wet kerrs [curs] I was the wettest and the most drooped — in other words, I felt like a _____ or tin cans or anything. So I sat out there in my camouflaged cart and waited for some one to wind me up. It takes two men to wind a 120 hp motor up so out they came and started to turn her over. Well, to make a long story short, she wouldn't go, and we worked from 10:30 A.M. to 2 P.M. with her and then wheeled her in by the hangars to get a little closer to civilizations and tools, etc. So I got back again and she ran fine, don't know what was wrong. Well, it was 5 P.M. then and I had to do some hustling, so I said goodbye to all and left in a cloud of dust and the old motor stuck to it and in one hour and 10 minutes, I made a landing in my own field, caught the motor and taxied to the hangars as big as life. It seems that my buss is a bit shy and don't like to show off, so there you have the whole story. Believe me I was glad to get back too. I got a letter from Uncle Russ and will write to him soon. I don't know when I'll get my leave or where it will be. I'm getting 6 or 8 hours flying a day here all formation work. We went up on 5000 meter patrol the other day and it was some cold. We also did a stunt formation yesterday morning. Can't tell you much about it, but its awfully interesting and very tiring work. I took some tobacco over to an aviation school nearby and dove down and dropped it with a message on it to the Frenchman who wanted it. He asked me for it one day when I landed there on account of engine trouble. Pretty classy way to deliver one's personal presents. What say you? Do you remember those people [the Normants] Q. Roosevelt and I went over to see last summer and I sent you a photo of their dining room. Well, one of the boys here was over there today and they want he and I to fly over there some Sunday and stay to dinner, so I'm going to try it next Sunday. Not a bad way to call is it? It is only about 30 miles away, and it won't take but 15 or 20 minutes to get there. Will tell you later if I go.

Well give my love to all the family and Althea and my best to all my friends and please don't turn over any more of my epistles, etc. to the newspapers.

Ever your loving son and brother,
Roland.

Monday 25   Moved over to Field 8 this morning. The barracks are full and I had to take an upper. Also there were no machines & we won't fly for a few days. Went to main camp this P.M. & stayed for supper.

March 26, 1918   Nothing to do today. Shot a few traps this A.M. and went to the main camp this P.M. Met [Dudley] "Red" Oultcalt at camp and bummed around till about 9:30 P.M. Then went back to camp.

Wednesday 27   Went over to the main field to fly our machines over. Met [Paul] "Bud" Sutherland from home. Flew the machines back and shot some traps this P.M.

March 28, 1918   Shot a few traps today and bummed around in general. Can't go over to the main camp so we just stayed over here. Havn't flown here as yet. Went to town tonight & bought a watch.

Friday 29   Wrote a letter to A. this A.M. and went over to the main camp this P.M. & sure enough got a letter from A. and a big box of hermits, great too, nothing like it. Saw Bud Sutherland & had tea at the ARC with him. Came back & went to bed.

March 30, 1918   Am leading a life of nothing to do. It is very rainy & muddy so we can't fly. We can't go off the post very easily either so we are more or less stuck here.

Sunday 31   Bummed around the post all day long. Not many here. Made some drinking chocolate out of cocoa, condensed milk & hot water this P.M., pretty good.

March 31, 1918.

Dearest Mother:

I have very little to say so I won't try to string it out. I have only flown once last week and that was when I brought my machine over here, from the main field. I've moved again and am on the last step of my training here. We have our own machines and three mechanics assigned to us over here, pretty nice, n'est ce pas? My machine is being lined up, painted up, cleaned up and made to look like a million dollars, it will be a shame to take her up for fear of getting it dirty. I spent Easter (today) very quietly in the barracks reading and writing and 'rithmetic, etc. Didn't find any easter eggs, but of course that doesn't make much difference. Don't forget to buy a birthday present for Coombsie and Emily on July 17, yourself on July 31st and Bobby on October 20th. I'm sending you $100 nearly every month. I put in for my leave again yesterday. Hope you have seen Uncle Ted by now, and received the little souvenirs I gave to him to bring to you. I can't tell you much about our training but here we are doing or will do aerial combat.

I received a big box of hermits and candy and chewing gum and a dandy book of connundrums from Althea the other day and we had a regular party in the barracks this PM. We still have a few left. I met Bud Sutherland over here the other day and sure was glad to see some one from home.

Well give my love to the family and Althea and my best to all my friends and lots of love to yourself, from your loving son,

Roland.

April 1, 1918   Walked over to field this A.M. & got one of my laundries. Shot some pigeons this P.M. Nothing much else doing.

Tuesday 2   Bummed around the post all day. Shot some pigeons & that's all.

April 3, 1918   Flew for ½ hr. this A.M. Came down on account of weather & I thought my machine was out of line it acted so funny, however I guess it wasn't. Went over to the main field this P.M. & this evening on official business.

Thursday 4   Bummed around all day. Shot a few traps & took a little walk this P.M. i. e. we were told to take a little walk. Some way to treat officers. The guard went wild this evening & shot about a dozen rounds tonight. Nobody hit.

April 5, 1918   Flew today aimed at a fixed target & maneuvered around parachute this A.M. Shot at fixed target & some parachutes this P.M. Also at "Mal" Boche plane [plane marked as a German aircraft] with a camera gun this P.M. had a good time. Played baseball this evening after supper.

Saturday 6   Did not fly all day. Went down town this P.M. & did some shopping etc. Suddenly 18 of us received orders to go to Cazaux at 5:30 P.M. leaving at 6:30 P.M. Some rush to get packed. We left Iss. on the train at 10:30 P.M. & stayed on all night changing at Limoges.

April 6, 1918.

Dearest Mother:

I just received two letters from you, one written March 10th and the other one February 24th. I'm awfully glad you have been to W. [Washington, D.C.]. and seen Uncle Ted and Tanta, and am glad Uncle Ted gave you a favorable impression of me but I'm afraid he greatly exaggerated in same impression, for I only saw him for a few hours the first time and for a very few minutes the second time. However, I'm glad it was a good one, but don't go into too many raptures, etc. about it, for that won't do anybody any good, and you know that kind of business don't suit me very much. I am enclosing a letter from my orphan Andre Le Gal. It seems that he never heard of me and doesn't know much of the benefits of our Society, so I wrote him again and explained to him how it was that I knew his address, and of course had to tell him how about the money, etc, which was a very uncomfortable proceeding, and also if he doesn't receive the money either in provisions or cash, to let me know right away, and I would look it up and see where the catch was.

I'm glad you liked the souveniers [sic], they weren't much, but I'm a bum one in selecting appropriate gifts, and I didn't want to burden Uncle Ted down very much. I suppose you saw the clock I sent Althea. Well I bought that quite awhile before Uncle Ted came over. Sometime before Christmas and after I bought it I didn't like it and felt very foolish for having gotten it, but I sent some over and Althea seems to like it so . . . . You asked some questions about our machines, which of course I can't answer, but we do have guns on them, you can be sure of that. I was shooting with a camera gun myself yesterday and havn't seen the results yet. I'd hate to think of going up over the line without a machine gun mother, so you can rest assured that we will have them. I've been at this field now nearly two weeks and expect to move to an aerial gunnery school down on the coast in a day or two, but nothing is definite and we will probably receive our orders to go about 1 hr in advance of the time specified to leave. From there we go to Paris awhile and get our machines and then off to the front. I'll try and cable you something about that time if I can. My opinion of the A.R.C. and Y.M.C.A. was changed a little in that they give you a place to buy candles, candy and chewing gum, etc. and the A.R.C. has a reading and dining room over at the main field for Officers, but they don't mind making one pay the price for such things.

Another thing the papers at home must be going crazy for some of the clippings we receive over here about "Our Aviators in France" are simply ridiculous, and it makes us kind of mad to think that you people are being told such abominable lies about us over here. Just for instance one clipping from a Boston paper talks about this Port [Issoudun] and comments on the wonderful work of the A.R.C. and Y.M.C.A., saying they have furnished baths and swimming pools for the boys, etc. Well, the only thing we have in the way of a bath is a room with about 10 or 12 showers in it, and we are allowed to use it between 4 and 5 P.M. gratis. That is fine though and is the best thing the A.R.C. has done in our Camp. Of course I only see one side of the game and the side of the little children in France I know nothing about, but if there is the same amount of truth in that there is in this other, why you can see why I feel the way I do. If any A.R.C. now starts telling you about swimming pools in the big Aviation Camps in France, you can call him a liar and sign my name to it.

Of course you hear lectures and reports of what is being done and what has been done in the camp over here, but when one hears something about the very Camp he is situated in that is nothing more nor less than a lie, why you naturally begin to get a bad impression of the party who does it.

Well after that little oration we can talk about something else. I went out "straffing" yesterday, that is flying low and diving on trains, farmers and wagons, etc. and had a great old time. That sounds pretty bad, but there is nothing like it to give one confidence in oneself and machine. I suppose you have heard what Lieut. Col. [Charles E.] Lee of the R.F.C. said about stunts, well that is very true but however I'd hate to try them in a Curtis, it is perfectly safe to do those things in the machine we run, so don't you worry.[4] I am now flying one of the fastest training machines there is. In fact this is the last type of machine one trains on over here, the next type is just out and is being used on the front. We will probably use them when we get there. A revised list of all those to go to the Aerial Gunnery School just came in and I'm on it. I don't know when we will go.

I get the magazines and papers quite regularly and they sure are a great help in keeping up with the times at home. I always look to the Glendale news to see what the Titus's and the Allen's are doing and all the people t'home. I don't suppose I'll get my leave for some time now, for it takes so all fired long to put anything like that thru that we never stay in one place long enough to get it. I put in an application again for it, but it hasn't come thru yet.

About the end of the war, well its pretty far off, and we have ceased to ever think about it, for it won't shorten it a bit, and we therefore would rather think about flying, etc. I sent the photographs I had taken of myself to you and Althea, eleven in all in three packages, so I hope you'll get them. They arn't very good, but they are the best I could do. Just keep on using my same address, only don't put any Paris on it, as it isn't necessary.

Please give my love to the girls and Althea and the family and remember me to all my friends (you ought to know that phrase by heart now) and lots of love to yourself.

Your devoted son,
Roland.

April 7, 1918   Arrived in Bordeaux this A.M. at 8:30 and went up town & had some breakfast. Lost 6 of the crowd on the train someplace. Had dinner here & left for Arcachon near Cazaux at 2:00 P.M., arrived at 5:00 P.M. Stayed in a hotel all night.

Monday 8   Took a 6:30 A.M. truck & arrived about 7:15. Had breakfast at Cazaux & then did some shooting with a 22 a French carbine & went out in a boat & shot at buoys with same. Had some deflection & machine gun lectures, then went back to the Hotel.

April 9, 1918   Took the 6:30 A.M. truck for Cazaux again & did some more shooting, more boating and had some more lectures today.We also shot a Vickers and a french machine gun at target in the water. Then we came back to the hotel & slept.

Wednesday 10   Took the truck again and hung around the hangars all A.M. Only 2 of us got a ride not me. The machines are terrible. This P.M. I & some others flew this machine. Tour de Piste PAS BON. Slept in our new quarters this evening. Very good & also good food at mess.

April 11, 1918   Went over to the hangars today & flew some more. I chased parachute around this A.M. & sighted on it. I didn't fly this P.M. Had a lecture on sights and came back to our new quarters at Cazaux Camp.

April 11, 1918.

Dearest Mother:

Just a short letter tonight to tell you that everything is O.K. We arrived at our destination the day after we left as you probably have seen by the post cards I sent you and Althea, that we did get our orders to leave the same day I wrote you. We received those orders at 5:30 PM to leave at 6:30 the same PM. I'm afraid you thought my last letter a bit pessimistic, but I'm really not, I just gave you a little change of diet, so to speak. Well, here we are down at an aerial gunnery school, we havn't as yet done any shoting from a plane, but we will either tomorrow or next day. The course is awfully interesting and I might as well tell you about it for I don't see that it is against censor rules, and if it is and they want to shoot me for a spy, why I'll have to die sometime, so what is the difference. That is the best attitude to take in a war anyhow, even a mean old war like this one. I really don't see why the Kaiser ever had a war anyhow, but even at that I could have arranged a better one than this.

Well when we got here we first had lectures on machine guns and deflection, then we shot French carbines at logs out in the lake. Then we shot a machine gun at same, then we went out in the lake in a speedy motor boat and shot both carbines and machine guns at logs. This was great sport, just like a vacation. We had lectures intermingled with this all the time. Then we went out on the flying field and had a tour de Piste, just to see the field and get our bearing. Then we took a parachute up and threw it out and sighted on it and maneuvered around it. This we did today. Next we will shoot at a big baloon [sic], then at a small one. Then we go up and shoot at a sleeve, that is pulled through the air by another machine, in these last two steps the holes are counted and the results shown the student. Then we do combat with camera guns, I think, then off to the front, maybe ? ? ? I have just found out that we are going to get dandy machines, just as good or better than the Spad, this of course is cause for much rejoicing among the crowd, for it would be very annoying to say the least, inconvenient to go over the line is a bum machine. You can readily see what a dandy course we are getting. Why I've had so much school that I feel as though I ought to be in the 8th grade by now, and as far as a machine gun, well I can take one apart without using an eye, both legs one hand and my mouth, also put it back together again. I fear I am boasting, in fact I'm quite the most conceited little cuss you ever saw, all aviators are, so they say. Well I havn't anything more to say, I havn't said much anyhow. Am feeling fine and everything is very O.K. We are on the go from 6:15 AM until 7:30 PM every day but Sunday. My love to the family and Althea and my best to all my friends.

> Ever your loving son,
> Roland.

Friday 12   Went up to the hangars today and I chased another parachute around & went up in another machine with two pairs of 2 baloons [sic] each & shotgun but I couldn't find the baloons [sic] when I let them out. Didn't do much this P.M. had a lecture on sighting again.

April 13, 1918   Flew this morning and chased a parachute around over the country. Had a lecture on Raillesonent [Reille-Soult] sights this P.M. and the class as a whole got a grand bawling out by [the] Major which wasn't all together called for on his part & which didn't do so very much good to us.

Sunday 14   Nothing much doing today, went to a lecture in the morning & bummed around all P.M. It rained today and so we couldn't go boat riding & had to stay more or less in the barracks.

April 15, 1918   Rain & low ceiling & general bad weather all day today. Went to many lectures today and learned about machine guns, deflection & synchronization etc. Our lectures ought to be nearly over now.

Tuesday 16   Flew today. Once this A.M. and once this P.M. Chased parachute both times, am getting pretty tired of chasing parachutes but it looks as though we will do it for quite awhile yet. Am pretty tired tonight stayed on field till 7:30 PM.

April 17, 1918   Bummed around the field all A.M. today but didn't fly till this P.M. when I chased another parachute. The Frenchmen think we are all crazy I believe for the foolish things we do out on the field & at mess but we have a good time out of it so who cares. (Chemin de fer)

Thursday 18   Flew again this morning & chased parachutes again. Some of the class has moved to baloons [sic]. This P.M. it was a little windy so they called flying off & we had a couple of lectures. Got a fine letter from A. today & sent $100.00 to mother. Everything O.K.

April 19, 1918   We didn't fly today for it rained nearly all day so we went to lectures etc. and came home early this P.M. and I wrote some letters and made my bed over again.

Saturday 20   I flew once this A.M. in an old machine with a motor that wouldn't throttle at all but a Frenchman took it up after me and smashed her up. Had lecture this P.M. and came home early & "saddle soaped" and chased rats after supper & crocked one.[5]

April 21, 1918   Got up late today and enjoyed life again. Had a general house cleaning today and then wrote some letters and chopped some wood for the fire. Most everybody went down town today so we had the barracks to ourselves. Killed another rat tonight.

April 21, 1918.

Dearest Mother:

At last I have time to sit down and write peacefully. I received your two letters of March 18th and 25th, and as usual was sure glad to get them. I received another letter from my orphan's mother saying, well I'll enclose it and you can see for yourself. I also sent you another draft for $100, which makes the third draft of that amount which I have sent you. I am going to send you as much money as I can, and you are to do with it as you please. I am glad you bought the sofa, and one can never tell but what I may want to use it some one of these days, you are a great old kidder all right. If you could though I wish you would save a little of it for me so that when I get home I'll have something to start on for it will be a long while before I'll be making this much money again. I can't understand about my letters not reaching you for I've written as regularly as usual and am sure that I've received all your letters.

I received a letter from Aunt Mabel [Richardson] yesterday saying that you had given Jim [Richardson] one of my pictures, so I guess they arrived O.K. I'm glad of that for you havn't missed asking for them in one of your letters. I sent 11 of them by three packages. Three to Althea and two packages of four each to you. Althea was to take her pick and then give the rest to you, or however you want to arrange it. They arn't very good but c'est la guerre.

I wrote to Mary J. [Johnston] and Maurice F. [Favier] not long ago so I'll probably hear from them soon. I did not take my leave, for they have a very inconvenient way of moving you just about the time something like that is coming off, so I no doubt won't get it for sometime now, not until after this new drive. This drive is very serious and it is going to be a long fight in which I hope we will come out on top.[6] I'm glad our soldiers are doing their bit, still there are so few of them that they can't do very much. It has been over a year now that we have been in war, and it does seem that we have done so little that I am getting ashamed of ourselves, with all our talk and boasting and then to have it simmer down and in a year's time to be doing so little and taking such a small part in this big war. Of course we are a long way off and as yet the people at home don't realize what war really is, that is very evident in all the newspapers we receive from home. It nearly makes me sick to read some of the statements made in our newspapers about conditions over here and elsewhere by people who either don't know what they are talking about, or are just naturally lying. Don't take what you read in the papers too much to heart.

Well as far as news goes, we are still here and may not go out for over a week, but I can't swear to anything more. I tell you I don't think much of these war marriages and I'm very glad that Hugh thinks the same way, for this war is too serious to start into with a wife, for the bride no sooner becomes a bride than she becomes a widow, or just as good as a widow. I know if I were married I'd have thought twice before I went through acrobatics at [Issoudun] and its darned few married men that get thru that stage of the game, not that its hard but that it looks dangerous. I have never heard from George Swallom, but goodness me I've got enough correspondents already and I don't want any more. I can just barely keep up now with the others. I write to you and Althea pretty regularly and to others whenever I can. It is too bad my letters havn't reached you and Althea, but I can't help it. Just blame it on to K. [Kaiser] Bill and our mail system, whichever it is.

By the way sell the shop as best you can and if you want to give it all to Joe [Hark] to sell and let him keep the money as a Christmas present (a little late) from me, for as far as I'm concerned I won't need it, either the shop or the money. Tell Joe to take it and do what he can with it, switchboard, motors, tools and all. Thanks for the "Ho to be a Soldier". It came the other day and sure is a crazy piece of literature.[7] About sending packages. You need not send any more knitted goods or clothing or newspapers for the latter make me more mad than otherwise and I still have enough of the former, but such things as candy, cookies, etc. go fine for we can't buy them any more in France. Chocolate goes well also. I chew quite a bit of gum lately, not because I care for it especially, but it helps to keep my teeth clean, so if you could send me a couple of boxes of Wrigley's Spearmint or Juicy Fruit, I'd be much obliged. I don't want you to do this if you feel that you can't afford it, but if you can I'd see that it wasn't sent in vain, so to speak.

I'm glad you feel the way you do about Althea, although I knew you did, for I feel that same way. She sure is a dandy girl and I'm awfully glad she cares for me.

Please give my love to the family and Althea and my best to all my friends. Lots and lots of love to you mother and don't worry a minute about me for it isn't worth while.

Ever your loving son,
Roland.

Monday 22   Had lectures all day today or rather were supposed to but it rained & the French kicked us out of the stands so we didn't do much of anything.[8] So we came home early very much disgusted with life in general.

April 23, 1918   We were graduated to the baloons [sic] today. But I took a trip in one of the new [Nieuports] 27's and had a good old time did renversements vrilles & vertical virages & had a peach of a time. Didn't fly on the baloons [sic] but will the first thing tomorrow, am next up.

Wednesday 24   I shot at the baloons [sic] today, went up 3 times, came down once on account of a jam. Pretty bumpy but I got up very close & let her have it, made 15 hits out of 18 rounds fired. 3 others claim to have shot at my baloon [sic] but I get the credit as it were. Will go on sleeve tomorrow not enough time on baloons [sic].

April 25, 1918   Shot at sleeve today — went up once & sleeve came down after I shot only 40 rounds. Went up again with Vickers 7 had a jam that I couldn't fix after 20 rounds, came down. Very bad results for the class on the sleeve.

Friday 26   Went over to the field today but didn't fly. Just as glad, for I didn't feel much like it today for some reason or other. Didn't do very much today but sit around and wait to go up. Took a bath this evening and sang songs at supper time. Bed at 9:30 P.M.

April 27, 1918   Took a walk this morning over to the ocean & took a swim it was pretty cold. Came back in time for dinner very tired. Went out to the field & watched some Frenchmen dive at sham trenches & be shot at by beach machine guns. Didn't fly all day.

Sunday 28   Flew this A.M. and shot 1 belt (100 rounds) at a sleeve, made 7.7% on the sleeve which is pretty good. Bummed around all afternoon and evening and went to bed at 9:30 P.M.

April 29, 1918   Went out to the field at 8:30 A.M. & had a lecture. Then some of the fellows went up & shot but not me. Went back again this P.M. & bummed around. Sleeve came down early & then called off flying. Had a big rat hunt tonight & got 5.

April 29, 1918.

Dearest Mother:

I just want to let you know that all is well. There really isn't any news, for we are at the same place, shooting at the sleeve now. Sunday three others and myself made hits out of 260, i.e. 7.7% about, which is considered pretty good. I shot one belt or 100 of the 260 rounds. The weather is fine now. Saturday four of us walked over to the ocean and had a swim, gosh but it was cold and we only stayed in about 3½ seconds at a time. We sure had a good time though, but it was quite a walk. Two hours each way and all through sand, which made the walking pretty bad.

It was fine flying Sunday, and lots of fun maneuvering around the sleeve, but I had a machine that dragged its left wing, so that every time I turned to the left, I could hardly straighten her out again, which was very disconcerning. However I had pretty good fun, and I had a good gun which is really more important than a good machine, so that I could get right up on top of the sleeve and unload in it. I could even see the tracer bullets hit it once in awhile. After I had fired my 100 I came down and wing slipped down to the field but at about 300 meters. It was too bumpy for any fancy stuff, so from then on down I came level, especially as my machine had such a feverish inclination to tip up to the left.

This is a great old place down here, but there is not much doing. If it wasn't for the rats around our quarters, we would find it hard to get along, but they afford enough amusement to keep up our spirits. They are really as big as cats and pretty slick old buggers too. Tonight we had a big rat hunt and got five, another fellow got two, and we two are now rated as "aces" for I got one the other day. It is a great sport and very hard on rats. It has the old "rough on rats" beat a mile, because it is so much more exciting to hit them with a club than have them just die.[9]

Please don't forget my cards, use the same plate and have my rank, etc. put on wherever it is the usual place to put it. I havn't had my leave yet. Heard from Mary J. yesterday. Hope you got the pictures O.K. Aunt Mabel said she had one, so I presume they arrived O.K. Buy Emily and yourself a birthday present with my money please when the time comes and see that Bobby gets herself a good engagement present and Althea's flowers for graduation all right with the $5.00 I sent her.

Heard from my orphan again. He sent me his picture. He is a nice looking fellow. He received a check for 50.00 Fcs from the_____ Society the other day so all is well on that subject. Still feel the same about the Y.M.C.A. The more I see of some of their Secretaries, the more I like our rats, so would you if you saw them, and what they do, the way I do.

Everything is fine with me over here and am getting fatter and rosier every day. Bought a "Gillette" razor and it is a lot better than my old one which is about gone. It has broken several times and I can't get any blades for it, and the old ones are so dull that shaving was a nightmare. Don't know when we will get rid of the shop. Give it all to Joe if you want to.

Well Mother, I guess that is about all there is to say. It isn't much, but I just want you to know that I'm very happy, busy and contented and I sure hope you all are too. Don't let Bobby get married until after La guerre.

Please give my love to the girls, Althea and all the family and remember me to all my friends. Lots of love to you mother and don't worry a bit about me.

> Your loving son,
> Roland.

Tuesday 30   Flew today went up & shot at sleeve but it came down soon & I only got about 40 rounds of Vickers at it, the belt jammed & wouldn't wind up so I came down.

May 1, 1918   Shot at sleeve again today & finished up, fired 100 rounds making total of 500 rounds at sleeve. Our class hit 6 the school record making 13½% (not me). Ready for exam tomorrow.

Thursday 2   Got through all exams all right & went to Arcachon after getting our orders. Slept there all night & took the 7:20 A.M. train next morning.

May 3, 1918   Went to Bordeaux this A.M. amid a great rush of ordering [?] baggage. Arrived before noon & left on the 11:00 A.M. train for Paris after getting paid at the Q.M. there. Arrived in Paris at 8:00 P.M. went to Grand Hotel.

Saturday 4   Stayed in bed late today. Went out & bought a helmet [?] tooth paste, razor blades etc. Went to the Casino tonight for shows. Rained this evening, no bombing yet.

May 4, 1918.

Dearest Mother:

Excuse this little note but I just have time to tell you that at last we are through at the gunnery school and are on our way back to [Issoudun] to await further orders. I am now completely through my training and am ready to go to the front. Am doing a little shopping in Paris before going down. We broke the school record for good shooting on the sleeve at [Cazaux]. However, I was not in the group that did it. My love to the girls, Althea and the family and I'll write you more in detail soon. Am feeling fine and hope you are well and happy.

Your loving son,
Roland.

May 5, 1918   Stayed in bed nearly all A.M. rode around the City this P.M. Nothing much doing up here.

Monday 6   Got up late & bought some silver Lts bars & bummed around all day, not much doing today.

May 7, 1918   Left for Issoudun this A.M. at 10:00. Arrived at about 2:00 P.M. & bummed around town till 5:30 P.M. & took train to Camp. Slept in barracks six tonight.

Wednesday 8   Reported this morning and bummed around all day. Went to bed early tonight for I felt kind of low grip I guess. Didn't sleep very well fever etc.

May 9, 1918   Got room on the Hill today. Still feeling bad. Went to the Hospital this P.M. and they kept me grip & fever. Slept there all night.

Friday 10   Stayed in bed all day today, fever gone & am feeling pretty good again. Ache a bit all over but that is all. Slept at Hospital tonight.

May 11, 1918   Stayed in Hosp. this A.M. & went out this P.M. feeling fine today & will get out tomorrow. Two fellows were killed here today.

May 11, 1918.

Dearest Mother:

Here I am back at the old camp arrived O.K. and didn't get bombed or anything like that. You would never know that Paris had ever been bombed. No sooner did I get there than I came down with the grip or something like that and after passing a very bad night in my bunk I went up to the hospital and Major _____ put me to bed with a little fever and all that but the next day, yesterday, I felt all right again and they let me up and out this afternoon. Here I am writing at the A.R.C. Club room on their paper. I am feeling fine now and will go back to my quarters tomorrow.

Well, the future looks pretty dull now and there don't seem to be any chance of us going out for some time, this is very discouraging, especially at this time when we feel that we are especially needed. The other day the officer in charge of training offered me a job of double control monitor for awhile and I've nearly decided to take it, although I hate to think of running those big old clumsy machines again and it is getting pretty low when one either has to do that or nothing at all, so I suppose I'll be doing some good anyhow.

Of course I may be a bum one, then I won't have to worry but it will help pass the time away and that is all we finished pilots have to do.

There is no news to tell you at all, so I'll tell you about the A.R.C. and the Y.M.C.A. at our Camp. The A.R.C. has a big building devoted to the officers, one end a library, reading room affair with books and magazines, tables and chairs, a piano and phonograph and is very nice by far the nicest part of the whole business. Then the other end is a dining room where they serve breakfast, dinner and supper for 50 Fcs. a week. The food is pretty good, not much of it though. They have just started trying to make us pay a membership fee to the reading room now so I really wonder if the A.R.C. won't be richer after the war than it is now and also really where the folks at home's money is going. Maybe I'm wrong but I can't see it.

The A.R.C. also has an enlisted mens' canteen reading room, piano, etc. where they serve hot chocolate, etc. The Y.M.C.A. has one big building with an auditorium business in it for boxing matches, movies, etc. and a canteen, reading room for the men and quarters for the staff. The only objection to that is that they charge too high for their stuff in the canteen. Well I'm not going to criticize any more.

I received two letters from you the other day that had come back from [Cazaux] and were waiting for me here, which I sure was glad to get. Glad you liked the pictures. I am going to try and send you some of me and the machine I've been driving lately, real aeroplane these.

That is all there is to say now. Sorry for such a short letter. Please give my love to the girls and Althea and my best to all the relations. Lots and lots of love to yourself.

Roland.

Sunday 12   Got out of Hosp. this morning and got my room up on the hill fixed this P.M. Slept there tonight.

May 13, 1918   Bummed around all day today between A.R.C. and room and didn't do much of anything at all. This is a hard life with nothing to do and very expensive to the government.

Tuesday 14   Got up late as usual today and went out today to try out for D.C. monitor. Had a ride in a 23 and it was awfull, never again. Then [William?] Farnum took me up & stunted the old buss & I nearly had a fit. Sure was glad when he came down. Ordered over to Field 8 today, good stuff.

May 15, 1918   Came over to Field 8 this A.M. Capt. gave us hell for being late, but the old boneheaded baby wouldn't listen to our explanation of not being able to get transportation & gave me confinement. Mal L. [Leach] hasn't gotten anything yet. Flew for awhile this P.M.

Thursday 16   My machine was on the bum this A.M. Oil stopped up somewhere in the motor & have to change motor. Didn't fly this A.M. got another machine this P.M. & aimed at fixed target for 1 hr. Came down at 5:00 P.M. All the bunch but Mal & I went out today to unknown parts.

May 17, 1918   Got up early this A.M. & went up to shoot at the fixed target with film. Then I went up to about 1200 m & did some virages & renversements etc. for awhile. Came down & got put on the ground for starting late. Motor wouldn't start but c'est la guerre.

Saturday 18   Flying again, went up and did line of flight with [Richard] Este for awhile then bummed around. At 10:30 I soloed and Mal Leech & I did some combat, this was very interesting and I need a lot of it. This P.M. I didn't do anything but bum around. This confinement is Pas bon.

May 19, 1918   Got up late and bummed around. Tried to play ball but it wasn't much success. This confinement is getting on my nerves. After dinner I wrote a few letters and bummed around some more. This is very bad.

Monday 20   Flew both periods this A.M. Never feel less like flying in my life than I did today. Soloed and dived on fixed target. Then this P.M. I soloed again, went over to Bourges & had a combat with Jim Osgood, he put it all over me. I sure am bum & need a lot of practice.

May 21, 1918   Flew first period this A.M. and did some line of flight . . . . Didn't fly the second period. Dr. [Brownell] not at post. Flew again this P.M. from 4:00 to 5:00 & took some pictures & film. Had a good time but still have lots to learn.

Wednesday 22   Flew all day. Line of flight this A.M. took some pictures second period. I dove on a big baloon [sic] till 2500 m & took 7 pictures of it. This P.M. I had a trial combat Mal Leech & I against two others. We met & had a very hot fight lasting nearly all period. Took 2 pictures.

May 22, 1918.

Dearest Mother:

Just received your two last letters of April 15th and 22nd, which I sure was glad to get, as usual. I also received two packages of S. E. Ps. and a Survey.[10] The S.E.P.s are very acceptable also the Air Service Journal, but you needn't bother sending the Survey any more. Thank you very much for the others, they certainly do help to pass the time away. I received a letter from Maurice Dubied and also Maurice Favier lately. Mary Johnston has left Cannes and is waiting to go up to the front in a French Hospital. I also received a letter from my orphan and his picture. He looks remarkably prosperous for a war orphan. I also received letters from Althea, Coombsie, Emily, Gramps and others. Most all these came in a bunch, so I don't suppose I'll get any more for awhile. I guess that is all of that kind of news.

There is nothing much to tell about myself. I am still over at Field 8 getting lots of flying and learning a lot. It seems that the farther one gets in this game, the less he knows, and the more there is to learn.

I had combat this AM with another fellow and learned a lot. I wish you could see the stunts one has to do in these combats. One never flies on an even keel, but either turns, flips around on his back, side, or any old place. You don't care what you do so long as you keep from getting directly in front of the other machine and try to get him in front of you. It is a great game all right. I also went up after a baloon [sic] today and took pictures of it. The old thing went up so fast that I could hardly keep up with it. Three of us were to dive on it and take pictures of it. Well one fellow never even got off the ground (motor trouble) the other had motor trouble up in the air and never got up to it, so it was left all to me and I got my seven pictures all right, but the last one was taken at 2500 meters and the baloon [sic] was still going up. I don't know where it landed. We don't start flying until 4 in the afternoon, for up until then it is pretty bumpy and disagreeable. We usually sleep, read or write between dinner and the afternoon flying period.

We are liable to be called out to the front or somewhere most any time now for they are sending fellows out every day and we or I should come sometime soon.

About Capt. [Allen ?] Eustis, he used to be Commanding Officer of the Headquarters Department Detachment here and all the fliers were under him. So as I was in charge of the officers' barracks at the time I had quite a lot to do with him. He was pretty nice to me, but he had some peculiar ideas about discipline etc. and soon left for other parts.

The big push has abated now as you know.[11] As far as we know way back here, there might never have been any push. We only heard about it through the papers we could get. It was some drive though. The Huns won't get very far is the general opinion over here. There are some of our fliers on the front who have seen active service and have done very well, looks pretty good for us.

By the way I wonder if Hugh is by any chance taking a course in Artillery Observation at Ft. Sill, they have such a school there I know. If he does it means that he has to go up in the air.

Am glad C. and E. are going to Wellesley maybe. That would be fine. Am sending you another $100 of this month's pay (May).

Was glad to hear from Margaret Kent. I'll bet she had a good time.

Well I guess that is all the news I can tell you this time for there really hasn't anything happened of importance.

My love to the family and Althea and remember me to all my friends. Lots of love to yourself from,

> Your devoted son,
> Roland.

May 23, 1918   Flew once today, had a group combat Leech and myself against [?] and [Alvin] Tread.[well]. We didn't meet till late but had a good fight. Mal left today for main field. I went over to see the dentist. All O.K.

Friday 24   Flew all day. Felt pretty good this A.M. Second period but this P.M. I had a combat with Treadwell & he put it all over me. I guess I'll never be a Chasse pilot. I can't seem to manoeuver [*sic*] fast enough, suppose I'll go bombing.

May 25, 1918   Went up first period this A.M. but found clouds at 250 m so I came down again only had to solo & no fun at 250 m. Went up again second period, ceiling same height but I stayed up and did cartoon flying. Wrote letters all P.M.

Sunday 26   Bummed around all day today. Went to Squadron ball game this afternoon was pretty good. Wrote a few letters & read and that's about all.

May 27, 1918   Bad weather this A.M. so didn't fly. Ordered over to main field this P.M. Moved & reported at H.Q. Det. Assigned to Barracks 8 as Casual officer. Went to movie at A.R.C. tonight.

Tuesday 28   Went up to see the Training Dept. this A.M. but they didn't know what was going to become of me. This P.M. I soloed again & found that I was on the bombing list for Clermont, not so bad but sorry I can't go chasse.

May 29, 1918   Bummed around all day today. Bought something at the Y & QM, had my picture taken for a pilot card for what purpose I don't know. Went down town this P.M. & got my picture.

Thursday 30   Big holiday today. Parade and decoration of graves in cemetery this A.M. in which we all took part. Held meet this P.M. which was a great success. Went to movie at Y tonight & then to bed.

May 30, 1918.

My dearest Mother:

Well, things have sure taken a change in my career, to make a long story short, I am going to be a bombing pilot and run the big planes instead of the little ones. Here is the way it happened. It is not all to my liking but after all it doesn't really make much difference.

Over at Field 8, after we came back from [Cazaux] aerial gunnery school, we had combat practice, and I wasn't very good at it, partly because I had a rather balky machine and partly because I never do catch on to things as quick as some other people do. Well, I thought all the time that I'd learn all right and it would come out all O.K., but here the difficulty, they really don't want [pursuit] pilots as much as bombers or artillery plane drivers so if they can find the least excuse they will send you bombing or something else, so they didn't give me time to catch on over there but sent me bombing right away after my 20 hours at Field 8 were completed and still I didn't combat to suit them, so here I am over at the main field awaiting orders. I put in for my seven days' leave again, this time to Bianitz [Biarritz] down near Bordeaux. I want to go. Bianitz is a good place and any place is better than here so I'm going, IF I CAN. Here also lies the difficulty, these leaves sound fine but they don't seem very anxious to give them.

Today was a Holiday here and this AM we had a big parade up to the cemetery where several addresses were made and the graves of all the students killed in training here were decorated with flowers. The percentage of fatal accidents is very low here. There have only been about 20 or 25 fatalities since the school started way back in October, that includes everything, sickness, falls and all. This afternoon there was a big field meet in which all the squadrons participated and after that a base ball game. It was a perfect day and everybody enjoyed it.

There really isn't much news to tell you for nothing of importance has happened around here. The Germans have started their new drive. I tell you this because you seemed to be very upset that I hadn't mentioned Fritz's last drive, but really there isn't much use in wasting ink and paper over such small details. We know he will be licked even if he does join a little territory. It seems to me very foolish that Fritz should start another drive for the ultimate outcome of all his driving is that he never really gets what he wants and always looses [sic] a lot of men. Of course there is a lot of blood shed up there but then its all in the game, c'est la guerre, que voulez-vous?

Rumors have come to me thru different sources that you, Mrs. J. C. Richardson Jr. is getting the over-seas work bee in your bonnet again. Well now let me tell you what I told you once before, just please get it out, this is no place for a woman with a family, such as you have to look after. Now Mother you worry me more than all the airplanes in Europe or the German drive or any of them. Just please take my advice for once and you will never regret it. I'll see to that. Really you can do more good at home where you are acquainted with conditions, people, etc. than you ever could over here, so you just please don't think of coming over here any more. If you did I'd sure send you back just as quick as I could. Its all right to be patriotic and all that but be it in good old U.S.A. and you can accomplish more over there than you can here. Not that I wouldn't like to see you, for that would be too good to be true, and then some, but when that time comes we both want to be behind the Statue of Liberty and not over here.

Now Mother, please don't start any more such rumors, you worry me, and one can't have any worries in this game. So you see, even talking and thinking about it is doing harm right here.

The weather over here has been good the last couple of weeks and we got in some very good flying. To date I have had 94 hours in the air, not so bad is it?

I received your letter of May 5th and am glad you heard from me while at gunnery school. Then I thought it wouldn't be long until I was at the front, but now I hate to say how long it will be. It seems as though I'll never get there, so I won't surmise any more. I had to laugh when you said "Do you know you've only been gone from home ten months?" Well of those ten I've been flying seven and am still in training, whereas if I were in the French or English Flying Corps, I would have been on the front four months ago. That's how long they take to train their pilots, although they arn't trained nearly as well as we are and one can't help but feel sorry for them.

Am glad to hear that . . . others from home will soon be over. I'd sure like to see them. I wish they would put all those good ideas of Uncle Ted's into effect over here, about rest etc. for the aviator, for it is all true and you have no idea what a serious strain flying is and one gets so little exercise to go with it, especially like at Field 8, where the Captain [Eustis ?] wouldn't even let us out of the camp and we stayed in our barracks for nearly two weeks of bad weather and couldn't hardly move and then when we did fly, good night, one half of the class busted up one way or another and that darned fool Captain didn't have sense enough to know why, but blamed us, you couldn't tell him either. Lots of these birds have funny ideas about flying, funny too they are the ones that don't care to fly, not even as a passenger, but luckily sooner or later they get bounced (Confidentially Capt. Eustis was that way, but he didn't last long). I'm just telling you these things so you will realize just what flying really means to a fellow, and you can't really understand it until you have flown yourself, for its so very different from anything else. Don't get scared at these things I'm telling you for as far as crashing goes there isn't much chance of my doing it in training any more for when one gets this far along, one usually knows all the tricks, etc. and there isn't much danger. But I can remember all right how I felt the day I went thru acrobatics, I didn't say anything to you at the time, for it wasn't over the bump yet, but I can talk about it now. They sit you in an old [?] of a machine and show you how to maneuver the control in the different stunts. Well up until then you have done nothing but straight flying to where they tell you to jerk the stick or rudder bar around. You have a pretty funny feeling around your gizzard, then you climb in a machine after looking it over to be sure that a wing or two won't come off in the air and you start up, you get up to the required altitude and throttle down to the required speed, and say to yourself

"Well lets see how do you do that?" Then you say "Well old top its about time you are jerking her around" then, "Well I can't stay like this forever so here goes", but nothing moves, gosh its awful and you have to fairly make yourself do it. Then of course after the first trick the next comes easy for you do several of the same kind each trip, but each new stunt starts the same feeling in your insides and believe me you are glad when its all over. Of course now stunts are an every day occurrence, but then — well I really can't explain what you really feel like, it is so absolutely different than anything else you have ever done. All this is to show you that aviators really need special and the very best of medical and mental attention.

In reading over your last letter, I see where you accuse me of saying that I might as well die one way as another. Well I must have said that in a very loose moment, for my thoughts and instincts are farther away from that subject and always have been, in this game, than anything else, and believe me and let me tell you right now so you can't forget it, if any aviator at all get back, I am going to be right there in the front rank walking on two legs and carrying two arms, my own too. Get that. Don't let there be any mistake there, for if you only knew what I do you'd know that the machines we are going to drive are the best ever and no German can catch them, let alone anything else.

Glad Mr. [Gilbert] Symons got back. Ask him if he received my letter, I answered a letter he sent me a long time ago.

I received another letter from Althea and am going to answer it very soon. I sure hope she gets along all right with her exams and graduates with many honors, it will come off now in a few days. She sure is an awfully nice girl and a peach about writing to me. You and she tie for first place on my correspondence list and I usually get your letters the same time. I sure was glad she could go on the boat ride and also that all the girls are having so many nice parties and dances to go to for even if there is a war, young people have to have recreation and old as well. Don't you miss a chance to have a good time mother, for it increases efficiency a lot.

Please give my love to the girls, Althea and all the family and remember me to all my friends. Please think over what I said about coming over and then don't think of it again ever.

Ever your loving son,
Roland.

PART TWO
To the Front and Home

At Orly Richardson tested mostly Sopwiths, an airplane that he heartily disliked. He found time to visit Paris frequently and to hone his fighting skills in mock combat. But he was pessimistic about the prospect of going to the front for real fighting. Then in August, quite fortuitously, he found himself assigned as a pursuit pilot to the 213th Aero Squadron, a unit in the Third Pursuit Group. Initially, the squadron was located at Vaucouleurs. At first his service came in rather routine patrols; often, though, his Spad was grounded because of mechanical problems.

But in September he and his squadron joined in the American offensive at St. Mihiel, strafing German troops, rail heads, and troop trains. He and two other pilots in the squadron shared in shooting down a German biplane. After the offensive ended, he continued to fly on patrols and also took part in some bombing attacks. With the coming of the Armistice in November, he moved from camp to camp, by train, ship and train until he reached Cincinnati early in February of 1919 as a civilian.

Chapter Four

At Orly: The Ferry Pilot

"I'm ... getting more discontented every day ..."

May 31, 1918   Ordered to Orly this A.M. Orderly woke me up at 7:00 & said be ready to leave at 10:00. So I packed & said good bye to everybody & left for Paris on the 12:45 train, arrived with 30 others & spent the night in Paris. Went to a movie before going to bed.

June 1   Went up to 45 Ave. Montaigne this A.M. just in time to miss the truck to Orly so . . . I bummed around town till 11:00 A.M. & took the truck. Reported out there but nobody knew why we came & as our baggage didn't come we went down again & spent tonight in Paris.

June 2, 1918   Got up late and bummed around Paris all morning. Went out to camp on 2:00 P.M. truck & found nothing doing. Baggage not there yet so came back to Paris & stayed in the hotel another night. Very expensive.

Monday 3   Did a little shopping this A.M. and came out to camp on 11:00 A.M. truck. Stayed to lunch & went out to Chateauroux to bring machine over but I didn't get one. Came back & found baggage & located myself for the night in a back room of Headquarters.

June 4, 1918   Moved to new barracks this A.M., wood floor, no lights. Took on new job as Asst. in Charge of Sopwith plane & had lots to do checking in incoming planes, etc. About 40 came in today. We also inspected them. Pretty tired tonight.

Wednesday 5   Went out to hangars at 7:00 A.M. and started again, lots of repair work to do. [Ish] Thurlow my boss left at about 10:00 A.M. & I never saw him again all day. Lots to do though. Several planes came in to be fixed up ready to fly. Tired again tonight.

June 5, 1918.

My dearest Mother:

Well of all things to happen to a person it seems that they all happen to me. Now that I've gotten that off my mind, or where my mind ought to be I'll explain.

The last time I wrote you was the evening of May 30th and I told you that I was going bombing and all that, also that I had put in for another seven day leave. Well, of course something had to happen for I never do get my leaves and I have only to apply for them to get moved or some such thing, so I knew something was coming. So next morning at 7 when I was just waking up an orderly came in and told me that I was to be ready to leave at 10 for where? why? etc? Well, I got up kind of bewildered like and went down to H.Q. at 8 and found out that we were to be sent near Paris as Transfer Pilots for I was moving with about 30 others, so I packed up in about ten minutes (I'm getting good at this) and at 10 we left. We arrived in Paris that night and were greeted by a couple of air raid scares, but nothing exciting, rather discouraging too for I've never seen one. Then we reported out at Camp but our baggage had not arrived, so we had to stay in Paris for three nights, which was very expensive. Then we moved out to the camp and sorted our baggage and we are now installed in barracks with no floors and no lights, so I can't write very much. When I got out here I was offered a job as Assistant in Charge of all one kind of machines on the field and it is a pretty good job too. Have been on it for two days now and sure have been busy, as we have a bunch of machines and they all need more or less repairs.

Now this place is a "pilot pool" in which all pilots who have completed their training come and do transfer work until they are called to the front, so we may go out any day or not for months yet. I can't tell what will happen to us, but we are one more step nearer the front, and that is something. This transfer work consists of driving planes that are brought in here from the factories out to the front or to the various schools in France. They drive all kinds of planes and drive them all over France. After awhile I'm going to take a few days off and do some of it myself, and see some of my old friends out at the front. Perhaps you have heard of Douglas Campbell, the first American Ace (5 Boches) whose training has been entirely American and what is better there are several others up there who are nearly Aces so it looks pretty good for us. Well, most of those fellows I know pretty well so I'd like to go out and see them and get some dope on how to exterminate the Boche.

Well I havn't anything else to say and it is getting pretty dark so I'll have to stop.

Please read this to Althea and tell her that I'll write to her next and I'll try and make it soon.

My love to all of you and best wishes to all my friends.

Your loving son,
Roland.

June 6, 1918 Worked all morning on the Sops [Sopwiths] Some more machines came in this P.M. I went down town & bought a pr. boots 3.75 pr. and left my watch at Tiffany's. Came home on 8:15 truck. Had a big raid at about 11:00 P.M. A "Gotha" [German bomber] came right over camp at about 1500-2000.

Friday 7 Went to work at 7:30 this A.M., got 4 Sops ready to go out, all tested and everything. They left this P.M. at about 3:00 and all got away in fine shape. Sold some shoes today. Wrote a letter to A. tonight.

June 8, 1918 Went out to hangars and bummed around out there. [Pilots] . . . from Clermont came up to get outfitted for the front, had a good visit with them. Worked this P.M. and got a few more machines lined up.

Sunday 9 Went out to hangars late today and worked all morning. Very hot today and not much doing. This P.M. we laid off and I slept and bummed around all P.M. Pretty hot. Went to bed at 10:00 same old time and slept like a log, as usual.

June 10, 1918 Went out to the field early this A.M. but came back to get dressed for town. Went in on 10:00 truck, did various shopping

& got my new boots. Came out and finished up work and put on new boots this evening. Everybody is very envious of them. They are some boots, too.

Tuesday 11   Worked on Sops all day today, didn't do very much. Got a few out to Tours & some more came in. Altogether about 100 on the field. Went to bed early tonight.

June 12, 1918   Worked on Sops again today, got some more off to Tours and more came in, the total about 100 remaining the same. It is getting kind of tiresome business but is better than nothing.

Thursday 13   Got some more Sops off to Tours today & more came in. Took a ride in a Sop today and they sure are funny old busses. They balloon along like an old boat. A liberty motored DH [DeHavilland] 4 burned up here today, it was too bad too.

June 13, 1918.

Dearest Mother:

Just a line tonight to let you know that everything is O.K. My new job as Assistant Flight Commander of the Sops, i.e. a certain type of airplane, keeps me pretty busy so I don't have much time to myself. Just keep on with the financial arrangements that you have made and buy as many Liberty bonds as you want, but don't forget that if you want anything, need anything or have to have anything either for yourself, the girls, or the house, why use my money and don't be stingy with yourself. It pays to get the best you know (I just paid 400 Fcs. for a pair of high lace boots). They are fine boots and are worth it to me. I sent you $150 not long ago and will send you money every now and then as time goes on just as I have been doing.

Well we are still outside of Paris waiting to be called to the front, but I'm afraid it will be quite awhile before that call comes. All our pilots on the front are doing wonderfully, especially well considering the planes they drive. The Germans have a new plane out now that is a peach and so far is the best on the front, but we have the advantage of better pilots.[1] If we only had planes as good as theirs we could wipe them out of the air. We will have them too if all goes well (in about four years).

I guess you think I'm becoming very sarcastic and I guess you are right, but they must be doing funny things over in the States when it comes to airplane construction. It is like a child with a new toy. In various air service magazines the fellows get over here, there are some very funny articles.[2] Two Senators talking about "combat" planes and "battle" planes, etc. We get a good laugh over it however, but seriously Mother this thing looks very bad. Why over here nobody knows what a "combat" or "battle" plane is. They seem to figure on building big planes, only where we come in I don't know, but we are hoping it will come out all right in the end.

I took my first ride in a Sop this AM. It is a big two seater but I didn't take up a passenger not the first time. Well, it was like riding a rowboat on a sea that has rather large swells in it. To begin with when I took off I didn't know when I left the ground until I looked over the side. Then began the waves. Gee it was some change from the planes I was used to running. To tell the truth I don't care much for them, they are such loggy old busses. The darn things fly themselves. I let go of the stick and she went along same as ever, same old buss.

Tell Althea that I got her letter with the gum in it and that I'll write her next. I havn't received any magazines with gum in them yet but am on the lookout for the same. I'm afraid you will have to make excuses to my friends and the rest of the family if I don't write as often as they would like, for this is the worst place for writing I've struck yet. I usually don't get done work until 7:30 or 8 PM making out reports, etc., and I'm on the job all day so when I'm not too tired I have to pull my trunk or somebody else's out in front of the barracks and write there until about 9:30. We havn't any light in the barracks. I'll send you a few pictures of moi like I sent you with photos of myself but I can't very well send you anything else, so you will have to be content with mine for awhile. I think I'll go down to Paris tomorrow PM and sport my new boots out and do some shopping. You ought to see those boots. I'll have someone take a picture of them with me in them for you. Just think of paying $75 for a pair of boots and then gaze fondly upon them. They are of the very best though c'est la guerre.

It is getting dark now so I'll have to stop. My love to the girls and Althea. I'll let you know when I go to the front by "Service" or some word if I can.[3]

Lots of love to yourself and remember that you are not only my onliest mother but the bestest mother that ever was.

Your loving son,
Roland.

June 14, 1918   Still working on the Sops. Went down town this P.M. and took my boots down to get stretched and came home for supper. Nothing exciting happened today.

Saturday 15   Still working on the Sops, are going to send a bunch to England and some more to the front which will be ready tomorrow. Two bunches are going to the front Monday.

June 16, 1918   Sent 5 Sops out to the front today. Tested one out myself and had a pretty good old ride. Sold another pair of Russet shoes today. Wrote a few letters this P.M.

Monday 17   Worked on Sops again today, getting rather monotonous. Took a Sop over to [Velizy-] Villacoublay. Mr. Honneur was my passenger. We saw a lot of new machines. Got some lining materials and came home again.

June 18, 1918   Worked on Sops again today but didn't do much.

Wednesday 19   Worked on Sops today this P.M. I went down town but didn't get my boots. Went around to Chatham Hotel & was sure surprised to learn that Mary Johnston was there. Had dinner with her and took her to the theater, had a good old talk with here about home and old times.

June 20, 1918   Worked on Sops this A.M. and P.M. Got some more out to Tours. Took a trip in the Nieuport Type 28. She sure does travel, did a few stunts but didn't like the engine very much but she sure is some buss to handle.

Friday 21   Worked on Sops this A.M. and went in town this P.M, bought razor & got my boots. Lost the razor but saved my shoes, and just caught the truck. Didn't fly today. Took Mary J. to supper & spent the evening with her. Had a very good time.

June 22, 1918   Got up pretty late & went out to the hangars. Got a bunch off to England & some to the front & Tours. Things are beginning to look a lot better in our department now.

Sunday 23   Didn't send any Sops out today, but we only did a Spad & Breguet [French bomber] landed here from the front today & heard some exciting experiences. Wrote a few letters this P.M.

June 23, 1918

My dearest Mother:

No mail this week, but then one gets used to those things over here. I've met Mary J. and had supper with her twice. She wrote you I think before this. We sure did have a good old time. She is the first girl I have taken out anywhere since I have been over here and I sure did enjoy it. It sure was good to see some one from home. I've been pretty busy lately so I havn't had time to do much writing. I wrote to Althea last and told her that I was enclosing some pictures for you, but of course I forgot them, but here they are, one for all of you.

There isn't any news to tell you. Am still in the Sop Department and we are pretty busy. Hope to go to the front on 220 HP Spads but can't tell, one never knows what one will do nowadays. I get to fly all kinds of machines up here and it is pretty good stuff. Had a letter from Ed Geohegan who is in France. He is still a Corporal. I'd like to go down and see him, but I don't know whether I can or not.

I see they are slowly moving the front our direction, so I suppose if we stay here long enough we will see some real action. We had some excitement today. A Spad boat from the front landed on our field and told us that he had brought down a boche this AM. His machine had a few bullet holes in it. He was an American in the French Army. Also a bombing plane from the front landed here and was lost. They had bombed a town across the lines and gotten lost in the clouds. The pilot was French and the bomber American. There isn't anything else to tell you exciting.

Receiving first installment of "gummed" magazines, very acceptable and a very good idea too.[4] Thank you very much. My love to the girls and Althea and my best to all my friends. Will write you more when there is something to say.

Your devoted son,
Roland.

June 24, 1918   Tested Sops all morning 4 in all and passed 3. Got pretty bumpy at last. Flew one to Villacoublay this P.M. with Mr. Honneur and back. Very bumpy. Was issued a bike today, pretty good stuff.

Tuesday 25   Tested some more Sops today. Took Mr. Honneur over to Villacoublay and left him there. Came back & bummed around. Went down town this P.M. and did some shopping and had supper with Mary J. and spent the evening with her.

June 26, 1918   Worked on Sops today, tested one this morning and 5 this P.M. Pretty bumpy. Took a Second Lieut. up for his first trip today and sure did get a kick out of it. The testing business isn't so good and I'll be glad when it is over.

Richardson by Sopwith, Orly, 1918.

Richardson in Nieuport 28, Orly, 1918.

Richardson and Mary Johnston, Orly, 1918.

Richardson in Spad XIII,
Vaucouleurs, 1918.

Richardson and Crew by Spad XIII, Lisle-en-Barrois, 1918.

Richardson's Spad at Foucacourt, 1918.

Jack Ogden by Spad XIII, Vaucouleurs, 1918.

Charles Grey by Spad XIII, Vaucouleurs, 1918.

John Hambelton by Spad XIII, Foucacourt, 1918.

Richard Phelan in Spad XIII, Lisle-en-Barrois, 1918.
(Phelan had recently crash landed his Spad but was unhurt, then was killed two weeks later)

Operations Office, 213th, Vaucouleurs, 1918.

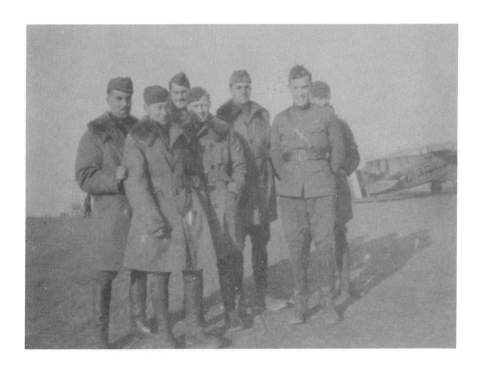

Richardson and Fellow-Pilots, 213th, Lisle-en-Barrois, 1918.

Richardson and Fellow-Pilots, 213th, Foucacourt, 1918.

Pilots and Staff Officers, 213th, Foucacourt, 1918.

Line of Spad XIIIs, 213th, Lisle-en-Barrois, 1918.

Pilot Officers at Field 9, Issoudun (Richardson in center), Christmas Night, 1918.

Thursday 27   Worked on Sops all day today. Took an artillery Lt. up this P.M. for his first ride and he sure got a kick out of it. Went down town & had supper with Mary J. & went to a movie. Stayed out in the Place de l'Opera during a very bad raid. It was one of the worst Paris has had. Bombs lit all around us.

June 28, 1918   Worked on Sops all day today. Got some more spare parts in. Mary J. & May Kale came out this P.M. and I showed them around the camp. Went up for a flight for the benefit of the ladies. Had another raid tonight on Paris.

June 28, 1918.

My dearest Mother:

Just a word to tell you that I am O.K. and everything is going along fine only I don't know any more about my future today than I did last time I wrote you. I've seen a lot of Mary Johnston lately, had supper with her several times and last night after supper we went to a movie, then watched an air raid from the Place de l'Opera. It was a pretty bad raid too. We could see the bombs dropping all around and see them too. They don't do much damage though, and as for demoralizing the people, there is nothing to it. Why it is the event of the evening, and everybody gets out to see the fun. You never hear a grumble from the people over here about the raids. They all have gotten used to it and don't mind it very much. Mary came out to Camp this afternoon with a friend of hers, and I showed her around and she took some pictures, and to finish it up I made a short flight, just to show her that I could do it. I couldn't take her up because it is against regulations, so I went up with one of the men on the field and flew awhile.

Mary came very near going home, for she got a telegram telling of Mardie's [Margaret Johnston] engagement and probable marriage in three weeks so Mary nearly went home. I encouraged her but she was too afraid she wouldn't be able to come back, so she finally gave it up. Mary saw all kinds of machines out here, nearly every kind we use on the front, even the new Liberty Plane. The latter is still in the experimental stage, but it sure shows up good for a large plane and can go like the dickens.

There must be a mix up somewhere in the mails for I haven't received any American mail for over two weeks, but I suppose I'll get a batch of it in a day or so. I hope to anyway. It is a pretty good night tonight, and I wouldn't be surprised if we had another raid. The planes come right over our camp and we can hear their motors just as plain as day. Ed Geohegan is over here, I believe I told you though.

It sure was good to meet Mary over here. I havn't been out with a girl since I left home and I was getting pretty stale and didn't know how to act so you can bet I was glad to meet her. Poor Mary gets pretty scared during the raids, she doesn't seem to like them very much. Well there isn't much more news to tell you so I'll go to bed for I have to get up at 6:15 AM every morning.

My love to the family and Althea and my best to all my friends.

Ever your loving son,
Roland.

Saturday 29 Worked on Sops all day today. Got some more off to England, 11 of them this P.M. General Pershing came out and we all flew for him. I flew a Sop three times and still I don't like them very much. Took a bath tonight. Letters from A & mother today. Photo from [A].

June 30, 1918 Worked awhile over at the hangars this A.M. Getting a new list of machines ready. After dinner I wrote some letters and bummed around not doing much of anything. Had a raid tonight.

July 1 Worked on Sops all A.M. Got my new list ready and tested a Sop but it was so bumpy that I couldn't do very much. After dinner I worked awhile then went down town and, did some shopping and had supper with Mary J. No raid tonight.

July 2, 1918 Flew a Spad, 180 HP this A.M. & let me say right here that it sure was great, they are some buss. Worked on Sops & talked about the Spad all the rest of the day. Got some off to Tours, got some more mail today. Flew a Sop with photographer P.M.

Wednesday 3 Worked on Sop today. Nothing much doing. Flew once today.

July 4, 1918 Worked all morning & went in town this P.M. had a great holiday today, the French nearly went crazy, lots of bull etc. passed around. Didn't fly today.

Friday 5 Worked on Sops some more, flew again today, very bad.

July 6, 1918 Took a Morane monoplane 120 HP down to Issoudun, had a forced landing south of Orleans and as luck would have it, I didn't bust up, got started again about 6:30 & arrived O.K. at 7:00 & didn't bust up again.

Sunday 7   Stayed at Iss. all morning, bought some gum and cigarettes in the A.M. and left on the 3:00 P.M. train for Paris. My feet are pretty
sore on account of my boots being pretty stiff. Arrived at Orly OK tonight.

July 7, 1918.

My dearest Mother:

Well, here I am back at the 3rd AIC [Aviation Instruction Center]
as you see by the reading (you know where that is, where I took my Nieuport
training), I'm only here for a day or so I'll begin at the beginning and
tell you about it. The evening of the 5th the transfer officer asked me if
I wanted to take a little monoplane from where I am stationed near Paris,
down here so I said O.K. Well I've never flown a monoplane, neither had
any of the other four, who were to take the rest down here so we expected
to have some time, and believe me I did. These little planes only have
one wing, very little surface and are just about the fastest thing there is.
They land at about 100 miles an hour. Well I tested my motor out before
starting and it ran pretty good for a new one, so I took off and she went
pretty good. I made a trip round the field and started off. Well if you get
out the map you can follow at Etampes the motor started doing funny
things, slowing down, then picking up again, etc. so I began to get a
little worried. You see I had never flown one before, and they are such little
speedy things that I didn't know how they would land, even if I knew my
field, so a forced landing would be nearly as bad as a smash up, so I was
really a little worried. Well I got down as far as Orleans and still the motor
was missing more all the time. I made a wide detour of the city and got
about ten miles beyond, just into the country covered with woods, when
the old engine gave her next to last pop. Well I'd never even had a forced
landing before, never, and I'd never even had a landing in the monoplane,
and I didn't know what kind of field I was going to have to land in, nor
even if there was one below, for I was over a woods. Well I nosed her
over and found a pretty good looking field, the motor caught again, but
I thought I'd better save it one with once for all, so I went over the field
and headed around into the wind and leveled out over my field. Well,
I went and went and went, motor stopped and she seemed to be fairly
gaining speed, finally I lit, hit again and bounced some more then I don't
know what I did but finally she lit and stayed lit and rolled along at high
speed, bounced some more and then stopped. Well I sure did heave a
sigh or two then I got out and looked her over and there wasn't anything
broken, not even a tire blown out. I tell you Mother, your son has horseshoes
around his neck, and from now on is living on borrowed time. It is the
luckiest thing I ever heard of, forced landings are bad enough in any
machine, but a machine you know nothing about and have it your first

forced landing to boot, well I consider myself the luckiest guy on two legs. I walked to the nearest town and telephoned for mechanics and in 3 hours or at 4 PM they were there and found the magneto 2 cogs out of time so they fixed me up and at 6:30 I took off again. The motor this time was O.K. i.e. enough to get me here, but not any too good, so I landed here all right, having had my previous experience in landing en route. I got away with it pretty good on this field that I knew. I sure was glad to get it here. I stayed all night with one of the doctors and saw all my old friends. Major Goldtwaite is a Lt. Col, by the way, and I am having dinner with him at the hospital this noon and will leave this PM for Paris. Some little experience.

I can go to the front in another month so they tell me and on a Spad too I hope. I see Mary J. quite often. Glad to hear that Uncle Ted is a B. G. I'll write him soon and congratulate him. He deserves it all right. Had an awfully nice letter from Uncle Russ, and right here let me bring to your notice that I do no more criticizing the U.S.A. or American Army. Things are coming over O.K. I only wish I could tell you how nicely everything is turning out, and really Mother the way you people at home are working for us is wonderful, just wonderful. Why everybody over here is remarking about it, and you have no idea how it helps keep us going over here. We are just as proud of you all at home as we are of our boys on the front. Everybody from the privates up. I could go on praising you people to the end of this letter, but you understand what I mean and I wouldn't say that if I didn't mean it, so I won't take up any more space doing it. I think you are the best of them all Mother. You must be doing about three peoples' work, so you need never worry about not doing enough, you may never hear the bullets whistle, but your work at home will keep hundreds of boys happy and unafraid of those bullets, just think that over and see if I'm not right. Sometimes I am right you know, even you said so once.

Got some more gum in three Air Service Journals and three installments of cards in letters, both of which I thank you very much for. I hear from Althea and you very often, got a whole batch the other day which made up for my shortage of the past few weeks.

Everything is fine over here. Paris was all decorated up on the 4th. I had to work in the morning so I missed the parade, but they say it was just fine. The people over here really think we are doing something now, and believe me we are too and no joking. We had a big time at our camp the evening of the 4th. A few Generals, Colonels, etc. spoke to us, so did some French ministers and we had three truck loads of A.R.C., Y.M.C.A. etc. American girls at our camp which made it very nice. We were busy showing them around and had a good old time.

Please give everybody my best and my love to you the girls and Althea, she sure is a nice girl all right, in fact the very nicest, she is awfully good to me. Please get Emily, yourself and Bobby a present when the time comes for your birthdays. I'll send you another $100 in another few days. I think I can afford it this month, although living up near Paris is pretty expensive, especially when one is equipping oneself for the front, but then I should worry about that and I can do it all right.

My very best love to you Mother and lots of it.

Roland.

July 8, 1918   Worked on Sops all day today, didn't fly though. The new inspection system is sure a balled up affaire and we can't get many machines through. Flew a [Nieuport] 27 today.

Tuesday 9   Flew this A.M. on an old Sop. And gosh but it was bumpy. This P.M. I went down town & bought some soap at the QM & gave it to Mary J. had supper with her & an English major, had a very good time.

July 10, 1918   Worked on Sops today same as usual. Got some more out & a few through the inspection dept. This P.M. it started to rain about 4:00 so we had to quit work & put the machines in.

Thursday 11   Worked on Sops all day today. Went down town and found that Mary Johnston was leaving so Jack Ogden & I saw her off to the front. Then we had supper & went to a movie then home to bed.

July 12, 1918   Worked on Sops all day today. Got a few more out & finally we are caught up with ourselves. We only have a few more to work on.

Saturday 13   Worked on Sops again. Tested one today & it flew pretty well. Got some more out & only have about 3 more to work on. Flew a [Nieuport] 28 this P.M. and sure had a good time.

July 14, 1918   Worked at hangars this A.M. Got dressed up this P.M. & went out to see a street in Choisy-le-Roi named after Pres. [Woodrow] Wilson and heard a lot of speeches & bull, also some good music.[5] Came home & wrote a few letters.

July 14, 1918.

My very dearest Mother:

Got a dandy letter from you today and one from Emily the day before yesterday, sure was glad to hear from you. Glad you got my check for

$150 am sending you another for $100 tonight. I am quite in favor of your buying bonds with my money as long as you have enough to go on, and the girls get their allowances. Be sure to keep some in my account so that if I ever want you to buy anything for anybody, you will have enough to do it. Don't forget your's Emily's and Bobbie's birthdays and please get something nice for yourself.

By the way that picture you sent is not me. I am returning it so you will know what I mean. I don't have anything to do with the observer's seat in an airplane and very little to do with two seaters at all.

I have no definite news about when I am going to the front, so that settles that question. Will be glad to get the gum as I am running low so I'll be careful about opening papers, etc. My work is pretty interesting here, especially when I get a chance to fly a good machine like a Spad or a Nieuport Type 28. I flew the 28 yesterday and it was relief after flying the loggy old Sops. You asked me what the ground looked like from the air. Well it looks just like it used to from a mountain, like we saw in Suisse, you remember that, the higher you get the more you can see.

➤ I wrote to Uncle Ted tonight, it sure is great that he got his B.G. He sure does deserve it. Gee, you people are sure tightening up on the food situation, is it really necessary to do all that?[6] There sure ought to be enough for everybody if everybody does as you people do. I wish you would take a vacation this summer Mother. I think it will do you a lot of good for you have been working awfully hard this year and you deserve a rest. Remember that a rest will raise your efficiency a whole lot.

We have had very good weather lately, just as bright and sunny as anyone could want, so flying has gone in great shape. Today the French had a big celebration, and we assisted at the naming of a street in a town nearby "Avenue du President Wilson" there was not much to do and speeches, parades, etc. in which we all helped. The French sure are like story things, and lots of talk and so forth, they are a great people.

We have a floor and lights in our barracks now so feel lots better. Also I have a Ford machine in our department, I mean for both my boss and I in which we run around in, in grand style. I went over to this little town in it this PM and got soaked, as it rained this afternoon while we were on our way.

I saw Mary Johnston off to the front Tuesday last. She went up all alone and seemed very glad to be going. Even I may get up there some day, who knows? You can't never always sometimes tell you know.

My 400 Fr. boots sure are great. You think me pretty extravagant and I guess I am, but there is nothing like having the best, and even that is none too good for war work.

If you want to read a funny article on Aviation read "Aces High" by Sgt. Pilot Harold D. Wright in the S.E.P. June 15, 1918.[7] He sure does sling the bull so to speak about himself and aviation in general, whatever you do though, don't believe all of it, for we have just read it and most

of the article is ridiculous. His figures are way off and the whole thing
is pretty much of a farce. It is a shame to misinform the public in that
way but it can't be helped I suppose. I am going to write Althea tonight
so you tell her to look out for a letter. Read her this one too if you will,
for I hate to repeat to her what I've told you, get me?

Well Mother don't overwork yourself now and go get plenty of rest
and please take a vacation this summer. It sure is great that the girls are
going to have such a good time. Please give them my love and also Althea,
she sure is a dandy girl about writing to me and you don't know how much
it means to me either. If anything would happen to her I don't know what
I'd do (You needn't tell that to everybody, that is between you and me).
Best luck to you Mother dear, and always think of me as well and happy,
having a good time, anxious to go to the front and all those things. I think
the war will be over by next summer.

Your loving son,
Roland.

Monday 15   Worked on Sops all day today until about 4 PM. We havn't
much more to do now for we have most of them fixed up & a lot sent off.
Went in town this P.M. with Warren Eaton and Jack Ogden & had supper
& went to the follies after, then home on the 11:45 truck.

July 16, 1918   Yesterday while taxieing [*sic*] a Sop, I stuck my elbow
into the dynamo prop, it sure is swollen up this A.M. Worked on Sops all
day & this evening. I got permission to fly a Spad to Issoudun. Some classy
rotating baffles. Went to bed early.

Wednesday 17   Took a Spad down to Issoudun today, had a forced
landing just north of Pandy. Motor trouble & ran out of gas. Got fixed
up & arrived O.K. at 4:15 P.M. Went over to Field 7 & saw Chick Nash
& stayed all night with Doc. Brownell.

July 18, 1918   Stayed at In. all morning, bummed around & saw all
my old friends. Had dinner at the A.R.C. and left this P.M. on the 3 P.M.
train for Paris. Arrived O.K. 7 came right out to camp.

Friday 19   Worked on Sops today, nearly all through. We got 4 Avros
in today. Pretty good buss. Flew a Sop around with photographer again
& flew an Avro this evening but had to come down on account of a bad
motor.

July 20, 1918   Flew another Avro but had to come down early on account of the gas pump stopping. Worked on Sops all day today. Sent a bunch out tonight after supper. Haven't had any raids for some time.

Sunday 21   Worked all morning & got off two more machines. Started to work this P.M. but they called it off for the Sop Dept. Took a Spad 220 to Saints [?] this P.M. Missed the car back so had to take the train, 4 hrs. en route arrived Paris 12 PM. Stayed in a hotel.

July 22, 1918   Got up late this A.M. & reported out to camp at noon. Went over to St. Cyr after dinner & flew a 27 Nieuport back here. Peach of a machine. I had a dandy trip.

July 22, 1918.

My dearest Mother:

Received your letter with the gum and cards in it. Thank you very much, the gum is O.K. and I sure am glad to get it. I suppose you think I am a regular gum artist, but it is the only bad habit I have, and once through this war I won't be bothered with it. The cards are O.K., suit me to a T, thanks muchly for same. Glad you heard that Mary and I had at last met. She has gone now as I said in my last letter, up to the front near Toul.

I think your summer plans are great. Sure am glad you are going away yourself. Don't see why you feel that you have to justify yourself for all your plans though, just go and do what you think is right, and if I were you I wouldn't bother with justifying myself about it. However, you are boss and running the business.

Believe me Mother we sure have the old Hun on the jump now, just pushing him right off the map. Yesterday I went up near the front in a new Spad 220 H.P. to deliver it to a Squadron, and the boys say that the front has been moving so fast that they can't keep track of it.[8] The Allies just picked off the Chateau Thierry salient at Riems and Soissons and captured all kinds of guns, men, etc. Guess we kind of fooled them that time. They are still going too. It took me 20 minutes to take that Spad up there and 4 hours and 30 min. to get back on the train. Some speed n'est ce pas? I've been riding around the country pretty much lately delivering planes, etc. I've flown all kinds of machines, Spads, Nieuports and others, but mostly the former. Brought a Nieuport 27 over here from St. Cyr. this PM and had a race with a Liberty plane [DeHavilland D. H. 4] over the field. He beat me 40 ways though. I didn't have a show. The Liberty is some plane, but it isn't the kind of a plane I want to go to the front on. I don't know whether exactly you people know just what kind of a plane a Spad is and what its duties are because Uncle Russ talked about wishing I could drop a bomb on the Kaiser, etc., in one of his letters. Well we don't carry bombs, wireless outfits or anything, but two machine guns mounted on the front of the machine so they can't move. They shoot through the propellor and can be shot together or separately, and to aim them, the whole machine has to be aimed at the target. Now at the front these single place fighters go up over the lines in formations of about five and patrol the lines, keeping German planes from coming over and fighting any German plane that comes in sight. That is all. That is all, except French straffing once in awhile, so you see we don't drop bombs or anything like that. It is the sporty branch of the Service, so to speak, that is what I've trained for, and that is the way I want to go over the lines.

There hasn't been any excitement here lately, so there isn't any news to tell you. Paris hasn't been bombed or bombarded for some time, and the old Boche are on the run. The Americans are doing fine. Gee, but its great to hear about it all. I'm only afraid that it will be all over before I get there, so I've been bothering the officer in charge of sending pilots to the front nearly every day to let me go up and I expect soon to get him so bothered, that he will be glad to get rid of me. If you can't get what you want one way, get it another, n'est ce pas?

I'm sending you a picture of a 220 Spad to see how you like it. Don't you think she is a peach? Look at those 4 [wing struts] on each side and all those strong wires. Regular bull dog stuff. Will you let your little boy go up in one of these here "heavier than air machines"?

Well I'll have to stop now as it is getting rather dark. Tell Althea that I am going to write her next in a day or so, and give her all the news in this letter S.V.P.

I think the war will be over by this time next year. What say you? Please give my love to all the girls and Althea.

Roland.

Tuesday 23   Worked on Sops all morning and went down town all P.M. had my pants fixed and bummed around doing small errands etc. Came home on the 8:15 truck.

July 24, 1918   Worked on Sops all day today, sent 3 out. Not much doing with us nowadays but we have to stick around Quand meme. Went down to Choisy this evening. Am trying to get out to the front.

Thursday 25   Worked on Sops all morning and this P.M. took a Spad over to Colombey les Belles. Landed once on main field to fix my map

& at Vinets to gas up. Had a good trip but broke a T.S. Shock absorber landing. Caught the 9:00 train at Toul & rode all night on it sitting up in a full compartment.

July 26, 1918   The train arrived in Paris at 9:30 A.M. It was an awful night. . . . I went up to the Y & had a shower bath, sure felt good too. Worked on Sops all P.M. Nothing to do, am pulling more strings to go out.

Saturday 27   Worked on Sops this A.M. & P.M. Flew a 28 Nieuport this morning and it sure went fine. Felt lots better than the other one did. After dinner I took a 24 bis up & tested it. Not much doing today. Went to some prize fights in town tonight & came out late.

July 28, 1918   Went out to hangars this A.M. and didn't do anything but at noon they decided to get some machines off to England. Had a goose dinner today. Worked all day on English order & didn't send any off after all.

Monday 29   Worked on Sops all day today and didn't do anything else. Got a few out but that is all.

July 30, 1918   Worked on Sops today. Flew an Avro twice & a Sop once. Panned the second time with the Avro in a potato patch. Got some letters today.

Wednesday 31   Worked on Sops all day today. Flew the Avro again today. Nothing much doing lately. Am still asking to go out to the front.

Aug. 1, 1918   Worked on Sops all day. Flew the Avro twice today and the old festive Sop once. Tried to get a ride in a Spad today but it had a flat tire & we couldn't fixed [sic]. Warren Eaton & I had a good old time up in the Avro today.

Friday 2   Thurlow . . . beat it this A.M. so I was left alone with the old Sops. Not much doing though. Tested two for wireless this P.M. and went to a dozen or two officers meetings off & on during the day.

August 3, 1918   Went to town this A.M. and left some clothes to be fixed up. Bought a dandy trench coat from the Q.M. and left my leather coat to be fixed. Came out on the 2:00 P.M. truck & read letters for awhile. Went to a Post dance this evening & enjoyed myself.

Sunday 4   Worked on Sops all day today. Sent out about 12 and worked till 6:30 tonight. I was the only one on the job tonight & all day. I was pretty busy & am pretty tired tonight. Will probably fly the Spad tomorrow.

August 4, 1918.

Dearest Mother:

Two very nice letters from you, one from Althea and Mardie's wedding announcement yesterday. How is that? Tres bons say I. Also the gum and some more cards. I have enough cards now for the duration of the war, or until I'm made a Captain or General, or some little thing like that, which will come about the same time or later.

Well, I'm still here and getting more discontented every day, and will keep on getting so until I get out to the front. Am enclosing a couple of pictures of one of my Spads and me. This was taken just before I took the photograph up in the same Sop to get some pictures of the Camp.

There isn't much news, except that I bought me a dandy trench coat from the QM for $19.80. which is some bargain, believe me. I havn't photographed the boots yet, but will some day and send you a copy. These planes I am looking after are SOPWITHS and there is no "L" in it. But please don't associate me with said plane, for I wouldn't take one as a personal gift from the King of Siam. Now you know how I feel on that subject. Sure am glad you are having such a dandy vacation. So far over here we have only had a couple of days of uncomfortable weather most of the time it is nice and cool. It has been raining here for the last couple of days, and, consequently, not much doing in the aviation line, except piling up machines to go out. This afternoon when it cleared off we sure did have to work for awhile. You never would have known it was Sunday, for I worked myself until 6:30 PM and the other flight commanders did too.

We had a dance out here last night. They brought out a bunch of signal corps telephone girls and Red Cross Nurses and Y.M.C.A. damsels and we had quite a good time. I fear however that my ability as one of Mr. Trepsicorian's (?) followers is fast leaving me, what little I had I mean. That is the least of my worries though and really doesn't bother me a bit for everybody else is the same way. I pity the girls at home when the war is over though, they will suffer agonies though or something like that for quite awhile afterwards. I received an awfully nice letter from Althea yesterday. She was then going up to Cleveland in Selser's car and about to have one grand time, which I hope panned out all right. She sure is one nice girl, in fact the nicest girl N'est ce pas, am glad you agree. Well you are probably back from your two weeks' with Aunt Mabel, and I sure hope you had a good time. Gee I'd give my new $75 boots and then some to see you all right now, wouldn't it be great. Well apres la guerre we will get together and you can ask as many questions as you like and I'll try and answer them.

My love to the girls and Althea and my best to all my friends and lots of love to yourself from your son.

Roland.

Aug. 5, 1918   Still working on Sops. Not much doing though. Went to town this afternoon and got my leather coat. Had supper with W. Eaton & Jack Ogden and came out on the 8:15 truck.

Tuesday 6   Worked on Sops all day today. Got some more in. Pretty bad weather lately so haven't flown the Spad. Am getting fat again, if I don't get out soon I don't know what will become of me.

Aug. 7, 1918   Worked on Sops today. Took Warren Eaton on for some combat, me in a 220 Spad & he in a 28 N. [Nieuport]. He put it all over me at 1000 m. Spad not very good, wing heavy.

Thursday 8   Worked on Sops today and got some more out & in. Not much doing here now.

Aug. 9, 1918   Took Warren Eaton on again. This time he had the Spad and me the 28 N. and I had him cold but at 2000 m. he could outclimb me. Worked on Sops same as usual. Went down town this P.M. & shopped.

Saturday 10   Big business today. Got some machines out & some more in. Took a Q.M. Lt. up for his first ride in a Sop today. He liked it pretty much. Am getting the Spad ready for another flight. It will be done tomorrow.

Aug. 11, 1918   Worked this A.M. Combat with Warren Eaton again he with 28 N. & me with Spad & he put it all over me. Spad still wing heavy. Came down because oil pressure quit. Didn't work this P.M. Wrote a few letters.

August 11, 1918.

Dearest Mother:

Your letter of July 14th from Michigan received. Thanks muchly. Sure am glad to hear that you are having such a good time with Aunt Mabel. It will do you a lot of good. I wrote to Althea this afternoon and told her that I was going up with another pilot and do a combat for some Generals, but they didn't come, so we didn't fly, much to my disappointment.

Well, what do you think, I have a Spad. I swiped it from the Spad Department and have it all fixed up. It isn't very good though for something is wrong with it, but it ought to be O.K. soon. I am writing on August 12th now, for last night I was interrupted by much loud talking and it happened all around my bed, so I quit. Well of all things to happen to me now, it has happened today, out of a clear sky. Jack Ogden, one of the fellows in Headquarters, called me up and asked me if I wanted to go to the front, and said that he and several others of my friends were on this list to go to the 213 Aero Squadron, which is in the 3rd Pursuit Group. Well I nearly jumped into the telephone for joy. So to make a long story short, I am really going out if nothing happens, and will be leaving in a few days. Will telegraph you SERVICE or something like that, so that you will know about it.

I am having some time writing this letter. It is the 16th now and I started this on the 11th, so you can see how busy I've been. I met Ed Geohegan today. He is stationed out near Paris and wrote me his address, so I immediately went out and looked him up and we had a good old time. He is a Second Lt. in the Field Artillery. Well we talked over everything we could think of and then some, but I had to leave at 2 PM, for we had a class then, but I am going to try and see him tomorrow. Well today our orders came to go out and join our Squadron and my new address will be:

213 Aero Squadron\
3rd Pursuit Group\
U.S. Air Service A.E.F.

How does that sound? I am afraid I'll have to stop writing to so many people or rather than I'll have to continue as I am and write to you, Althea and then others if I get time. So please explain to anybody who might feel that I owe them a letter, for it is too much for one guy to do, not that I wouldn't like to keep everybody posted, but the list grew too long. I received two letters from Althea and one from Emily and Gramps lately which I am going to answer as soon as possible. Just now I am busy packing up to go out tomorrow. I don't know where we are going nor much about our future, but I will tell you as soon as I do.

Well I'll have to finish this Mother or I never will. Please give my love to the girls, Althea and the family. It sure is good of Aunt Mabel to give you such a treat.

I will write you later about our new situation, when I know something about it myself.

Well lots of love Mother to you and I hope we can finish this war soon. There are rumors that if no leave is taken for 18 months, we get 20 days HOME. I hope that is true, for it is only five months more for me. How would that suit you? Good night Mother and lots of love.

Your son,\
Roland.

Monday 12   Am going to the front, 213 Aero Squadron. Worked on Sops today or rather got the Spad ready to fly this P.M. Got her all lined up and ready to fly this P.M. Combatted again with W. Eaton who had a 28. At 2900 m. he put it all over me. The Spad isn't right yet. I don't know what is the matter with it.

Aug. 13, 1918   Combatted again with Eaton, me in N. 28 & beat him. Took a Spad out to Saints this A.M. had dinner out there and flew a 28 N. back. Saw a fellow get killed today in 28 N, dove into the ground. Went to town this P.M. for supper.

Wednesday 14   Worked on Sops today. We have the R's [Avros], Caudrons, Farmons & Capronies now. S. O. S. Combatted with Eaton again today both in N. 28's, he beat me again but not very bad. Had a good flight. Flew type 21 N today for awhile.

Aug. 15, 1918   Tested a Sop this A.M., then took up two more passengers for a ride. Worked on Sops all day till 4:00 P.M., then went down town with Jack Ogden & saw an English show. Had an air raid tonight.

Friday 16   Went down town this A.M., looked for a dentist but couldn't find one. Went out to Vincennes and saw Ed Geohegan. Sure had a good old time. Our orders came to leave today. Got my clearance papers & am packing up tonight.

Aug. 17, 1918   Packed up and went down town this A.M. Did some shopping but couldn't get my boots. Met Ed Geohegan and we went out to Orly & I took him up in a Sop. Had supper & went to a movie with him. Slept at the Chateau Hotel.

Chapter Five

At the Front: The Fighting Pilot

"Gee but it was exciting."

Sunday 18　　AT THE FRONT　　We left Paris on the 8:08 train and rode all day till about 5:00 when we arrived at VOID. Went by truck to our destination, just outside of Vaucouleurs. Very pretty camp in the woods and everything sure is great. We will have 220 H.P. Spads.

Aug 19, 1918　　Got my machine all ready today. Am assigned to Spad 15804, it is a pretty good machine too. I made a few changes in it this A.M. and took it for a hop this P.M., little wing heavy. Charlie Grey is our flight commander.

Tuesday 20　　Worked on my machine all day today, fixed the carburator, wing and other smaller things, turned the motor up this P.M. 2100 RPM — very good. Didn't fly. Made a map and got settled in our barracks also today.

Aug. 21, 1918   Worked on my Spad all morning. Lined the guns up and shot them. Took her up on a test flight this P.M. went fine. Came down, landed, wheel collapsed and she turned over. Wing, prop, rudder broken. Bad day.

Thursday 22   Took the top wing, prop, radiator off my Spad today and she looks like a wreck sure enough. The new wing is a round tipped one which isn't as good as the new type. Worked on it all day today. She ought to be ready in a couple of days now.

August 22, 1918.

Dearest Mother:

Well here I am out at the front at last. Arrived here Sunday evening. I can't tell you much about our location or where I am, but we are in a very pretty camp and everything is fine. It looks more like a summer camp than an aviation camp on the front. We are pretty close up to the lines and can see the observation baloons [*sic*] and enemy planes surrounded by the smoke of anti aircraft shrapnel almost every day. At night they bomb all around us which makes it quite interesting. I have a peach of a machine, but as yet havn't been out on patrol with it because it took two days to get it in shape and then yesterday I took it up for a test flight and brought it down, landed it and had rolled along the ground for 50 or 75 feet when my left wheel just collapsed and over I went and landed upside down with gasoline, oil and water trickling down all around me. Of course the belt held me in while I was going over, but I lost no time in undoing it after we stopped moving, for there is always danger of fire but not very much, anyhow I dropped out of the seat, lit on my head and crawled out. It is a very unpleasant sensation to go up on your nose and then all the way over on your back in a plane. This is the first time I ever broke a machine up so I feel very chagrined about it. However, there wasn't much broken on it, the top wing was cracked a little, the prop and rudder broken and that was all, as far as we have been able to find out. In fact it is quite remarkable that there wasn't more broken, but it didn't go over very fast and didn't hit very hard when the tail came down again. O, yes, the left wheel was a mess, looked more like a large pretzel than a wheel, this incidentally was the cause of it all, for everything went along fine until the wheel broke, then, oh my.

It all goes to show now that I have no machine at least not until they get mine fixed again, which will be a slow process I'm afraid, because of the lack of tools and spare parts, in the meantime my flight goes merrily over the lines and I stay at home and hear about their adventures when they get back. No one has gotten any boche yet, and no one has gotten hit yet, but there have been a few scraps in which the odds came out about even.

I'd like to tell you all about our organization and everything else more in detail but it is forbidden, so you will have to be satisfied. News has just now arrived that some one in our group has just gotten a boche, not so bad is it?[1]

Thank you very much for the box of double mint gum. It arrived O.K. and sure was appreciated. Please give the girls my love and tell them that I received their letters and will answer them when I get a chance. I wrote to Althea day before yesterday, but give her my love anyhow. Will write you soon again, in the meantime lots of love from

> Your son,
> Roland.

Aug. 23, 1918   Worked on my machine all day today. I need a prop. now and about another days work on it and it will be finished. Nearly took [another pilot's] plane on a patrol this evening but he arrived just in time & I stayed home. Food not so very good here now.

Saturday 24   Went over to Colombey les Belles this morning to get a plane with Dick Phelan, had dinner over there and got the two planes ready & it started raining so we came home on the truck again. Got some wire to lock [?] with and some spark plugs.

Aug. 25, 1918   Went over to Colombey les Belles this A.M. again. Got some more wire & we flew our machines back to our field and landed OK. Machine very good. Worked on my machine all P.M. Rode one to Amanty and bummed around for awhile.

Monday 26   Worked on my machine all day today. All it needs is a prop. and a rudder and she will be O.K. I don't know how the round tipped wing is going to work but I hope it will be O.K. Went out in the woods & shot awhile this evening.

Aug. 27, 1918   Went out to the range and shot pistols again this A.M. Then worked on my machine awhile doing little odds & ends. Chic Nash & W. Eaton came up today. They are in the 93rd. Pasted some photos in my album this evening.

Wednesday 28   Shot the pistol again today and didn't hit much. Worked on my machine awhile today and made a few more improvements, etc. No rudder in sight yet. Dick Phelan broke up tonight so they lent me his wheels & rudder so at last may fly tomorrow.

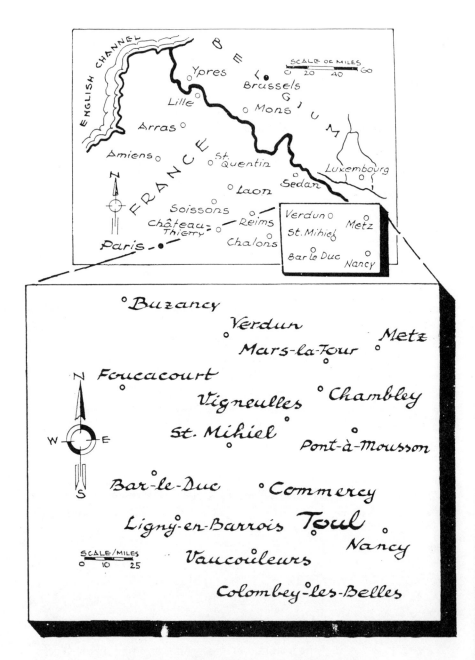

Toul Sector: The 213th at the Front, 1918.

Aug. 29, 1918   Rain this A.M. it stopped about 10:30 so I took my machine down to the range & lined up the guns to the sights. Flew this P.M. but had to come down on account of throttle rod coming off. Went on patrol today had to come down on account of loss of oil somewhere.

August 29, 1918.

Dearest Mother:

Well at last I've been over the lines. I didn't want to write you until I had so now here goes. To begin at the beginning after I turned my Spad upside down they had a hard time fixing it on account of not having the parts to do it with, but last night another fellow broke up, but the parts I lacked were still intact on his machine, so they transferred them and so put me in shape to fly again. This AM I got up to go out on an 8 AM patrol only to find it raining, but it cleared up about 10:30 so I took my machine down to the range and lined up the guns with the sights, which is very necessary, as you can imagine. Maybe you would like to know how that is done. Well the machine is put up in line of flight, that is level, a certain distance away from the target and the tail of the machine moved around until the right gun is lined up with the bull's eye of the target and when fired the burst is around the bull's eye. Then the left gun is lined up by moving the gun this time so that the burst, i.e. a burst of shots, hits the target at the same place as the right gun's burst did, then the sights are lined up with the holes in the target made by the guns, see. Well this morning I did that and this PM about 3 bells and a demi, I took her up for a test flight and rose to about 400 meters, when all of a sudden the engine dropped from about 2000 R.P.M. to 1300 R.P.M., which is not enough to keep in the air. Well, I tried to open up the throttle and nothing doing, so I tried to close it and she kept right on going and no matter where I pushed or pulled the throttle to, the engine kept right on going at 1300, all this time though I was losing altitude, but I had turned around towards the field and saw that I was going to make it all right, so I kept the motor going and stopping alternately with the magneto switch, for that was the only way I could stop her. Well, I finally made the field and caught the motor after I had landed, but it wouldn't pull me along the ground, so I stopped her and got out to see what the trouble was, and found that just as I had expected, the rod leading from the throttle to the carburator had come off at the carburator end so it wouldn't work. Well, as I had a regular patrol at 6 I didn't go up again, but had the mechanics go over the machine very carefully so that it would be ready in time. At 5:30 I warmed the engine up and got ready to go up, loaded the guns, and gave the signal to the mechanics to pull out the blocks from under the wheels and then I taxied out into the field, a mechanic on each wing and turned around and took off. (This sounds like one of Harold Wright's stories in the S.E.P. "Aces High" I believe it is called) Well, if you read those articles, don't believe them. I guess you know now how he was exposed and the real truth about his career in the French Army came out.[2] I believe he had the sum of 13 hours over the lines and never was in a fight. Well, to go on with my story, I knew that a little oil leaked out where a gasket was broken where the water pump in bolted on to the crank case, but it wasn't enough to keep me down, so I went up all right. I was the first one off and we were to circle the field to the left and our flight commander was to circle to the right, and at 500 meters we were to pick him up. Well, all went well until the patrol was formed there were seven in it. I was second to the right. Now the trouble begins. The oil started leaking faster and faster, but I kept on for I had 5 gallons in the tank, then we reached the lines and started patroling up and down. The anti aircraft fired at us awhile, then a lone Spad from somewhere joined us, and believe me he lost no time in showing us his colors under his wing. Well about that time the oil was a regular lake in the cockpit and all over me too and getting worse all the time, so I finally decided to break away from the patrol and come home for there were seven of them and they didn't need me there as bad as they needed my machine for other patrols so I didn't want to risk running out of oil and burning up my motor so I came home and landed. Well it all goes to say that at last I've been over the lines, even if it wasn't for very long, so now I feel that I can write you without making excuses and giving alibis about not doing any active service. There is lots to say but I can't tell you anything about what we are doing up here anyway, this war isn't going to last much longer, take that in your pipe and smoke it, for we are here now and the English and the French have the Boche on the run, and I hope the U.S'ers will too again soon. Well I've about talked myself out. We have a dandy squadron and a dandy C.O. and everything is fine. My next patrol comes day after tomorrow and I sure hope my buss will be ready. It is a fine old buss too, the new top wing works fine.

Please read this letter to Althea. I will write to her next after I have some more news to tell for I am all out of breath now.

My love to the girls and Althea and lots and lots to yourself. I am sending you $150 tonight, do as you please with it. Buy Bobby a birthday present for me and keep up the girls' allowances and don't be stingy with yourself. Anything you need why get it and pay for it with my money, remember them is my orders.

Ever your devoted son,
Roland.

Friday 30   Worked on my machine all A.M. Shot a little with my pistol. Went up on a trail squadron formation, didn't go yery well. Came down again & found thermometer on the bum.

Aug. 31, 1918   Bad weather today so we didn't fly. Tried to go to Nancy this P.M. but transportation failed to appear. Went to a dance at Toul hospital tonight and had a pretty good time. Came home about 1:00 A.M. Sunday morning.

Sept. 1   Off all day today went over to Nancy this afternoon and had a good bath and a swim in a pretty good pool, had a good dinner & bought some candy etc. Came home and arrived here about 10:00 P.M. went right to bed.

Sept. 2, 1918   Worked on my machine and played ball this morning. Had a pretty good game. This P.M. we had another squadron formation. Went pretty good today. Went up on a patrol at 5:30 but mag. [magneto] fell apart and I had to come down, too bad.

Thursday 3   Got my machine ready this A.M. but found my mag. wouldn't work so they had to put a new mag. in. Got it in about 2:00 P.M. and my machine worked fine. We are on special alert all P.M. Played ball and had a good time. Went over to the 93rd this evening to visit.

Sept. 4, 1918   Had a patrol at 8:30 this A.M. Dick Phelan, Charley Grey and myself were to be in it. We all got off but Charley & Dick had to come down so I patrolled by myself. From St. Mihiel to Verdun to Flirey. Then came down. Saw nothing on alert all P.M. Nothing doing. Saw the Archies [anti-aircraft fire] bring a plane down in flames.

September 4, 1918.

My dearest Mother:

Two nice letters and a cable from you, sure was glad to get them. I guess you received my SERVICE cable O.K. Well, as yet I've seen very little service for my machine always seems to have something wrong with it. The day before yesterday I started out on a patrol and one of my magnetos fell apart. I wrote to Althea about it, she will read that part to you I know, funny she doesn't read you all of my letters, isn't it? How queer, I suppose you all think "they aint as they should be", but they are all right and I have my doubts if I would read you all of her letters to me. How's that, tres bon I say.

Well just after I finished writing to Althea yesterday morning in came a cablegram from her, gee but I was glad to get that. Wasn't she a peach to send it. She sure is one fine girl (that is between our family only).

The girls too have sure been good about writing me, where I really don't deserve it, for I havn't written to anybody but you, Althea and Mary Johnston (who by the way is down near the Swiss border at Epinal, or some place like that) for a long while. Gramps wants a letter very badly and so do lots of others, i.e. I owe them letters, but it is getting beyond me to keep up my correspondence, get three meals a day, keep my machine in condition, go on a patrol now and then and get some sleep. Please explain this to them all for truly I am down at the hangars nearly all day working with the mechanics on my machine and at night we have nothing but candle light and on a good night, no lights at all for fear of being bombed out, so there you go, c'est la guerre.

Please thank Frances R. [Richardson] for her letter that you enclosed in yours. She is a dear little girl to remember her cousin over here. That sure is good news about Mr. [William] Procter. Gosh, but I sure would like to see him. Be sure to give him my new address and ask him to try and look up our organization and I sure will be glad to see him.

Well you people sure have had a fine summer at least while you were away. I can't tell you how glad I am that you all got away for awhile and had such a good time. Too bad Althea couldn't go visit C. [Coombsie] in her camp, but I guess she was right after all. E. sent me some pictures of herself, you, Frances, Jim and Aunt Mable. They all looked fine. The picture wasn't so good of you though, you seem to be watching the "Archies" burst around a plane about 4000 meters up in the air, or maybe it is an observation baloon [sic], or an enemy formation, the last two seem to be the most probable, don't you think so. Are those the shoes I gave you for a birthday present, if they are I think I am a pretty good chooser. I like your pins too, very patriotic idea, you see what a detailed examination I made of your picture.

So Angeline Loveland is at last engaged, well it is a good thing. Please congratulate her for me. I sent you $150 not long ago, so you can be on the lookout for it. Do as you have planned with it and don't stint yourself by all means promise me that.

I just got back from a patrol this AM about half an hour before I wrote or started to write this letter. It was scheduled for 8:30 AM, so we all got up and ate, and down to our planes at 8. Only three of us were to go up over the lines, but all of us were to start out in case some of us had trouble and had to come back. Well I was first off and was to take the lead in case our flight commander, or the fellow on the right couldn't keep up, so I circled around the field, picked up the second flight commander, our regular one had to land on account of a broken oil pipe well. The two of us started out and got as far as the lines and Dick Phelan, who was then leading, turned around and headed for home. That left me all alone, so I followed him down awhile, then picked up another man who was waiting in reserve, then it was up to me to lead, so I started back again, and got as far as the lines again at about 3000 m. and the other man dropped out so that left me alone again. Well my machine was running O.K. and as our orders were not to cross the lines under any circumstances, I decided to go on by myself at about 4000 m. and half way along our sector the air pressure in the gas tank started to go down slowly and I happened to glance at the magneto that had been changed the day before and it was wobbling around in fine style, the bolts holding it down on the motor plane had come loose and so there it was. Well the motor was still running O.K. so I thought I might as well keep on. Believe me I was keeping my eyes open too. About this time I saw a plane in the distance so I climbed up on its level and went over to get a look at him. He was coming right into France from Germany. Well, I got up as close as I dared, still out of range of his guns and saw that it was a friendly plane a Breguet bomber so I went on up the lines to the end of our sector still swerving around and looking above, below and on all sides, but saw nothing save a few "Archies" that fell very short. I was pretty far inside our lines too, for it isn't safe to go near them alone, especially in our new sector, which is pretty active in the aviation line. Well, when I turned to come back down again, my motor cut clear out so I switched on the reserve tank of gas just in time to catch it before the propellor stopped turning over, which was quite a relief for it is no joke landing with a dead stick on unknown territory. Well the cause was that the reserve in the gas tank had dropped to zero, so I switched off the motor air pump and pumped her up again with the hand pump and then turned on the main tank again and started down the line again or rather continued. However, I had to keep pumping every so often to keep the pressure up for it was the motor pump that was leaking. I got back to the rear end of our sector all right, now about 4800 m. up in the air, some high n'est ce pas? I like altitude though for the higher you are the safer it is, for no matter what happens you can always come down, but you can't always go up. Well, I monkeyed around awhile and went half way back up the sector again, fired my guns awhile to break them in and came back again, fired my guns some more, and nearly hit another Breguet bomber, which passed right in front of me, then as it was getting near time to come home and the pressure was leaking worse and worse, I shut off the motor and came in. Coming down I had to use the reserve tank altogether as the pressure refused to stay up any more and in making the field I had to use my motor and it was on a high horse, ran awhile, then stopped then ran some more and stopped, keeping me in cold perspiration all the while, which was most annoying, for this is the worst country to fly in I ever saw, all hills and woods, so one has to depend on his motor altogether. Well, I got in all right and taxied up to our hangar and the mechanics are now setting me O.K. again.

I have to go to dinner now so good bye for the present. Please excuse all the "I's" in this letter. My love to the girls, Althea and the family and whole lots to yourself.

> Your loving son,
> Roland.

Thursday 5   Worked on my machine awhile this A.M. Bummed around & tried to dodge the rain. Went to Loire with the C.O. this P.M. Had a pretty good supper and bummed around the town till the C.O. came for us in the car again. Had a wild ride home in the dark.

Sept. 6, 1918   Got up late this A.M., made breakfast and bummed around the hangar awhile then pasted some photos in my album. After dinner worked down at the hangars till patrol time. Rained so didn't go. Went to bed early.

Saturday 7   Had an early patrol this A.M. at 6:00 A.M. I was the substitute but finally was the only one that met Charley [Grey]. Stayed out for 1.15, came in with missing motor, was shot at by "Archies." Didn't go up this P.M. as it wasn't my turn. Had my carburator fixed this P.M.

Sept. 8, 1918   Got up early or rather late this A.M. and shot my machine on the range. Went up on patrol 10:15 clouds too low, 1000 m. So we went over the lines once, then practiced formation flying etc. Didn't do anything much this P.M. Have patrol tomorrow A.M. Rained this P.M.

Monday 9   Rained all day today. Went to Nancy with our C.O. this P.M. and had a good supper and a little shopping. Our auto broke down on the way so we didn't make very good time. Bought some candy, grapes, etc. Came home late & hit the hay toute de suite.

Sept. 10, 1918   Rained off & on all day today. Sure is bad weather. Didn't do much of anything today. My machine is all O.K. now and just itching to go after a Hun. Had a vaudeville show at the "Y" this evening and it sure was great. All enjoyed it.

Wednesday 11   More rain off & on all day today. No patrols. Bummed around the hangars this A.M. & P.M. Got an Aldis sight this P.M. and showed them how I wanted it put on. Nearly patrolled this P.M. but it rained again. Bad weather for flying.

Sept. 12, 1918   The drive began today. St. Mihiel to LeMont, Pont a Mousson at 12:45.[3] After being on alert all A.M. we went out & straffed

a road, which we successfully did, & a railway station & some troops.[4]
Came home O.K., went out again this P.M. but didn't get on Patrol, never
formed.

Sept. 12, 1918

My dearest Mother:

I only have time to write to you and Althea now and very little at
that for today the drive started and we are on "alert" from sun up until
sun down. Believe me Mother dear, I passed one of the most exciting days
today that you could ever imagine. At about 12:30 after being on alert
all this morning, we were sent out to "straff" a road in Germany and hinder
the enemy's retreat. Well we started out in a pouring rain, joined our patrol,
five in all, and went on over. Well the infantry had chased the Huns way
into Germany, and we didn't know which were American and which were
Boche, but we flew along at about 600 M. (pretty darned low too) and
to put it mildly, we sure did give the Boche H---l. Gee how they did run.
We fired on a railway station, some troops in fields and everything we
could, and the air was filled with American planes. We were all over them
and the old boys were sure on the tear. We didn't get machine-gunned
very much, but we could see shells bursting all around us on the ground,
gosh but it was exciting. Well, after it was all over we came on home
and believe me I was glad when I set my old machine down on our field.
Oh, good old motor, you sure did stick by me today. I tell you you sure
have to take off your hat to the infantry, those boys are there without a
doubt, I take my hat off to them every time. Why they pushed those Huns
back so fast that nobody knows where anything is any more. Well we went
up again this afternoon but it rained so hard while I was up waiting for
the rest of the patrol which never came, that by the time it quit I was
about out of gas, so I came down. That is all there is to tell about tonight.
Now I'm going to get some good sleep. Will write some more tomorrow
night.

Friday 13   Went out this morning to shoot up a road at Mars-la-Tour,
did so successfully & came home, were heavily archied and shot at by
machine guns etc. from the ground. Went out to shoot up Chambley-Mars-
la-Tour road, did so, ran into 2 Foker [Fokker] monoplane, attacked me
but I got away. I flew between them, it was a close shave. Climbed up
and came home.

September 13, 1918.

Went out on two patrols today, first one we shot at troops retreating along a road and were heavily "archied" and shot at by rifles and machine guns, the machine gun bullets sure did come close too. They just missed me for I could see them going past, i.e. the tracer bullets and hear them zip too. Very uncomfortable around too. Also the archies they go WUFF, WUFF. Also very uncomfortable for when you can hear them like that, they are too close for pleasure. This PM we went out again and attacked artillery retreating along another road. After I had dived and fired on them, I was circling around to pick up my formation, when I saw two machines over and a little higher than I was, so I went over to see them, when low and behold they were two German fokers [sic] monoplanes. Well it was too late to turn around and beat it and I was all alone, so I just went right between them, then they dove on me and I did all kinds of things keeping them off my tail and I couldn't get a shot at one, for I had to keep an eye on each to keep out of danger myself, so finally I got away from them, after one dove straight down on me going in the opposite direction from me and I dove out of his way, then I climbed away and looked on and I saw a very good dog fight. My motor was missing so I came on home, and believe me I was glad I got there too, I tell you. The U.S'ers sure are pushing the Huns back. Guess you are reading about it. Wherever it tells about the retreating enemy being harassed by our planes, you can say that you know somebody who is doing it. By the way, we got the Boches, there were others though and a few of our men are missing.

Sept. 14, 1918   "First Boche." We were wakened up at 5:30 A.M. & told we were on alert from 6:30 on. Well we didn't go up till about 1:00 P.M. Charley, [S. P.] Gaillard and myself & spied a red Foker [sic], went over & dove on him and shot him down, put in for confirmation. Went to the show at the "Y" this evening, pretty good.

September 14, 1918.

Another big day. They got us up yesterday morning at 4 AM and found it was a mistake, so when they came around at 5 AM this AM we didn't quite know what to do, but they were pretty persistent, so we got up and went to the field after breakfast, arriving there about 6:30. We were not scheduled to be on alert until 9, so we waited around until then, but no call came. As soon as were off duty I took my machine down to the range to line the guns up with my new sight, which is a peach. It took until noon to do that, then we were told that we were to go out at 12:30 on a patrol, so I rushed up to the mess hall and ate as much as I could in as little time as possible, which is very bad for the stomach causing indigestion and internal eruptions at times, you know. Well we took off, three of us. Our flight commander, Lt. Grey and a Lt. Gaillard (Gilly) and myself. Well we went over the lines at about 2200 m. and looked around until finally Gilly spotted a Boche. I didn't see him. Well we pointed him out to Grey and we made for him. All the time there was a big formation above us which we didn't know were Boche or Allied but this red Fokker monoplane sailing along right under the clouds was too good a shot and we just about had time to take a crack at him and get away. So we dove on him and Grey shot at him then I did. I guess I fired about 100 rounds at him and he tried to turn but fell off on a wing straightened out again then I pulled off and Gilly fired about 75 rounds at him and the last we saw of him he was going down in a "vrille" or a spinning nose dive. Well we all pulled away, and I picked up a Spad and found it was Gilly and we beat it for home. We got here all right and soon after we landed Grey came in. Well we talked it over and are pretty sure we got him so we put in for confirmation on him. I think that if he crashed a baloon [sic] or a ground observer would have seen him, so we ought to know in a day or so, whether we got him or not. This is the first Boche plane gotten by our squadron, and I am sure glad I was in on it. This is interesting work, but believe me you have to keep your eyes open for things happen awfully quick. You have no idea how quickly things do happen. They sure had me scared yesterday afternoon but it is all in the day's work.

Well the big all American push is coming along in great style. I think we will soon have old Fritz's goat. I wouldn't be a bit surprised if we had Metz soon, for we are headed that way. I'll write you some more tomorrow, or I guess I'll send this tonight and start a new one tomorrow. My love to the girls the family and Althea and lots of love to yourself.

Your loving son,
Roland.

Sunday 15   Got up late today and went down to the hangars. On alert till noon. Played a little baseball after dinner then the bunch went on patrol at 4:15. I couldn't go on account of a pipe being broken on my machine. Got confirmation on our Boche this evening from a french balloon observer.

Sept. 16, 1918   Got up late again and bummed around all morning. Had first patrol at 2:00. I went up but couldn't keep my motor cool and it started to vibrate so I came down. Went up on 5:45 patrol and managed to stay up all right. Came down at 7:20 & landed in the dark. Took a bath this evening.

Tuesday 17   Got up late this A.M. and bummed around the hangars till 10:00. Put a new prop on my plane, went up on a patrol, bad weather, rain, clouds, etc., couldn't keep behind the leader, started home. Got to St. Mihiel & got lost. Clouds very low & landed at Commercy found myself & took off. I got here about 6:45. Bummed around all P.M. Show at Y tonight.

Sept. 18, 1918   Got up late again. Bummed around all A.M. Had a hurry up patrol at 12:15. I had to lead it. About 10 machines got off & when I got to Commercy 4 were there. I had to come back, new carb. wasn't adjusted. Only 3 made whole patrol. 2 more of our men are missing, Dick Loomis & Dave McClure.

Thursday 19   Dick is all right, no word from Dave & Jack Ogden is missing in my machine.[5] Went up to the front today & got more confirmation of our Boche. Got a lot of Souvenirs, rifle, ammunition, helmet, etc. Got out of St. Maurice just as they started to bombard it. Had a great old time. Some sound, a whistling shell passing over head. Got home at about 9:15 P.M.

Sept. 20, 1918   Bummed around all day today. Weather pretty bad, no patrols. Jack Ogden is missing in my machine, went out yesterday noon. Went to Neufchateaux & bummed around part of the day. Packed up to move tomorrow. Going up to near Bar Le Duc. Sorry to leave this place.

Saturday 21   No news from Jack Ogden yet. Was sick last night & this morning, shot my lunch etc. The whole group is moving, everything is disorganized & we finally left with machines about 3:00 P.M. All our flight arrived O.K. Found no accommodations for men or pilots at our new field, only hangars. Slept at Bar le Duc tonight on public beds at the Town Hall, not so bad either.

Sept. 22, 1918   No news from Jack O. yet. Had an early patrol but couldn't fly on account of rain. Bummed around most of the day with nothing to do. Moved into billets, all but Gilly & I, we are out of luck. Will sleep in CO's room tonight. Ate with the men in the corner table today.

Sept. 22, 1918.

My dearest Mother:

Well, lots of things have happened since I last wrote you so I'll begin at the beginning and give it to you chronologically. First of all, thank you very much for your last letter, August 5th. I have heard from M. Favier lately and I wrote him lately. He is out with an air artillery battery. Everything is fine over here, the drive is over and we are taking life a little easier than a week ago. I tell you that was one strenuous three or four days. I bet I lost ten pounds during that time. How we straffed woods etc. Well you probably read it in the papers, so my letter will be stale when it reaches you, however it will be first hand news. Last Thursday my machine wasn't working very well, so the C.O. sent another fellow and myself up to the front to get some more confirmation on our Boche. You know that I am credited with a Boche plane officially now. Well I tell you the three of us who jumped that red Fokker, the one I wrote you about, are all credited with him, one third of a Boche, how is that, I am getting very conceited as you can see no doubt. Only Boche in the Squadron. Well we went up to the front to get this information, and I went along to do the Parlez-vous stuff and also to get some souvenirs. Well we arrived at one of the towns evacuated by the Germans, and rummaged around and I got a German rifle, helmet, bayonet and post cards, etc. All kinds of junk, am enclosing some German picture show tickets that we got, give some to the girls if you like. Well we sure did load that car up. You just ought to have seen the mess the gunners left. They must have just grabbed up what they could and beat it. The towns were all shot to pieces of course, and all in all it was very interesting. We passed through several roofless towns like you see in pictures. Of course the Germans have had this salient since 1914, and they sure were well trenched and fixed up. They left immense ammunition dump with the shells, cartridges, and everything all kinds of supplies. Well, after we got about all the souvenirs the car could carry we went up on the top of the hill near this town the name of which is on the tickets, top right, look it up on the map, to see the baloon [sic] observer who saw our plane go down. He wasn't there, so after much talking, etc., we finally found another man who saw it fall and he wrote us out a confirmation and we came back. All this country used to be in the German's hands, so it was awfully interesting. We weren't more than four or five miles from the front lines then and every once in awhile we would hear a gun boom and a shell would go over our heads and hot off on another hill. They make a funny noise when they are going through the air. Well, then we came down to the same town again and started to rummage around some more. There were four of us in the party, driver and three officers, so we each picked a house and started through. You see nobody lives here. The Germans took all the able bodied people with them, so the towns are empty, and the houses full of shell holes. I had just gotten well started on my third room, when I heard a gun boom and shells gurgle, and, well, it gurgled very loud, until finally it hit the house next to me and made an awful noise scattering bricks and stones everywhere. Well, you ought to have seen me clear out. I bet I was going 60 miles an hour when I got into the street. The rest of the crew were beating it towards the car, and in about two seconds we were a miles down the road. I never did step so fast in my life, funny too that the same idea occurred to us at the same time, very peculiar. Well we stopped well out of the town to get our breath, and to give the air a chance to fill in the vacuum we left behind us, and you ought to have seen what the Boche did to that town. They dropped a dozen or more shells in it, and, well, we didn't go back to see what it looked like, for it was no place for me. The farther away from those shells I am, the better I feel, for they sure do hit hard. It was then about 4:30 PM, so we hit the trail for home. We wanted to get home a different way and get another look at the old trenches, so we went along a very nice road, when it passed the third line trench, just stopped being a road, and became an expanse of shell holes and communication trenches, so we had to turn around and come back. This was no man's land, the road was just chopped off and about one half mile farther on it continued again on the French side. No man's land is sure a mess, nothing but holes, barbed wire and holes. There were shell holes of all sizes all over the territory gained in the drive. There was one that was about 50 feet. It made traveling on the road very inconvenient. Well we finally got home at about 9 PM. My, but that was an interesting trip.

Friday afternoon we were told to pack up and that we would move the next morning so we did and the next morning about 3 I felt like the last of the Mohawks, in other words, I was sick, only indigestion and all that goes with it, well to make a long story short between 3 and 4 that morning I went through a marked physical change, and wasn't the same man afterwards. Usually you feel better after such a change, but I didn't, and, consequently, didn't feel like moving, anyway I didn't have any machine for Jack Ogden took my machine out the day I went to the front, and to this day we don't know what happened to him. Well we hung around camp all morning and at noon I felt two or three hundred percent better, so at 3 PM I flew Jack's machine over here to our new field. I can't tell you where it is though. Well we got here last evening, it was only a short ride and the trucks had all gone on ahead, but our new post consisted of hangars and a small house that our squadron lost when lots were drawn. We didn't have anything to eat, no place to sleep, no mechanics and nothing but our planes. It just looked as though somebody else agreed and nothing else was thought about it until we all arrived. Anyway no preparation was made for us. So we went into a town about ten miles away and had something to eat and then searched for a bed, which we at last found in the county jail, or some place like that. They were all public beds, free of charge, but weren't half bad at that, a strain tick (free of cooties) and two blankets, so to cap the climax, we were informed that we had a patrol at 6:45 AM ten miles from the hangar and a patrol at 6:45 AM. Well we reached the point when we didn't give a [damn] about anything, so we didn't have any patrol anyway. We arrived in camp about 7:45 and found that someone during the night they had changed the order, and we had an 8:45 patrol, so we went after some breakfast and found some bread and jam and coffee, and beat it back to the hangars. Mechanics had just arrived all tired out from riding trucks all night and having no food, so we were in a fine mess.

❧ We found some gasoline and loaded the machines up and about 8:45 it started to rain. We didn't sing any rain, rain go away songs either, for it saved the day. Then we went looking for billets, or any kind of quarters. Some of the fellows and myself tossed up for room for five and of course of the seven of us another fellow and myself lost out, and I don't know where I am going to sleep yet, but it is only 3:30 PM. Our kitchen is cozily situated between two dominating manure piles in the court of a French peasant's mansion and as long as the odor from the kitchen is synchronized with that of the two manure piles, all is well, but well, far be it from me to describe it otherwise. I don't think it will be there very long however. Well that is all the news up to date. Enclosed please find two railroad tickets, these are the ones I came up to the front on, you can have them as souvenirs if you want them.

It is too bad about Jack Ogden, he was an awfully nice fellow. We came out here together. I don't think he landed in Germany, for the last that was seen of him he was heading towards home after dropping out of the patrol, in my old machine too, No. 23, I think we will hear from him soon. The weather is getting pretty bad now, rain, most all the time, so we havn't flown much lately. Please buy Bobby a birthday present for me. I will send her some money too. Hope you get the $150 I sent you lately. I am going to write Althea a little later, in case something turns up, please tell her and give her my very best love. My love to the girls and the family and my best to all my friends. Lots and lots of love to you Mother, take good care of yourself and the girls and don't be stingy with the money I am sending you. If you can help the Fords in any way at all with it, please do it, and let me know and I'll try and send some more, this is confidential between you and me.

Ever your loving son,
Roland.

P.S. All my money is in the Guaranty Trust Co. 1 & 3 Rue des Italiens, Paris.

Monday 23   Had an early patrol this A.M. but didn't fly on account of rain. Not much doing out here. Gilly, John [Hambleton], [John] Aiken & Jack Lee & myself found a room in the mayor's house. Moved in this P.M. Good room, fireplace, electric lights, etc. Had tea with the mayor & his wife this evening after supper. Pretty nice too.

Sept. 24, 1918   Had a patrol at 8:45 A.M. but couldn't go on account of the weather. Bummed around all morning and P.M., didn't do much of anything. Weather cleared up this P.M. and a few patrols went out. Sat around our fire after supper & enjoyed life. No word from Jack as yet.

Wednesday 25   Got up late and missed breakfast. Bummed around all morning and had dinner at 11:30 to go on patrol at 12:45, went, clouds at 500 m. Saw some A.A.A. & that is about all. Bad day to fly. A new drive is about to start. CO gave us a talk. Have to fly in any condition now.

Sept. 26, 1918   Didn't fly all today. My machine needs new radiator & gas tanks repaired. Bummed around the hangars all day. A few patrols went out this P.M. but the weather was pretty bad. Came home tonight & enjoyed a fire. My long lost boots came tonight.

Friday 27   Didn't fly this morning. My machine is O.K. now. This P.M. at 12:30 flew, tried to make patrol but was late 7 missed it so I flew up towards the lines. Came home. Went up on another patrol. Stayed up till 5:00 P.M. Saw a few Boche & nearly got lost. Came home O.K. Machine runs pretty good.

Sept. 28, 1918   Got up at 3:45 A.M. to go on patrol at 5:30. Went up, saw nothing. Went on another at 10:00. Got chased by 5 Fokers [*sic*]. Went up on another at 12:30 to bomb a road. Went only 20 of us, met & surprised 7 Fokers [*sic*]. I guess we got nearly all of them. Dropped our bombs before going into the dog fight.

Sunday 29   Flew on a patrol this P.M. I led it. We saw what I thought were Spads but some of the others thought were Boche. On alert all A.M. Came down this P.M. with nothing special to report. Had a pretty good patrol. Went to bed early tonight. Nothing doing much around here.

Sept. 30, 1918   Went up on patrol this A.M. Clouds low, saw nothing, lost [Clarence M.] Bellows. This P.M. Lt. Hambleton & myself went up on a reconnaissance patrol over into Germany to see if the Boche were retreating & sure enough they had. It was very exciting to me, flew very low, were archied a little bit but inaccurately.

Oct. 1   Bellows was killed yesterday. Were on alert all A.M. Tried for a patrol at noon but leader had to come down & I did too. Went up this P.M. over old sector, Grey and myself. Oil pressure went down & I panned near Naviant, plane O.K. Stayed all night at C.A.S. [Corps Air Service] 4 Corps. Couldn't telephone Squadron, will try again in morning.

October 1, 1918.

My dearest Mother:

We are on "alert" this morning from 7:00 to noon I suppose, so I have little time to write. "Alert" means that all pilots stay up at the hangars, the machines out all lined up ready to start up at a minute's notice. We are supposed to be ready to take the air ten minutes after the order is given. Just now it is very foggy and we are not at all likely to have a call. We have been working pretty hard lately, two and three patrols a day. The other day we had three before dinner. The second one we were chased back in our lines by six Fokers [sic]. We went over to bomb a road. This is a job not meant for Spads at all, but we do it all the same. Well we went over about 20 of us and just about as were going to dive down through the clouds and drop the bombs 7 Fokers [sic] appeared out of the clouds below us. Well we all dropped the bombs anywhere and went to it. The Huns didn't seem to know what was going on, they stayed all bunched together and didn't even try to get away which they might easily have done. Well by the time I arrived on the scene, there were so many Spads in action on the Huns that I stayed around above looking for a straggler, but none came out. The fight lasted about five minutes, and I think only two of the Huns got away. That was the third and last patrol we had that day. During the second one, a fellow in our flight dropped out. I didn't see him go. We didn't hear from him for two days, then finally got word from a baloon [sic] company that he was safe with them. He got home yesterday and sure did have some experience. His motor stopped and he headed towards our lines and in doing so had to dive through a formation of six Fokers [sic] who followed him down to the ground. He turned in behind a woods, hit once and swiped his landing gear off and hit again and turned over. He climbed out, Huns still shooting at him, and ducked for a woods where a dough boy greeted him. O pleasant sight, and told him to lay low as the boche were sniping the woods. Well he found he was way up among the contact patrols, about 500 yards from the German outposts. He stayed there all night, scared to death, then walked back to the baloon [sic] company where he got a telephone message in. All the time the barrage, etc. were lighting all around him. He said that he "flopped" so many times on the road that he soaked up all the stray wind thereon. This sounds like the stuff you read in the S.E.P. By the way did you read Sgt. Pilot Harold E. Wright's articles in the S.E.P. Well that was a fine line all right, but all the Lafayette men in our group that knew him, know also that after about 30 hours over the line with the French, he was discharged out of the French Army for cowardice. He would leave his patrol and come home when they reached the lines. So much for him, just spread that around.

Yesterday was rather busy. We had a patrol in the morning about seven of us. The clouds were at about 800 m. so it was a rather unpleasant one. We didn't see anything but a couple of our own observation machines and a lot of artillery fire. If we had ever had to land due to motor trouble, it would have been pretty bad, for the ground was filled with trenches and shell holes which make landing rather difficult. Well we lost one pilot on that trip, he is on our side of the lines, but as yet we havn't heard from him.

Yesterday afternooon our C.O. of our Squadron came in to where we were sitting around, and asked me if I had a good reliable machine, to which I answered that it was pretty good, so he told me to come on. We went into his office and he showed me what we were to do. It was a special mission to fly over Germany about 8 or 10 miles, and try and find out if the Boche were retreating. Well we warmed up and off we went, had to fly low, so over we went. Gee but it was exciting. The Germans had already retreated it seemed so we could see the dough boys advancing to take the outposts they left to cover their retreat. They fired on us a little but very inaccurately, so it didn't bother us much. Well we flew around over Germany for about 20 minutes, then came home. It was a great experience all right and pretty good fun.

Well I'll have to quit now and get warm. It is getting pretty cold over here now. Don't forget Bobby's birthday present for me please. I sent her some money besides. Please give my love to the girls and Althea and to all the family besides, I won't name them all but you know. I'm feeling fine enjoying myself all your letters and everything. Received the Air Service Journal and gum. Merci. Doesn't the war news look good though. We may get home soon, who can tell?

Lots and lots [of love] to you Mother dear from your son,

Roland.

Oct. 2, 1918   Had a good nights sleep and got up about 7:30 A.M. had a good breakfast & tried telephoning to camp again but couldn't get it. Finally got a side car to take me back to the camp. Arrived O.K. Will go after my machine tomorrow probably. Didn't fly any today. Heard of Bellows death today.

October 2, 1918.

P.S. Just as I finished the letter we were called out on a patrol. Three of us in our flight. Well, I got off but one dropped out before we formed and then the leader went so fast that I could hardly keep up with him. We just got over the hill and over the lines, when all of a sudden my motor began to act funny, so I looked at all the gauges and found that the oil pressure had dropped to zero so I cut the motor and started down. I headed south to make sure of landing in our lines and finally landed near an air-drome under construction. I just didn't make the field however and landed in another along side. There was no telephone there, so I borrowed the Captain's car, after putting a guard over the machine and drove down to the nearest town with a telephone, and there I tried and tried to get our group but couldn't. Finally I had to stay there all night in a billet, good one too, and this morning I tried to get the group again and couldn't. So finally I got a side car and he took me back to the airdrome, about 60 miles ride, very dirty and bumpy, but believe me I was glad to get here. Will go down after my machine tomorrow morning. I think the oil pump broke I hope I didn't burn the engine out, but I don't know yet.

Say doesn't the news look good though. Bulgaria out and internal trouble in Germany and the Allies pushing on every front. Great news isn't it? I tell you I'd like to see the end but see it end the right way, and that is the only way it can end now. We may get home by Christmas you can never tell. By the way we got our Boche officially confirmed by wing headquarters, so it really means that we got him. Well I'm taking a rest now, no machine and nothing to do, shaved all up and am feeling pretty cocky. They had an awful barrage up on our front this AM, or rather at noon. You could hear the guns pretty loud, I guess the "dough" boys are going right through them.

We are going to have some kind of a Y.M.C.A. show tonight. It will be pretty good I think. Anything is good over here as long as it is distract-ing that is a pretty near necessary thing. Well, I'll have to stop now. My love to the family, Althea and yourself and my best to all my friends.

R.

Thursday 3   Went out after my machine today. Arrived at the place at noon after a very interesting trip along the old St. Mihiel-Apremont line. Found that the pump shaft was broken & couldn't be fixed, so I was about to get quarters when the CO arrived and took me along. Left the machine and came home via Toul. Arrived 11:30 P.M.

Oct. 4, 1918   Got up late today. Bummed around till 10:30 then patrolled at 10:55 till 12:25. Protected some Breguets. C. Grey got a Boche. We saw some Fokkers but they had the advantage so we didn't bother them. Went way into Germ., all went well. Tried again this P.M. but the pressure line broke & came down.

Saturday 5   Flew in a patrol above the clouds this P.M. 11 of us started out & 4 of us ended up. We dropped some newspapers on the dough boys down pretty low under the clouds. Saw no boche. Started on another patrol but couldn't make it. Motor trouble. Am getting a new machine, one from the 1st flight, new motor.

Oct. 6, 1918   Got up at 3:45 A.M. to patrol at 5:00 A.M. My machine wouldn't go. Gee but it was dark & chilly. My machine wouldn't go for the 8:30 patrol either. Putting my new motor in #11. Flew new machine back here from Bar le Duc. Peace negotiations are opening maybe. I hope so too.

Monday 7   On alert all morning. Had a patrol at 12:45. I flew 23, pretty good ship. Clouds closed in under as we came home by way of St. Mihiel. Saw no Huns. Had another patrol at 3:45 but the weather was too bad. Dick Phelan & I are off tomorrow. Will go to Bar le Duc maybe.

Oct. 8, 1918   Off duty today. Stayed in bed till about 8:30, got up cleaned up & dressed up. Went to hangars and bummed around awhile. My new Avro de Chasse isn't quite ready yet. Went to Bar le Duc this P.M., did a little shopping then ate supper & came home. Went to bed early to get a good sleep.

Wednesday 9   Got up early this A.M. for a 6:15 patrol but had no machine. On alert all AM, very foggy so didn't fly. Fog cleared up at about 12:30 so at 2:00 we went out to protect some bombers, were attacked by 7 Fokkers, surprise, dove away. Dick Phelan went down in flames but came out O.K., tank blew out. All of us got home all right.

Oct. 10, 1918   Got up early this A.M. 5:30 but couldn't fly on account of having no machine. My new machine isn't ready yet. Didn't fly all day. Some of our bunch were in a scrap & Bill Munn got a Boche. War news sure looks good today. Will discuss peace when Germans are out of allied territory.[6] We may get home yet, who knows.

Friday 11   Got up at 5:00 A.M. and spent the day at the hangars, 6:00 AM — 6:00 PM. Weather foggy, didn't patrol. I went out alone this P.M. to see how thick it was & it sure was thick. Played cards, read & tried to get my machine in order. The oil don't circulate in it for some unknown reason. Had a good supper tonight!

Oct. 12, 1918   Got up early this A.M. for a patrol at 7:15, went up but I had to come down on account of motor trouble, others saw nothing. Went up at noon to chase Fokkers away from attacking our troops. Foggy & raining all of us got lost but we finally got back, very foolish sortie. Didn't do much else this P.M. My new machine is O.K.

October 12, 1918

Dearest Mother:

Thanks muchly for your letters and gum. Please thank the girls too, for they sure have been good about writing to me, and not being answered. The reason is that we are on the job 100% of the time, staying up at the hangars from 6 AM to 6 PM, and the only time we can write is between patrols or during an "alert", and I can't seem to write a good letter at those times, but here goes.

I just now came down. We had a patrol at 7:15 AM, I went up, but just as I was getting into position in the formation one of the magnetos cut out and I found that a wire had come off, I fixed it and another one came loose and started sparking, very intensely, so I turned around and came back. Two more have returned. We have been having pretty bad weather lately but have been flying anyhow and the strain is beginning to tell on the fellows. We are all about all in and all of us have colds, or this new fangled disease Spanish Influenza or "Flu" as it is called, so all in all we are a pretty punk bunch of pilots.[7] However, it isn't as bad as you might think, especially with all the good news about peace that is going around. I tell you President Wilson certainly is on the job and we are all behind him too. Wasn't his reply to the German Chancellor's peace note fine though, he will never get caught by those Hun diplomats as long as he keeps that up.[8] One of our men just came back from Paris and he says that the people there talk of nothing else but that reply and President Wilson is the most used word in the French language at present.

Tell Althea please that I received her "picnic" letter just after I wrote to her last and will answer it as soon as I get time again. I wrote to her the other day and told her of a one sided fight we were in over the lines when about seven Huns attacked four of us and chased us some, get her to read that part to you. Tell Bobby to be on the look out for a draft from me for $50 for her birthday maybe and probably she has already received it, for it was sent quite awhile ago. Don't forget to get her something else either will you. I'll send you some more money soon which you can use "comme vous voulez". By the way, will you please send me some "Valet" auto strop safety razor blades, a couple of dozen or more if you can. I can't get any in the town here and can't get to Paris. I have enough to last me for a month or so, but will then be out. Maybe peace will be fixed up by then, who knows, gosh I hope so. We are making lots of advances over here and the old Huns must be getting pretty tired of it all. A couple of our men caught Hun machines the other day. The enemy has increased their aviation on this sector lately and we see formations of Fokkers all the time, they don't do much good though unless they get you by surprise, which isn't very often. I got a look at a Fokker yesterday, one that was brought down on our side O.K. and it sure is a clumsy, crude looking affair. I don't see how they can be so good in the air still they can maneuver better than we can, but we can always outdive them, which is a great satisfaction if they surprise you. Do you remember I spoke of meeting a red headed fellow from U.C. a S.A.E. [Sigma Alpha Epsilon] named [Dudley] Outcalt, a red headed fellow. I saw him at (s.s., [?]), well, I saw him again yesterday, he is at the 1st Pursuit Group, just arrived as a replacement pilot. He and Geohegan are the only fellows I've seen over here.

You ought to see your little son sew; why I'm a regular seamstress, pants, pockets, hats, buttons and anything from these up and down, just as though I'd done it all my life and you know I havn't now don't you? Not that I care particularly for it, but necessity is the mother of invention and I've invented a new way to sew, it's slow but always sure, why it would take a team of horses to pull off a button that I sewed on. I'm not really as conceited as I sound to be though so don't worry. Glad to hear that Emily is having such a good time, I received her letter with her pictures in it, thanks very much. Please give my love to the girls and Althea as usual and also the family in general and remember me to all my friends. Lots and lots of love to you Mother and believe me I'll be home soon

> Your loving son,
> Roland.

P.S. After eighteen months service abroad one can get a furlough home, but maybe they will call it off while they are advancing like this. We will see though.

> R.

Sunday 13   Got up early this A.M. for all A.M. alert 6:00. Very foggy. Went to Bar le Duc to get a machine. Good news. Germans accept our peace terms.[9] Gee but that does sound good. I hope they will get out of France, toute de suite so we can get home. Foggy all day today. Don't know whether we will patrol any more or not. Probably will.

October 14, 1918   The orderly woke us at 4:00 A.M. but it was awfully foggy so I just went back to bed again so did everybody else. Went to Bayonne & got that machine today. Weather very bad. Ceiling about 150 ft, finally flew back this P.M. & have been mad ever since. The war isn't over either, damn it! This is a bad day all right for everybody.

Tuesday 15   Got up for a 6:00 A.M. alert this A.M., but it was still very foggy and we might as well have stayed in bed. Bummed around all morning on alert and didn't do anything. Did a 15 min. test flight in my new machine and a patrol of 50 min. this P.M. at 3:45. Clouds very low & foggy, saw nothing, got lost & lost the formation.

Oct. 16, 1918   Got up late. Bad weather so we didn't fly all day long. Bummed around the hangars all morning. Took a bath & a shave this P.M. & cleaned up around our room a little after supper. We sat around & read the papers.

Thursday 17   Got up late again. Weather still very bad, fog & rain & low clouds. Didn't fly all day today. Gen. [William] Mitchell inspected us today and we were sure a muddy crew. Took some pictures of the machine & mechanics. Played cards all P.M.& bummed around reading the paper after supper.

Oct. 18, 1918   Got up late. Nobody woke us. Weather still bad but showing signs of clearing up. Played cards all A.M. On alert this P.M., weather good. Went up to protect some bombers. I couldn't keep up on account of my motor, had to come down. War news very good tonight. Bummed around after supper.

Saturday 19   Had a patrol at 7:00 this morning. Clouds at 1000 m. Saw nothing but finished the patrol. Went up again to test the weather but didn't stay long. Saw a big explosion the first time. Ammunition dump I suppose. Bummed around the rest of the day. Weather got bad again.

Oct. 20, 1918   Got up late, weather very bad, rain & low clouds. Didn't fly all day. Sat up in the barracks & played cards etc. all day long. It rained all day. The news isn't as good as it was. Suppose the war will last all winter but it will end well when it does end.

October 20, 1918.

Dearest Mother:

Just a few lines to let you know that all is well. Thanks very much for your letters and gum enclosed.

Lately we have had such bad weather that I really havn't any news to tell you. I have only made one complete patrol this week. We started out on some others but had to come back on account of the weather.

It looks as though the war wasn't over after all doesn't it? Well after all it is a good thing for it ought to be finished once for all now, so we will never have a war again. I took some pictures not long ago that turned out pretty good. I will send you some as soon as I get the films printed. By the way could you send me two or three rolls of films for my kodak? Size 3A (Post card) also a couple of dozen of Auto strap "Valet" safety razor blades and some prophylactic tooth brushes "stiff and large".

That is all I can think of now that I need. I have all the clothes that I need just at present. The news sure is great. Ostend, Lille, Thielt, etc. in our hands and by the time you get this the Boche won't have any outlet on the Belgium Coast, that means not so many submarines. The French, British and Belgians and some Americans have been doing work and gaining lots of ground, etc, but we have had probably the hardest fighting yet, this is a great strategical point and the Germans are sure loathe to give it up, but they will have to soon. I bet we have half the German aviation down here on our little sector. At least it has looked like it lately. I received a letter from Uncle Russ the other day. He sure is a peach to write to me and I appreciate it very much. I answered your questions about the kind of plane I fly. It is a single seater, just remember that. I havn't flown a D.H. with a Liberty motor in it and frankly I don't care if I never fly it, the old Spad is pretty good, just about the fastest machine on the front.

Don't let anybody tell you that the machine equipped with Liberty motors are faster than the little Spad, that is what we read in one article, I don't remember where it was. The Liberty motor is all right, it is fine but there has been lots of exaggeration about it. Somehow or other the fellows who fly the D.H. 4 over the lines don't like it very much. They say the motor is all right but the plane isn't good enough for it. We go out and protect them quite often, and believe me they have nothing on us for speed.

I am still living in a billet, it is pretty nice too, better than a barracks, warmer, dryer, etc but farther away from the field.

Today is Bobby's birthday, please wish her a happy birthday for me even if it is a little late, this is the right time to be thinking about her anyhow. I hope she got the $50 I sent her and also that you got her something besides. I am enclosing a letter from my orphan over here. He tells me that he received the money this term and thanks, etc, and also that his bicycle is on the bum, so I sent him a check for 100 francs when I answered it, was that all right? I don't want to spoil him. Please subscribe for him again when the year runs out for me. Also buy as many bonds as you can, but don't stint yourself if you ever need anything.

Well I guess I'll have to stop now as it is getting pretty late and there "aint" no artificial light. My love to the girls, the family and Althea and thank you all for all your letters, also the photo you sent me. Best luck and lots of love to yourself from your loving son,

Roland.

P.S. If anything happens to me, write to The Guaranty Trust Co., 1 & 3 Rue des Italiens, Paris, France for my money. I told them to send it to you.

Monday 21   Got up early and went on early patrol, 5:45. Got out to the line & ran into a heavy fog & had to come home. Weather clouded over later & we didn't go on a later patrol. On alert all P.M. Weather fine but we weren't called. Played football & cards most of the day. Went to bed early.

Oct. 22, 1918.   Got up early this A.M. on alert, were called out to protect some bombers over Buzancy at 7:30, went up & found weather very bad and no bombers. Coming out we were very badly shelled. I got a hole in my wing. 7 Fokkers chased us for awhile. Had motor trouble & landed at Clermont. Came home in a side car.

Wednesday 23   Got up & shaved this A.M. Bummed around all morning & heard that my machine at Clermont had a very bad crack in it. Didn't do anything all day but nearly went on 2 patrols, 1 low bombing one. My plane will have to be hauled to me on a truck. Only got 2 real patrols out of it, too bad. Bar le Duc was bombed tonight.

Oct. 24, 1918   Got up early today, weather very bad. Didn't fly at all. Bummed around playing cards & kicking the football most all day. Some of us went down to Bar le Duc & shopped a little. I got my pictures down there. Came home & went to bed. Tested weather this P.M.

Friday 25   Got up at 4:30 A.M. for a 5:45 patrol which we didn't have on account of bad weather. Didn't fly all day today. Wrote some letters etc. & tested out my motor this P.M. it vibrates pretty bad but doesn't knock. Hope that it will turn out all right. Got our washing tonight, was done pretty good too.

October 25, 1918.

Dearest Mother:

My pen is on the bum, so please excuse this pencil. I am writing this to send you my Christmas parcel label, which you will need to send me a package. It is a pretty small package and I guess I'd better tell you a few things to get for me, for we will have to economize on space. Some of these things I've asked for in another letter, so if you can send them in another package, but if that isn't possible put them in the Christmas one. Two dozen Auto strop valet safety razor blades 4 or 5 prophylactic tooth brushes, stiff and large. A small size Waterman's fountain pen. That is all I can think of just now. Any chocolate that is very acceptable. If you can think of anything else all right, but I have about all the clothes, etc. that I need and I don't need any food stuffs.

Just received your letter of Sept. 25th in which you told me of your visit with Uncle Ted. Gee but that was fine, I sure would have liked to have been with you. Glad you got a look at some real aeroplanes, and particularly a Spad, was it a 150, 180 or 220 H.P. Spad that you saw? ours are the latest 220 H.P. they are a little bigger than the other two. By the way I am sorry Uncle Ted was disappointed in that I went Pursuit instead of Bombing, but really I don't think he understands just what Pursuit Aviation is. That is the trouble over there in the U.S.A. The general opinion is that a single seater pursuit is out of date, etc., and they seem to worship the D.H. 4 with the Liberty motor, when really the bombers, observation and all other branches of aviation would be helpless without Pursuit. We have to protect them and clear the way for them, as well as knock down enemy planes. That is also the reason why we have so few planes. The Spad order in the States was cancelled by some blockhead that thought this D.H. 4 Liberty was going to revolutionize aviation.[10] Well we won't dwell on our mistakes, for it doesn't do any good, but they sure have made enough of them in the Air Service. It will all come out all right I hope. I suppose you know by now that it was the St. Mihiel drive that we were in when I wrote you that diary letter, and now we are in the other drive, you have no doubt read about it. The country is awfully hard to fight in and our troops have really done wonderfully well. I don't see how they did it and are still doing it. Yesterday I went down town and got some photos I left to be printed and developed and am sending you some. By the way please send me some 3A films too if possible. I'll write explanations on the back.

We still are on the job from morning until night, not doing so much flying because of the weather, but still we can't take advantage of our spare time as we would like to do. I busted my machine the other day. The day the piece of shrapnel went through my wing. I wrote Althea about it. The motor went on the bum. Only got two patrols out of it, they took it apart and hauled it some distance on a truck and are putting it together again, putting on a new wing. I'll have to fly any old kind of machine now until they get a new motor in mine. Nothing like having your own machine in commission, it makes flying over the lines a hundred percent better. I nearly went on a low bombing mission the day I wrote Althea, but the machine I was to fly wasn't fit so I didn't go. Everybody got back O.K. though, thank goodness. A regular patrol isn't bad, but excuse me from these low flying bombing and straffing raids, especially as these machines arn't made to carry bombs. I wish they could put the Liberty motor in some kind of a single seater. They say the motor is O.K. and very reliable, that would be the stuff all right. I don't know what they are going to do though now. They may be going to spring some new machine on us. I hope it is as good as our old Spads.

Please give my love to the girls, family and Althea as usual. I'll let you know if I find out anything else about a furlough in January. I'm afraid the _____ of advance will be out of luck for anything like that though, but we can try.

Best luck and love to you Mother dear and don't worry about your getting too old for me, that is a foolish worry. I had to laugh when I read that letter.

Your loving son,
Roland.

Oct. 26, 1918   Got up early for an alert this A.M. Weather very bad so didn't fly. Had a patrol this P.M. 3:00 weather cleared up a little. All took off but didn't all form on account of mist & clouds. I got lost & landed at Varennes. Got dark & I came home in a car. Missed a good party here this P.M.

Sunday 27   Got up for an 8:00 patrol. My machine was ready. Went up but had to come down again, pump line broken. Went up again at 11:00 but motor was missing badly so came down. Went on a bombing mission this P.M. Got back O.K., dropped 4 bombs, saw a plane go down in flames. An American Spad. My machine will be ready tomorrow.

Oct. 28, 1918   On alert all A.M., but didn't go out. Played ball & bummed around. We had two patrols this P.M., our flight in second. Had a Scrap first thing on the line. My motor was bad so I didn't get in on it. Saw lots of Boche, a plane & baloon [*sic*] go down in flames. Came back. Grey & [P.H.] Mell each got a Boche.

Tuesday 29   Didn't make a patrol today. My machine is no good & all the others were taken. Made a test flight in my buss but it still vibrated awfully. Bummed around all day, weather very good, a little misty though.

Oct. 30, 1918   Flew my plane on another test flight but it is as bad or worse than ever. I didn't go on day patrols today not having any machines. Went to Chalons this P.M. Very good town, did some shopping and had a good supper. Nearly froze coming home in the car.

[October 30, 1918.]

Dearest Mother:

I am sending you these four pieces of lace that I picked up in Chalons, France while visiting there. Please give a piece to each of the girls and one to Althea for a Christmas present with my best wishes and a Merry Christmas.

I havn't found a suitable present for you yet, so I'll send you some money that is better anyway.

Merry Christmas to you all and lets hope to be together this time next year at least.

Ever your loving son,
Roland.

Thursday 31   Still no machine, didn't fly all morning, took No. 23 up for a test flight after dinner & it vibrates, pretty bad but not like 26. Took it out on a bombing mission this P.M. and it got much worse. Dick Phelan & Art Weirick are missing tonight. I am darned tired of the war now.

Nov. 1, 1918   On alert all A.M. Planes loaded with 4 bombs each ready for a special mission. The new attack started today. Weather bad so didn't go. Went on a 11:30 patrol, came back with bad motor, landed in fog at 1st Pursuit. Stayed there till 3:30 P.M., then flew home. No word from Dick or Art W. as yet. Pretty bad.

Saturday 2   No word from Dick or Art yet. Slept late this A.M., went up & couldn't go on 9:45 patrol. No machine. Weather cloudy. Nothing doing on front. Had a bombing mission this P.M. but didn't go on account of rain & fog. Bummed around all day. My machine is fixed up now. It goes fine on the ground.

November 2, 1918.

Dearest Mother:

Just a word to let you know that all is well. We are still working pretty much all the time and nothing of very great importance or interest has happened since I last wrote you. Yesterday noon we started out on a regular patrol in a dense fog. We met above it just three of us and started out towards the lines. I, unfortunately had to drop out, due to a missing motor and come on in the direction of home at about 2000 M. up above the fog. When I got to what I thought was our field, I went down into the fog and was very much surprised to find that the fog went clear down to the ground. I nearly hit trees and houses and had to climb up over the hills and go down in the valleys to see the ground. Well, I followed the road and finally saw an aviation field in the distance. I went over it and lost it then luckily found it again and landed just making the field and just missing a hangar. I bent an axle on landing, but otherwise was all right.

I found that it was the 1st Pursuit Group Field, they are about 6 miles east of us. Well I had dinner with them and hung around, got my machine fixed up and telephoned the squadron and waited until it cleared up which it did about 3, so at 3:30 I left and arrived home O.K. The two that I left in the formation attacked 11 Huns and knocked down three and only left the fight because they ran out of ammunition so just see what I missed.

Just got a letter from Welly Morse and he sends his regards to you and the girls. He is in Belgium with an infantry company. By the way please send me a small diary book for 1919. I have kept one all last year and I want to continue it. It certainly is great to hear about all that is going on at home in the way of preparedness for the war etc and the people certainly are backing us up and believe me it makes a difference over here too. Just keep up the good work and the war will soon be over. You have made no mention of the St. Mihiel drive that the Americans made and carried through so successfully. That was our first all American drive. Our group did road straffing and regular patrol work then and had a great time. I wrote you all about it then, so I won't repeat it any more. We are fighting in very difficult country now, especially for the infantry for it is all hilly and wooded country, and the Germans have thrown in all the reserves they have to try and hold us so you see it is no joke. Also the best German Aviation is down here and there is quite a lot of it too. The Richthofen [Flying Circus] and all of them so every patrol is interesting and we usually have a fight, or could have if we had advantages.[11] I tell you all this aerial combat work you read about is quite different from the real fighting. By the way how did these "Wild Cat" cock fliers get along that were to tour the States?[12] We heard over here that a couple of them were killed in the first few days. What kind of machines did they fly? They certainly are brave boys!! To tell the truth about this flying over the front, acrobatics and all these skillful maneuvers you read about are very seldom used, the main things are to see all there is to be seen and to keep out of the Boche's way and to try and get an advantageous position on him, i.e. get between him and the sun or behind clouds and always above, then attack and pull away again, and if they surprise you just stand the old Spad on her nose and let her go down and they can never catch you.

Well Mother I'll have to say goodbye and go to dinner. My love to the girls, Althea and the family and my best to all my friends. Will send you some more money soon again.

Lots of love Mother and don't you worry about me at all in any way.

Your loving son,
Roland.

P.S. Enclosed find an article which gives you a good idea of the training at Issoudun.

Nov. 3, 1918.   Got up for a 7:00 alert this A.M. went out with bombs to bomb & machine gun woods north of Buzancy. I didn't go because my machine wouldn't go. Went out this P.M. on a bombing raid to Suippes [?] with 93rd & 103rd & 28th. . . .

Monday 4   Got up for an 8:00 patrol but didn't go on account of the weather. Tested #26 again today but it still misses. Tried for a patrol with 23 but had to come back. Got some Chocolate & doughnuts at the ARC this P. Got lots of mail tonight.

Nov. 5, 1918   Got up for a 7:00 alert and had a bombing mission over Mouzon at 9:20 at 4000 m, participating 1st D. B. G. [Day Bombardment Group]. I started out & as usual had to come back, magneto trouble. Got a new machine today, a Belleville. Some class. We move to Foucacourt tomorrow morning.

Wednesday 6   Had an early patrol this A.M. but didn't go, weather. Packed up to leave, flew on a 9:30 patrol. Had a scrap. Lost Treadwell & got one Boche. I had motor trouble all the time & couldn't get in very far, landed at our new field. I didn't fly any more today.

Nov. 7, 1918   Got up for 7:00 alert with bombs. Very foggy & stayed so generally all day long. Played cards & bummed around all day. My new ship is getting ready. She runs fine. Good war news today. Fixing up the Armistice terms and all looks well.

Friday 8   Got up late this A.M. Very rainy & low clouds at noon. We were called out to bomb & straff a road, went out 500 m & didn't see a hun on the roads as per usual, so we bombed a town. Every bomb didn't drop, anyway our troops had just taken the town. Jack Ogden is a prisoner.

Nov. 9, 1918   Bad weather all day today so we didn't fly at all. This P.M. 6 of us went off to Chalons but the car broke down & we ate supper at a french camp & they took us into town where we couldn't find a bed so we all separated & [L.] Lamb & I slept at the M.P.s, had lots of blankets so it went O.K. although it was pretty cold.

Sunday 10   Had 2 breakfasts this A.M. as we couldn't get enough at one place. Met the car at about 9:30 A.M. Came on & left chauffeurs with the Fiat & came on home in time for dinner. On alert all P.M. Went up to bomb some towns later 7 had to come back with motor trouble. Everybody landed in the dusk. Very good news tonight, Germans accept terms.

Nov. 11, 1918   The Armistice was signed this morning and hostilities ceased at 11:00 and maybe we weren't glad. Didn't fly today. Lots of rejoicing. Bummed around all day. It really seems hard to believe that the war is really over. Maybe it isn't but we will see. I think it is but when will we go home?

November 11, 1918.

My dearest Mother:

Well, maybe you don't think I am happy. Hostilities cease at 11 this morning and it is now 10, and very foggy, so we won't be doing any more flying during the war. What do you think of that? Of course this is all ancient history to you when you get this. It seems too good to be true doesn't it. I guess and hope I flew my last time with hostile intention yesterday PM when we went over to bomb a town and it doesn't make me a bit mad either. You see it only took me and [Ferdinand] Foch about three months to end this war, that wasn't bad was it? Well, I won't dwell on it any more, but you know how I feel.

I sent you a box with some lace collars in it for the girls and Althea, which I found in Chalons. I don't know whether you can use it or not, or whether such things are in style, but it has gone now, so there you are. I am also sending my German helmet to Althea, just as a souvenir. Also I am sending $100 for you to buy a Christmas present for yourself and for the girls and Althea, if you think you want to make an addition to the lace.

Excuse this pencil, but my pen is "pas bon". We moved again about or nearly a week ago, but the weather has been so bad that we havn't been doing much flying. However we are still operating on the same sector with the 1st Army, and you know where that is. We sure have been working and giving the old Huns H--l, as they say in the newspapers. Our news is only recent. In fact we know from the papers what we have been doing only the day after, that is pretty good though. I am going to try to cable you right away, so that you will know that all is well with me, in fact it couldn't be weller. I was feeling pretty low lately because we lost so many men and such nice fellows, but then c'est la guerre. I didn't want to say anything about it to you, but of course now that is all over and I can tell you such things without being afraid of worrying you.

I received Bobby's and E's letter, thank them very much for me please, it sure is nice of them to write to me and I'm afraid this will have to be their answer for the present at least. I sure am a bum on letter writing. I don't seem to be able to write worth a darn, don't have anything much to say. Did you ever get the letter I wrote you about the St. Mihiel drive.

I wrote you a regular diary on our activities then, but you have made no mention of it yet, and have even asked me to tell you what kind of fighting we have been doing, so I guess you havn't gotten it yet. I received your last letter, October 6th yesterday with the gum in it the gum arrives O.K. and sure hits the spot.

Glad to hear that you have had some more lights put in. Too bad you wouldn't let me do it when I had the time and material was cheap. Well we won't cry over spilt milk, especially now that the war is "fini". Gee but it will be fine to get home and have a good old talk with all of you. Won't it be just too grand though? I don't know how soon we will be home, but it ought not to be too long now. I certainly am glad that Althea likes U.C. so much, it would be a shame if she didn't, and I don't see how she could go there and not like it. I'll be darned if I know what I want to do when I get back. In the first place I will be very lazy, and then everything that I knew of constructional value is about forgotten and all I've learned lately is of destructional value, so there you are.

My love to the girls and Althea and all the family and lots and lots to yourself.

Your loving son,
Roland.

Chapter Six

Returning Home

"Well such a meeting as we did have."

Tuesday 12   Got up for an 8:00 practice patrol, but weather was too bad. We are going to have practice practically every day now. I am in the 3rd flight till C. Grey gets back. Flew this P.M. & led the formation, did some stunts. The Armistice terms sure are great. The old Hun is fine now. We will be here all winter now I suppose. No word from Treadwell yet.

Nov. 13, 1918   Had a 9:30 patrol this A.M. I didn't go, motor trouble. Had a practice group formation this P.M. and I didn't go on it either. Bummed around and didn't do much today. Fini la guerre and Hurrah.

Thursday 14   Went up on a practice patrol this A.M. but had to come down with pressure trouble. Didn't go up this P.M. Had a muster. Went to Bar le Duc this P.M. but got there too late to get a bath. Had supper & then went home. Had an awfully cold ride but all went well. Got 2 letters tonight.

Nov. 15, 1918   Got up for a 8:00 practice patrol, but my wagon was not in commission. So I didn't fly. Bummed around all day & didn't fly this P.M. either for my machine was still on the bum. Got awfully cold and windy today and very uncomfortable this evening.

Saturday 16   Got up late this morning and gee but it was cold. Didn't fly all day but just hung around and thawed out. It was awfully cold and windy all day. Sent some picture cards home today. Not much doing now days but lots of rumors going about. Pretty bad again tonight.

Nov. 17, 1918   Got up late this A.M. and bummed around all A.M. Pretty cold, was cold all last night. Went up to the hangars but my plane is still out of commission. Went for a walk this P.M. and had chocolate at the Red + wrote a letter and went to bed. Still pretty cold.

Monday 18   Didn't fly today. Weather very cold today. First flight made a trial formation. Bummed around all day. Went out to the Red Cross & had chocolate & doughnuts this P.M. Came home & bummed around some more.

November 19, 1918   We didn't fly this A.M. It isn't so cold as it was today. Went up for a trial formation. Had to try it 3 times. My machine went on the bum so I had to come down & take another. But didn't find the formation. Didn't go so good. CO was peeved.

Wednesday 20   Got up late this A.M. and had a lecture on Avrons. Regular school boys now. This P.M. we had a practice formation with the 103rd. I had another mag. go bad & came down. Went to Bar le Duc this P.M. & bummed around, came home & nearly froze. Pretty cold tonight.

Nov. 21, 1918   Got up late again 8:00 & bummed around all A.M. Tried to sew my "A" on but didn't make much progress. There is a rumor now that we take them off. Flew this P.M. but mag. went bad again. Came down. Took a walk & got a letter from A. tonight. Pretty cold again.

Friday 22   Got up late again as per usual. Had a Squadron sortie with the 103rd this P.M. I had mag. trouble again and had to come down. Had chocolate at the A.R.C. and bummed around. Went to bed early. Went to Bar le Duc & back.

Nov. 23, 1918   Went down to Moulin near Ligny en Barrois with 1st Bombardment Group to visit. . . . Came back OK. & had chocolate at A.R.C.

Sunday 24   Got up early to fly over to Metz, went out & 3 of us started out but my pressure wouldn't stay up so I had to come down and couldn't go. Bummed around all day and had chocolate at the A.R.C.C. Grey & I came back. My name went in the Group to go to the rear and maybe home?

Nov. 25, 1918   Bummed around all day and didn't do very much this evening. We got our 3 day leave & left for Paris at 6:00. Caught an 8:00 train out of Bar le Duc & spent the night on the train. It was pretty cold but we all had seats.

Tuesday 26   Arrived in Paris at 5:30 A.M. Found rooms in Chateau Hotel at 9:00 & shopped etc all day long. Had a grand time, took a bath & had good room. Went to the Opera & saw Monna Wanna or something like that.[1] Went to bed & slept O.K.

Nov. 27, 1918   Shopped & bummed around all day today after having breakfast in bed etc. John A. [Aiken] & I went to the Follies tonight and it was a pretty good show. Dick [Loomis] took a friend & me to dinner.

Thursday 28   Shopped & went to Charleroi to get our passes stamped and purple card at the M.P's. Ate at King's Carriage, got down to the Champs Elyesses. Had dinner, went to Casino tonight, rather slow. It was a cold day.

Nov. 29, 1918   Took the 8:50 train out of Paris and sure was sorry to leave, left about 100 dollars behind. Spent all A.M., ate dinner & till about 2:00 P.M. on the train. Came out to camp tonight in the machine and slept there.

November 29, 1918.

Dearest Mother:

Well, so much has been going on in the last few days that I havn't had time to write anybody. I'll have to make this a family letter for I owe one to all the girls as well as to you. To begin with, I have just come back from a three day's leave in Paris where three of us put up in a good hotel and a bath, breakfast in bed and all the comforts of home and then some. Well I havn't seen a bath tub for about three months or anything else pertaining to a city so we really splurged a little and they sure do know how to take your money in Paris so we emerged today with only our pocket books suffering. Before I went to Paris, they sent in five names of men in our Squadron to be sent to the S.O.S. [Services of Supply] and then probably home, and they picked these names from men who had been in the squadron longest and who had the most time over the lines and luckily I got on it so I may be home very soon, how is that. I am very mad about it myself. Just now I am down at the Y.M.C.A. officers' club at Bar le Duc writing this letter, for we just arrived from Paris, and for all I know our orders to go home may be waiting for us at camp. I'll telegraph you as soon as I know anything definite and if it is possible, but things are so indefinite and telegraphing sometimes hard to do that you may hear from me as arrived OK in New York. Just keep my place at the Christmas dinner table and I'll try and make it. How would that be? I am all excited about it myself and so darned anxious to get home that I'd do anything to hurry it up a bit.

I received your letter of October 27th just the day I left for Paris, the one with the red leaf in it. That sure reminds me of home. By the way that "plan" you proposed is strictly against censorship rules, and if I did it and got caught I'd be liable to about "steen" courtmartials, etc.[2] So you see, I won't use it. You see the Army isn't like civilian life, that is one of the reasons I am anxious to get out of it.

I received your's and Althea's gum regularly and it is fine. If you want to you can stop sending it now, for I won't be doing any more flying to speak of and therefore won't need it, and now that the war is fini, I will want to loose [sic] the habit which is none too good.

I tell you you will have to give me instructions in all kinds of things when I get home especially the society arts principally table manners, etc., for I fear that I am very crude at present.

By the way my friend Jack Ogden never came back. He is a prisoner in Germany, and has been ever since he took my plane out and didn't return. You must have read my letter wrong or something, anyway, he is safe. I havn't received the package yet, but am on the lookout for it all the time.

Well I'll have to stop now for our transportation to camp will be along in awhile and I don't want to miss it. My love to the girls and Althea, and tell her that I am going to write to her next and soon. My best to all my friends and lots of love to yourself.

Your devoted son,
Roland.

Saturday 30   Got up and bummed around all morning. After dinner went up to trenches in Argonne forest and sure saw some interesting things. Orders are for me to go to Issoudun for duty.

Dec. 1, 1918   Packed up today and finished up all business in the Squadron and had all our pictures taken by the official photographer. Left after supper for 11:00 P.M. train for Paris, but it arrived at 2:15. It was loaded & I stood up all the way to Paris till 9:30 next morning.

Monday 2   Got off the train feeling pretty low. Washed and shaved at Grand Hotel lobby & found room at the Chatham again. Brought own luggage over and checked it to Issoudun and had a good dinner & supper. Saw an English show after supper, then to bed & O, my,!!

Dec. 3, 1918   Got up at 8:30 and went down and took a 10:30 train for Issoudun. Arrived there about 3:00 P.M. Got a truck out to Camp, reported and found a bunk in a barracks. Back to the old life again. No rumors yet.

Wednesday 4   Went up to see the Med. Board & made a date for my exam. We all have to take a physical exam and Class D go right home & Class A follows right away. I get mine tomorrow. Very muddy & bad down here as usual. Looks kind of bad but I'll see.

Dec. 5, 1918   Took my exam today, nerves, eyes, all those things. Am afraid I'll be in A Class. Met Major [I. W.] Patton who examined me in Wash. He took me to see Col. [William] Wilmer who told me that we would all get home very soon, pretty nice, not very good quarters.

Friday 6   Got up late and bummed around all morning, didn't accomplish much. This P.M. we went down town and got some rooms in a hotel where we will try and arrange to stay as long as we are here. Played cards with Lt. [Henry] Loomis & went to bed early.

Dec. 7, 1918   Got up for 8:00 formation. Bummed around all A.M. and finally got permission to live in town. Packed up & went in. I've met Wallace Innis going out to Colombey. Sure was glad to see him. Ate & slept in town tonight, Hotel de France.

Sunday 8   Stayed in bed late and bummed around all day. Ate a good dinner & supper and went to bed early. Absolutely nothing to do now, no new dope and no rumors.

Dec. 9, 1918   Got up late, had breakfast & went out to camp, had dinner, bought a meusette & some eats from Q.M. Took a bath and came in for supper. Had a chicken supper, very good. Played cards with Dick L. a little & went to bed. Got a letter from Mother today.

Tuesday 10   Got up late & missed breakfast. Bought some butter for dinner & bummed around all A.M. After dinner we went out for a walk and spent a good part of the P.M. that way. Ate at the hotel tonight, pretty good.

Dec. 11, 1918   Got up late and bummed around all morning. Haven't a thing to do so it is a very lazy life. Ate at Mathers & had supper at the Hotel de Commerce. Went on to Camp this P.M. Got a package by mail from Harrods London from Mother and Althea.

December 11, 1918

Dearest Mother:

Received your letter with the razor blades sewed in the handkerchief all right. That was a good idea for they never slipped once and arrived in good condition. The handkerchief came in handy too, for I am right in the midst of a regular "runny" cold you know, and with the uncertainty of getting washing done, because we can't know how long we will be in any one place, well it makes it rather uncomfortable at times. However, I am coming along fine and havn't a thing in the world to worry about now that the war is over.

I wrote to Althea the other day and told her of all the news there was, but I am afraid it was a pretty discontented letter, for there was a gang in our room all talking at once, and in the meantime I was trying to write. Anyhow here is the situation: five of the oldest men in our squadron, including myself, were sent back to the S.O.S.i.e. [Issoudun] to go home we thought. When we got here we found it was to take a physical exam, similar to the one we took on entering the flying game. This was for statistical reasons only, to see what effect our flying on the front had on us physically and mentally. This by the way was done by a board of doctors sent over by Uncle Ted for the care of the flier of which he had no doubt told you all ready. They are doing fine work too and are a fine bunch of men. Everybody that has had anything to do with them says the same thing, and all the fliers are very much in favor of the idea and of the work they are doing, so you can tell Uncle Ted that at last his goal has been successfully reached and if they would have let him have his way before many lives would undoubtedly have been saved, but such is the Army.

Well they were to class the man as A. B. C. and D. according to their physical and mental fitness and furthermore they were to go home the reverse of those letters, i.e. the As. last so we all were very desirous of being put in class B. or C, just to get home soon. Well as luck would have it I drew an A, but I ran across a Major Patton who had examined me in Washington to get into the Service. Well he and I had quite a talk and he took me in to see Colonel Wilmer who is in charge of the board and he told me that the latest news was that we were going straight home as soon as they could collect all our records, etc. and get out the orders, so here we are, still at Issoudun waiting. They gave us permission to live in town so a bunch of us are living in a hotel, a rotten place but better than living out at camp, where we would have to answer roll calls, do calisthenics etc. That is all the news there is, only this morning the Captain in charge of the Provost Marshall [sic] station where we report at 9 AM and 3 PM everyday said, that a bunch of orders were coming through in a day or two.

I think we will be leaving inside of a week, so really you need't bother to answer this letter, or write any more, for strange as it may seem I think I'll be home before they can get to me anyway I hope so. Doesn't it seem just too good to be true though to get home, gee I can hardly believe it. It has been nearly a year and a half since I came over, so you can imagine how glad I'll be to get back and also to get OUT of France, gee but this is an awful country to live in. I don't ever want to see it again never of all rotton [sic] dirty, smelly, absolute behind the times, etc. countries, this one takes the lead. As one fellow said about the French "When they arn't robbing you, they are in your way." Of course that must sound pretty bad to you, but after one has spent one and a half years here and seen all that I have, it is easily understood.

Don't get too optimistic about my coming home, for it may be a month yet, but we will hope not anyway. I think we ought to be sure by the first half of January.

I am still on the lookout for packages, but as yet none have come. Hope they get here before we leave, but it will probably be just my luck that they won't. Guess you think I am getting pretty pessimistic, well I'm not, I am just getting homesick. To wait a month now with nothing to do seems years to me, but I suppose I'll have to be patient and take my medicine the way it comes. That is the only thing you can do in the Army, so here goes.

Please give my love to the girls, Althea and all the family and my best to all my friends and lots and lots of love to yourself.

Your loving son,
Roland.

Thursday 12   Got up late again and bummed around all morning. Got lunch at the Hotel & supper at the Hotel. Then took a walk with Lt. Loomis this afternoon & visited the waterways, etc. went to bed early after playing Rummy with Lt. Loomis.

Dec. 13, 1918   Got up late and didn't eat any breakfast. Am eating too much & getting fat so I'll have to slow down. Took a walk this A.M. and visited the foundry this P.M. Saw them pour some castings, pretty interesting. Gerry Barnes had supper with us tonight.

Saturday 14   Got up late as per usual & ate a little breakfast and bummed around all morning. Had a cheap dinner at Mathers & went out to Camp right afterwards. Got some mail and met Buck Freeman, sure was glad to see him, just got back from Germany. Came back on the train & went to bed.

Dec. 15, 1918   Got up late and bummed around all morning. Had dinner at Mathers & then Bill Munn and myself went out for a walk. The weather was pretty good so we had a good time, visited an old lime kiln and saw the practice trenches. Came home, ate supper & went to bed early.

Monday 16   Got up late & went out to camp. Got a haircut and dinner at camp. Asked for a 5 day leave. Got a bath and had a dinner there. Saw Buck again. Bummed around the rest of the day. Saw some wild flying with a 28 N & some 27 N. Came home on train & went to bed.

Dec. 17, 1918   Got up earlier than usual today and went out to camp to see about our 5 day leaves, had to sign some property slips etc. & found one couldnt get on leave as our orders are about due. Ate dinner at camp, in on 2:15 truck & played cards till 11:30 tonight.

Wednesday 18   Got up late this A.M. as per usual. It rained all day so we didn't do very much. Played cards, wrote letters and read all day long and played awhile after supper.

December 18, 1918.

Dearest Mother:

Received your letter of November 10th yesterday and was glad to get it. The box from Harrod's came in good shape. I wrote Althea about it the other day for I owed her a letter. It is all gone now but the soup and we are going to have a can of it today so it will be one half gone by tonight. Never mind sending anything more, for I think I will be home soon, anyway that is all we are waiting for now. I don't know anymore about getting home now than I did the last time I wrote you, so there isn't any more to say on that subject.

By the way, I sent you my Christmas package certificate about November 1st, it was late I know but they didn't dish them out until that day, so there you are. I hope you got it, but now I am afraid we will be gone before the package reaches you. I really don't need anything but a tooth brush, but some milk chocolate would sure go good. It is worth its weight in gold over here, for we can't buy it anywhere for love or money. In fact you can't buy anything much any more. I guess they are saving it for Christmas. By the way I've found out what the trouble is with my pen, it is all right but the ink is no good. Thank goodness we soon will be back where we can buy decent articles. How these French ever live in comfort is more than I can see, but we won't elaborate on that unpleasant subject any more.

We are still living in the Hotel and doing nothing at all. It sure is a lazy life and it gets on your nerves. If they don't send us home soon we won't be worth much when we do get there.

That certainly must be interesting work you are doing with the A.R.C. and also your volunteer nursing. Don't work too hard now Mother and get yourself sick or overworked, because when I get home we want to have some real family rejoicing, and believe me it is going to be some tall rejoicing for yours truly.

Gee won't it be good to get all the family together again like we used to. Well that time will come very soon I think, but nevertheless it seems a long way off.

By the way I met Wallace Innis over here at camp the other day. He was on his way out to the front, or rather to the 1st Air Depot that used to be the front. He is flying D.H.4s. I don't know why they are sending men out any more, but maybe it is just to relieve the old men in the squadron, that is how we got relieved.

Well Mother I really havn't news of any kind to tell you. All I've been thinking about lately is getting home, and believe me I sure do want to get there.

Please give my love to the girls, Althea and the family and remember me to all my friends and take good care of yourself and them always. Lots and lots of love from

> Your loving son,
> Roland.

Dec. 19, 1918   Got up late and after our "petite dejeuner dans la chambre" we went out to camp where we got the mail, all the new dope which was most discouraging etc. and heard a jazz band at the "Y" & came home. Had a can of our soup for supper. Pasted photos after supper.

Friday 20   Got up and went down to the M.P.'s this A.M. pasted some photos, etc. this A.M. and P.M. Had lunch and supper at "Mathers". Dick & I took a walk out to a chateau near us this P.M. Went through an awfully pretty garden. Got a letter from A. tonight, not very good news, she wants to go out and work !

Dec. 21, 1918   Got up pretty late this A.M. and went out to camp. Took a few pictures out there and saw a Caproni come in. Had dinners at Mess #6 and after bumming around a little came in. Had a good chicken supper and ate a lot. Played cards till 10:30, then to bed.

Sunday 22   Got packed up this A.M. and the Field 9 water truck picked me up at the hotel bag and baggage and took us out to the field. Got there about 1:00, had a fine dinner and got settled in our new quarters this P.M. All is well and we are glad of the change. Had a good supper & went to bed.

Dec. 23, 1918   Got up for a 7:30 A.M. breakfast. Bummed around camp and went to the main field this A.M. Bought some galoshes and a pair of boots from a Frenchman. Had a dandy dinner. Believe me the meals are great here and bummed around this P.M. Went to the Y this evening & then to bed.

Tuesday 24   Got up late this A.M. had chocolate at the "Y" and bummed around till dinner. Afterwards went out & watched them fly a little, played basketball & played ping-pong. After supper the 3 of us gave a little talk to the men in the "Y" about our experiences at the front and then went to bed.

Dec. 25, 1918   Got up for an 8:00 breakfast. Bummed around camp and took a walk, went to church before dinner at 2:00 P.M. Sure was grand. Best Xmas dinner I ever ate, from soup to French pastry, it couldn't be beat. Went to the "Y" this evening & saw some movies, etc.

Thursday 26   Got up medium time and I went down town to get rid of the boots I bought the frenchman. Got a 48 hr. pass to Paris for Dick & myself. After lots of rushing I managed to make the 3:00 P.M. train, it was 2 hr. late had a long ride, supper on the train & arrived in Paris at 10:00 P.M. Got a room at the Chateau hotel & slept.

Dec. 27, 1918   Got up at 8:00, had breakfast and shopped all A.M.& P.M., bought presents to bring home etc., went to a movie & saw an English show this evening, was very good. "General Post" at the Theater Albert.[3] Will probably leave on 10:00 A.M. train tomorrow morning. Had two good meals today.

Saturday 28   Got up, ate breakfast and left for station to get 10:00 A.M. train back to Issoudun. Had a long unjoyful ride, ate dinner on the train and arrived about 2 hr. late as per usual.

Dec. 29, 1918   Got up late this A.M. Not feeling very good. Read all morning, had a good dinner and wrote letters and bummed around all afternoon. Had supper and read for awhile, then went to bed.

Issoudun, Dec. 29, 1918.

Dearest Mother:

Received your letters of November 17th and 24th, for which I thank you a lot. Awfully glad you received the cable. I was kind of afraid to send it first for fear that when it arrived, you might think it was a cable telling you that I had been bumped off, so you see you nearly didn't get it.

Well, here it is after Christmas and we are still in France. I thought for awhile that I might be home by the 25th, but no such luck. However, we had a dandy time Christmas, so I'll tell you about it.

In the first place, two other fellows and myself decided to move out to field #9 here at camp where one of the other fellows had a friend, for it was a little too expensive living in town in a Hotel. Well, this field is noted for its goodness, so were glad to be able to come out here. All we have to do is eat and sleep, so we went to the best eating place in camp, not so awfully hard to comprehend is it? Well in the first place I received your last two letters Christmas morning, a dandy Christmas present, so the day started off fine. Then came dinner and it was some dinner too, soup, turkey, vegetables, salad, French pastry, cake, ice cream, nuts, etc., everything and all you could wish for. It was really a remarkable dinner for the A.E.F., and we all gorged ourselves. We didn't have any supper, didn't want or need any anyway, but spent a great part of the afternoon at the "Y", where they had movies, gave presents out to the men, etc. First time I ever saw the "Y" give anything away. Also Christmas morning I went to Church at the "Y", something like our own, only simpler. This was the first time I had gone to Church since I left the U.S.A., and I sure did enjoy it. So passed the day. December 26th I found that it was possible to get a 48 hour pass to Paris, so another fellow and myself beat it up there that same afternoon and stayed all the next day and until 10 the next morning. We didn't stay all of our 48 hours, but we had nothing more to do after we finished our shopping and various business, so we came home, and here we are back at field #9 again.

Some of the fellows have been ordered out of here lately, among them three of our bunch, two of whom arrived here after I did, but that is the way in the Army. You can't ever depend on anything or ever count on getting a square deal. That is one of its faults and one of the reasons why I want to get out of it as soon as I can. You asked me what my plans were, well the first one is to get discharged, and then darned if I know what I ought to do. We will talk it all over though when I get home.

I wouldn't be surprised if I were ordered out of here to Angers pretty soon, and then in a week or two to a port, probably St. Nazaire and then home, so I may be home by Feb. 1, 1919. That wouldn't be bad would it? Gee but I do want to go home. It has been nearly one and one half years since I left home and it seems like so many centuries to me. I have it all doped out now what I am going to do when I get home. I want to spend the first evening with you and the next with Althea, and after that I don't care what happens. Just remember though that my first two evenings home are engaged, very much so. Does that meet with your approval?

By the way I, I am not sending any more money but will bring all my money with me. Also, I sent my Red Cross Christmas label quite awhile ago, about Nov. 1st or thereabout. I really don't need anything, but only wanted some real milk chocolate, maybe you have sent some already. I received the papers with the tooth brush, razor blades and gum, all in good condition. Never mind sending anything more, for by the time it would reach me, I may be gone, maybe home, who knows. For goodness sakes, don't go to thinking about coming to France now, nor ever. You stay right home, what do you think I am coming home for, to play boats in the bath tub, no sir, you want to be there when I get home.

Well, that is all the news there is so I'll have to stop. I am going to write to Althea next soon. Received an awfully nice letter from her yesterday. Not the illustrated one but one written since then. Please give my love to her and the girls and the family in general. Also received a letter from Uncle Russ, it sure was nice of him to remember me. I'll write him soon.

My best to all my friends and lots and lots of love for yourself.

Your loving son,
Roland.

Monday 30   Got up for breakfast this morning for a change and played around all A.M., went to town after dinner to get my boots fixed and to take some laundry in. Made out my qualification card and saw lots of orders but none for Loomis & myself. Came out to camp, saw a movie at the "Y" & went to bed.

Dec. 31, 1918   Got up for breakfast again this A.M. and went out and flew Type 28 N. with a 120 H.P. Rhone in it, had lots of fun and didn't mind the change a bit. Went down town after dinner and got my boots etc. and found that Dick's & my orders are here and will leave any day now.

Jan 1, 1919   Got up for breakfast. My Christmas box came today and I sure am glad to get it. Had lots of nice things in it. Had a regular dinner today and bummed around this P.M. Flew a 15 M. type 27 N today. Sure was great. Wrote some letters & went to bed.

Jan. 2   Went out to main field and found that our orders ready so we packed up and went down town at 2:30. Ate dinner there and left on 5:27 train. Stayed the night at Y so we wouldn't have to stand up all night on the train.

Jan. 3   Got up early, had a french breakfast and got the 7:40 train in Tours. Stood up most all the way. Killed two youths on way over they got in the way of the train. Sure was a shame. Changed at Tours and took express. Stood up all the way, arrived at A [Angers] at about 2:30 P.M. Reported at camp and slept on a brass nite bed tonight. Pretty good camp & lots of officers here. It is a casual officers camp, no dope on going out at all.

Jan. 4   Woke up with a regular old backache today. Our luggage came thank goodness and we got settled today. Dick & I went down town tonight & had supper there, brought some cake home, came back on the street car. Saw Jack Ogden & Dave McClure yesterday.

Jan. 5   Had a good sleep. Got up & went on sick report. Doc gave me some pills for my back. Kidney trouble. Bummed around all day long. Wrote letters and packed my trunk again. Went to bed early. Not much doing over here.

Jan. 5, 1919.

Dearest Mother:

Well, lots of things have happened since I last wrote you. First, the Christmas box came on New Years day and it sure was fine, everything in it was great, and I thank you one and all. I am using the pen now and all the eats are gone. Those dates were fine and went pretty fast, so did the chocolates and nuts. Dick Loomis and I have a parcheesie tournament on now and at present are even. I havn't tried the [?] or other things but will as soon as I need them.

The day after New Years Dick and I got our orders to go to Angers to the Casual Officer's Camp so we went along and arrived here day before yesterday and are all settled now to await assignment to a boat, when I don't know. We sure are glad to shake the mud of Issoudun off our feet, that sure is a muddy hole. By the way, speaking of mud, it has rained for forty consecutive days over here, and still going, not all day every day, but a good part of the day. Last year they said the rain was caused by the artillery etc. up at the front, maybe that was so but I'll be darned if they can explain the reason for it this year. I suppose it is the lack of said explosions, anyhow, it is sure wet and sloppy. So here we are at Angers in a big camp, stone buildings and pretty good quarters, not a good mess and about 1000 officers just sitting around doing nothing. We have three roll calls — 7 AM, 11 AM and 4 PM, and that is all we have to do. Dick and I went down town to Angers yesterday PM, and it is a pretty nice place. If you remember we came thru here when we were with the Benedicts and saw a big Chateau. Well, here I are again, Chateau and all. I think I'll go see it again if it ever stops raining. I don't think it will, so probably I won't see it.

I don't know how long I'll be here but I don't think it will be very long, it is just another step towards home. Well anyway I had my mail sent home, so I won't get any more. It is so uncertain that I thought that was the best thing to do, so you may get some letters of mine before I get there, anyway just save them for me.

I saw lots of fellows down here who were prisoners in Germany. Jack Ogden, McClure and others, who were in ours or other squadrons, sure is good to see them too.

I'll have to go to dinner now so goodbye and good luck and hope to see you soon. Best love to all.

Roland.

Jan. 6   Got up for breakfast this A.M. and bummed around till Roll Call at 11:00. Went down town for dinner and went sight seeing afterwards. Saw the Chateau and Cathedral. Came home and bummed around till supper. Went to the movie at the "Y" then played cards at W. Eaton's room, then to bed.

Jan. 7   Got up for breakfast. Bummed around till roll call. Went down town & bought some doilies, etc. Came home for 4:00 roll call and had supper. Went to the movie at the "Y" afterwards.

Jan. 8   Bummed around all morning till 11:00 Roll Call. Went down town and got a bath before lunch. Came home for 4:00 roll call and went down again to the movies with Dick's cousin. Walked some in the rain. Walked around town today and ate at a new place. Food O.K but rotten service.

Jan. 9   Got up late this morning & didn't get any breakfast. Bummed around all day and didn't do much of anything. I got bawled out by a "Kewie" Captain for wearing my roll call coat.⁴ Gave 100 fr. to "Y" lady for some poor children in a Hospital. Played cards up in Warren Eaton's room till 9:30, then went to bed.

Jan. 10   Got up for breakfast. Am in Co. "G" on parade grounds. Ate dinner at Camp and bummed around till 4:00 Roll Call. Didn't go to the movies as was planned as there weren't any. Played cards awhile with W. Eaton's gang & went to bed.

Jan. 11   Had breakfast & went down town after roll call. Bought tickets for the movies. Had dinner & bummed around till 4:00 roll call. Had dinner at camp. 390 men left today for Bordeaux & Brest. Pretty good. Eaton & [L. E.] Cauffman were in it. . . . Rained.

Angers Jan. 11, 1919.

Dearest Mother and Girls:

Well here we are still and will probably be here for a week or more. It isn't a bad camp though and the town of Angers is pretty nice, only it has the usual drawbacks of being an Army Post.

I have been here just about a week now and am in Company "G", one hundred men in a company, so you can see how many are ahead of me. Tomorrow I think 250 officers will be ordered out to Bordeaux, where they will board a boat right away, that is the rumor around here anyway, but maybe we will have to wait there too. Everything is so indefinite that it is hardly worth while telling you about anything at all.

So far I have seen none of the Glendale or Cincinnati boys that I knew before the war. I guess there are few of them in the air service, and probably the boys who joined battery "E" have gone up with the Army of Occupation, so there you are. Funny I havn't seen any of them isn't it? I guess I'll be over here to get my third service stripe all right.⁵ I only have until January 18th before I can put it on. Believe me I wouldn't care if I never got it if only I could get home and get there quick.

Hope you arn't thinking of coming over here any more. I cabled you to stay at home and also told Althea to tell you not to come and to even think about it any more. For once please take my advice and stay right at home, where you can be one hundred percent more useful. I'd hate to have you connected with the Y.M.C.A. I'm afraid they have a black eye over here. They have done lots of good, but they have done lots of harm to themselves by their methods, prices, etc. You ought to read some of the articles in the home magazines about them giving doughnuts, cigarettes, etc., away, it is the biggest line of propaganda ever put over. Well I won't waste any more time on that subject for you don't like it I know.

I think this sure is a lazy life over here at present, and it must cost the Government quite a lot to keep paying us and not getting any service for it, but c'est la guerre when there isn't any "guerre", so there you are. I think we will go to a movie tonight, how does that sound? We will have to walk home afterwards, only about two miles and it will probably rain, it usually does, but anyway it is worth it. The "Y" had a show last night, but it wasn't much good and the room was so full of smoke and so empty of ventilation that you couldn't see what it was.

I wish I had had my mail sent down here now, but at the time we thought that we would be here only a few days and then go right out and sail. It was a sweet dream but had its usual ending and here we are "sans letters". I guess you will be getting back your letters soon, darn the luck, they won't do you a bit of good will they? Well just keep them for me in my desk or somewhere and when my desk gets full sometime in June or July, why start in the dresser and so on. I'll have a fine time reading them. You can open any packages that come and devour the contents thereof if you so desire. Well I'll have to say goodbye and get some food. My love to Althea and the family and lots of love to yourselves.

Your devoted son and brother,
Roland.

Jan. 12   Got up late. No breakfast. Bummed around all morning. The camp is closed & no one can go down town, 40 men couldn't be found last night at the time of leaving. Went out to an airdrome & saw a pretty nice looking biplane, a new type.

Jan. 13   Got up late again. Walked out & visited a slate factory that was shut down. After roll call John Aiken and Jack Lee left for Brest tonight. I guess we will be seeing some movies at the "Y" tonight.

Jan. 14   Got up for breakfast. Have been ordered to stand by for orders. Went down town took a bath & got my pictures etc., came back & bummed around all PM packing etc., all cleared up & orders to be given out at 10:30 P.M. Got our orders & walked around till 2:30 A.M. Then rode down town in trucks.

Jan. 15   Got down town at station at 3:00 P.M. and waited there till 5:00 P.M., then we left on 3rd class train. Rode all day on the local and ate what we brought with us and unlit at 12:00 that night.

Jan. 16   Rode till 3:00 A.M., then arrived at Brest where we reported and walked out to a camp where we got a bunk & some blankets and slept till 8:00, got up, ate breakfast at the "Y" hotel and then walked out to Camp. We all reported again and were given quarters, blankets & some food. Bummed around camp all P.M. Bought some Hall Krown mint. Hell of a camp. To bed early.

Jan. 17   Got up at 7:30 A.M., went to breakfast. Meals pretty good. Then walked down town after 9:00 A.M. Roll Call to sign property clearance air service papers. Got milage and bummed around Camp till 12:00 Roll Call dinner, bummed around all P.M. Came in after supper and played cards. Read till time for bed, 12:00.

Jan. 18.   Got up for breakfast and bummed around all A.M. and P.M. doing not much of anything. Rained all day. Hopes pretty low now, won't get out for 3 or 4 days is rumor. Played cards this evening & went to bed early.

Jan. 20   Got up, breakfast & bummed around all A.M. Rained all the time. Played some cards this P.M. and Dick and I took a little walk but got caught in the rain as usual. Lots of mud & rain and not much hope of getting out of here.

Jan. 21.   Got up for breakfast and bummed around all morning. Took a walk this P.M. and had a pretty good time. Came home and after supper Dick & I volunteered to go second class if necessary. Went to bed early as per usual.

Jan. 22   Got up for breakfast as usual and bummed around all A.M. A list of about 150 was posted but neither Dick nor I were on it. Went down town this P.M. & had a good visit with Harry Brown. Went home & found that I was on a 2nd class list for the Adriatic. Dick isn't on it, too bad. Got packed etc. & am to leave tomorrow morning at 7:00 A.M. Hope they don't change their minds before then.

Jan. 23   Went down town at 7:00 A.M. Reported & marched down to the dock and here we took a small boat over to the Adriatic and soon we boarded her. Got our quarters & seats at table & and sailed at 4:00 P.M. Some feeling to be going out on the way home. Went to bed early tonight. Good food & quarters and a good end in view.

Jan. 24   316 miles. Got up late & had a bath and good breakfast. We bummed around all day. H. Brown is on the boat so it is pretty nice. Bummed around the boat all day, read, played shuffle board etc., ate & enjoyed life. Went to bed early this evening.

Jan. 25   382 miles. Got up early & went over to the gym and worked a little & am a little constipated and my back is bothering me again. Took a Turkish bath this P.M. and felt rotten this evening. Took some A.O. pills this evening and went to bed feeling "Pas bon".

Jan. 26   390 miles. Got up late and relieved myself etc. feel pretty bad yet. Bummed around all day and felt rotten while doing it. Don't know what is wrong with me. Constipation, Back ache & all bad all over. I guess the sudden change from life in camp to this was too much for me. Had a chiropodist fix up a blister on my foot today.

Jan. 27   367 miles. Got up feeling a lot better this A.M. Back all right but still a bit constipated. Took some oil this P.M., maybe that will help. Played shuffle board & walked today. Read some and felt a good deal better. Have had wonderful weather all the way but it fogged up a little this evening. Went to bed early this P.M.

Jan. 28   361 miles. Got up for breakfast. Feeling fine this A.M. and felt so all day. Weather pretty cold today. Getting toward home. Played shuffle board and read today, also walked around awhile. Had a concert after dinner this evening, was pretty good too. Went to bed afterwards.

Jan. 29   380 miles. Got up as usual and bummed around after breakfast. Made out my pay voucher and declaration of property for duty. Read a little this P.M. Had a good supper and went to bed early.

Jan. 30   364 miles. Got up same as usual and bummed around all A.M. Played cards etc. Walked around all P.M. and didn't do much of anything. The trip so far has been wonderful. No rough [seas] & little bad weather. Remarkable for January. Watched them auction numbers at pool & sang a little after supper.

Jan. 31   373 miles. Got up for breakfast and packed up this A.M., getting ready to get off. After dinner we saw lots of boats and sighted land about 3:00 P.M. Then as we got close it looked good. Arrived in quarantine at about 4:00 P.M. and then sailed up the river to the turn of a land and a boat along side. Saw the Statue of Liberty and felt fine. We docked at a little after 5:00 P.M. and were told we couldn't get off. Well there was nearly a revolution but they read a lot of orders & regulations. We get off tomorrow A.M. No S. B. belts and march to Hoboken. We could see nobody on the pier & nobody could see us. Some men had families from Wash. to see them. DAMN orders & their originators, it is really a shame but we can't do a thing. It is just the Army all the way thru. The "returning heroes" are treated like a bunch of irresponsible children.

Feb. 1   Got off the boat at 8:00 this A.M. Went over to Pier#2 Hoboken, reported, had a physical exam, received orders and got pay vouchers, money changed and stewards fees etc. for trip, $10.00. Then came back to Pier 5 and got hand baggage & arranged other baggage, all O.K, had lunch & reported to Garden City as per orders.[6] Got leave to stay in NY till Monday A.M. Will take physical exam tonight & get discharge finished up. Went to a show this evening. Wired Mother again & Uncle Ted. Stayed at Hotel York.

Feb. 2.   Got up late. . . . Walked around town all A.M. . . . Will go out to Garden City tomorrow A.M.

Feb. 3.   Took the 6:40 train out to Garden City this A.M. and got first in line for my physical exam. Started this at 9:00 and went off till I reached Major Patton who sent me over to the other field with 50 others to take a rebreathing test which took all P.M. Came back too late to do any more this P.M. and could get nothing definite from the damned major. Went to a show tonight, pretty good. Three Faces East.[7]

Feb. 4.   Came out to camp on the special 6:30 train this A.M. and couldn't get my medical release. The major wasn't there & wouldn't be till 9:00 so I had to wait & lost my place in line & he didn't come, finally I found that some Captain had forgotten to release me last night so that was the trouble. Finally I got in line and just reached the discharge desk when it was time for dinner. Came back & passed thru desks 4, 5, 6, 7, 8 & saw the colonel to be re-rated and then to sign out at desk 10 for *discharge papers* at 5:00 PM. I was paid off for the last time, paid milage etc., then went back to New York. Saw a show & bought some candy this evening.

Feb. 5.   Got up at 7:00 A.M. and ate breakfast, went over to Pier #2 and got my baggage but the taxi broke down & had to get another so I was pretty late getting there. Called up & said goodbye to Dick Loomis & had dinner with W. Eaton & wife. Boarded the train & left at 4:00 P.M. for home. Whew! but it sure is good to be really on the way.

Feb. 6.   Got up, had breakfast etc. and bummed around getting more and more impatient all the time till finally train pulled into Cincinnati, then got off & the folks were all there. Well such a meeting as we did have. Althea and everybody. Gee but I was glad to see them all . . . . Everybody was so nice & interested. Sure made me feel good, and Mother and I stayed up till 2:45 A.M. talking. Then went to bed.

THE END

Feb. 8, 1919   Became engaged to Althea this evening. Sure am a happy man.

March 3, 1919   Started in work at the Richardson Paper Co. in the Sales dept. at present but expect to go into the mill soon maybe.

May 20, 1919   BOUGHT Althea engagement ring today, stone 1.07 carat mounted tiffany — $479.00.

Notes

INTRODUCTION

[1] Maurer Maurer, *The U.S. Air Service in World War I* (4 vols., Washington, D.C., 1975), I, 17. When the United States entered the war, the Aviation Section of the United States Army Signal Corps was directing air operations of the army. In June of 1917, the Air Service replaced the Aviation Section, taking over all aviation activities from the Signal Corps. Maurer, *Air Service*, I, 52. For various aspects of training and equipment, see Maurer, *Air Service, passim.*

[2] The biographical details on the Richardson family come from several sources: Stephen F. Stieritz, "Air Force Logistics Command Oral History, Interview #11 of Roland W. Richardson," August 1 and August 28, 1978; Ritchie Thomas and Carl Becker, "Interview of Elizabeth Kurlin," September 28, 1990; Elizabeth Kurlin to Carl Becker, February 7, 1991; Carl Becker, "Interview of Elizabeth Kurlin," February 28, 1991.

[3] Becker, "Interview of Elizabeth Kurlin."

[4] Roland Richardson, "Standard Daily Reminder, 1913" (hereinafter abbreviated as "SDR"), in possession of Elizabeth Kurlin.

[5] "SDR," January 8, 1913; July 11, 1913.

[6] "SDR," April 7, 1913; September 7, 1913.

[7] Stieritz, "Interview of Roland Richardson," 1.

[8] "SDR," May 16, 1913.

[9] "SDR," July 26, 1913.

[10] Unfortunately, neither Roland Richardson nor other members of the family know exactly where Annis Richardson intended to go in Germany; and no family records deal in any way with the subject.

[11] James J. Hudson, *Hostile Skies: A Combat History of the American Air Service in World War I (Syracuse, New York, 1968)*, 4-5.

[12] Stieritz, "Interview of Roland Richardson," 3.

[13] Maurer, *Air Service*, I, 97. See also H. A. Toulmin, Jr., *Air Service: American Expeditionary Force, 1918* (New York, 1927), 294.

[14] Stieritz, "Interview of Roland Richardson," 5; Kelly Wills, Jr., "Richardson's Remembrances," *Cross and Cockade*, No. 2, 6 (Summer, 1965), 103-120; Gene Gurney, *Flying Aces of World War I* (New York, 1965), 154. Though noting his trips to Issoudun in his autobiography, Rickenbacker made no reference to Richardson. Edward W. Rickenbacker, *Rickenbacker* (Englewood Cliffs, New Jersey, 1967), 88-89.

[15] Wills, "Richardson's Remembrances." In a memorial biography using some of Quentin Roosevelt's letters, Kermit Roosevelt described Quentin Roosevelt's relationship with the Normants at Romarantin. Neither Roosevelt mentioned Richardson. Perhaps

referring to Richardson, Quentin Roosevelt, who also scoured the countryside for building materials, complained that only he and one other officer at Issoudun could speak French. Kermit Roosevelt, *Quentin Roosevelt: A Sketch with Letters* (New York, 1921), 112, 51-52.

[16] Maurer, *Air Service*, I, 94.

[17] Stieritz, "Interview of Roland Richardson," 6.

[18] For a description of the functions of the Air Service, see Toulmin, *Air Service*, 1ff.

[19] See this view in Maurer, *Air Service*, I, 105.

[20] One may read of the Penguin in James Norman Hall, *High Adventure: A Narrative of Air Fighting in France* (Cambridge, Massachusetts, 1918), 25ff; Thomas R. Funderburk, *The Early Birds of War* (New York, 1968), 18, 60; and Frederic Oughton, *The Aces* (New York, 1960), 234.

[21] Warren J. Brown, *Child Yank: Over the Rainbow Division* (Largo, Florida, 1977), 214. Bert Hall, who served for a while in the Lafayette Escadrille, wrote that "Issoudun must be a bastard of a place." According to Hall, students became so inured to deaths in accidents that at every report of such a death they sang the irreverent "Worm Song." Bert Hall and John J. Niles, *One Man's War: The Story of the Lafayette Escadrille* (New York, 1920), 287, 342. Probably the muddy runways at Issoudun caused accidents. As an airplane took off, its wheels threw mud and stones into the propeller; nicked, the propeller might later disintegrate in the air causing the airplane to crash. Quentin Reynolds, *They Fought for the Sky* (New York, 1957), 268.

[22] Maurer, *Air Service*, I, 110. For a brief statistical analysis of deaths in training, see David K. Vaughan, ed., *An American Pilot in the Skies of France* (Dayton, 1992), 9-10.

[23] Stieritz, "Interview of Roland Richardson," 9.

[24] Wills, "Richardson's Remembrances."

[25] Earlier in the war, the Czar had sent two brigades of Russian soldiers to France in exchange for guns and ammunition. Even before French troops mutinied in 1918, the Russian soldiers, fired by revolutionary rhetoric of the Communists, were creating a baneful effect on the French poilus. The French, seeing that influence heighten during the mutiny, isolated the brigades in rear areas, among them Cazaux. S. L. A. Marshall, *World War I* (New York, 1971), 285. One may find an account of the Russians and the mutiny in "Les mutins du soviet de La Courtine," *Le Monde*, August 30, 1987.

[26] Stieritz, "Interview of Roland Richardson," 12.

[27] Ibid., 15.

[28] Toulmin, *Air Service*, 168.

[29] The 213th was on the *Tuscania* when a German submarine sank it off the Irish coast in February of 1918. At least five men of the squadron died. For a brief history of the 213th, see Kelly Wills, Jr., "History of the 213th," *Cross and Cockade*, No. 2, 6 (Summer, 1965), 121-134.

[30] The Third Pursuit Group was a unit within the First Pursuit Wing. Composing the Group were the Twenty-Eighth, the Ninety-Third, the 103rd, and the 213th squadrons. The Wing was a part of the First Army Air Service, the first "concentration of American air forces under its own commander." Maurer, *Air Service*, I, 301-302.

[31] American pilots often voiced the complaint, probably with some cause, that the French gave them the "leftovers" from their stock of Spads. See, for example, Rickenbacker's comments. Edward V. Rickenbacker, *Fighting the Flying Circus* (New York, 1918), 148.

[32] We derived these figures from a review of Richardson's diary for the period.

[33] Richardson to Annis Richardson, September 12, 1918. One may read the orders to the 213th during the offensive in Maurer, *Air Service*, III, 157-158, 278-279, 289, 379. See also Toulmin, *Air Service*, 360.

[34] Stieritz, "Interview of Roland Richardson," 39.

[35] Richardson to Annis Richardson, November 11, 1918.

[36] See James R. McConnell, *Flying for France: With the American Escadrille at Verdun* (New York, 1917), 96-97. In less elegant language, McConnell also declared his commitment to a cause in a letter to other pilots opened after his death: "God damn Germany and *vive la France.*" Paul A. Rockwell, *American Fighters in the Foreign Legion* (Boston, 1930), 253.

CHAPTER ONE

[1] Probably Richardson used "U.S.M.S." to refer to United States Merchant Ship. The *St. Paul* was a merchant ship taken by the United States government for wartime service on October 27, 1917.

[2] Though submarines were a menace to shipping, Richardson may have magnified their threat. At least at the time that he was writing, they were exacting a declining toll of British merchant ships. For the week ending April 22, 1917, they sank fifty-five British ships. The weeks thereafter saw the number declining until by the week ending July 15, submarines sank but eighteen ships. New York *Times*, July 12, 1917; July 19, 1917.

[3] Clearly Richardson was describing a Sam Browne belt. Once worn by officers of the United States Army, it was a sword belt with a supporting strap over the right shoulder. Policemen, guards, and army officers in other nations sometimes wear it. The name comes from its creator, General Sir Samuel Browne (1824-1901).

[4] Charlie Chaplin was a comedic genius of the budding film industry. Richardson could have seen him in any one of three movies released in the first half of 1917: *Easy Street, The Cure,* and *The Immigrant.* David Robinson, *Chaplin: His Life and Art* (New York, 1985), 718-719.

[5] A comfort bag or kit usually contained pencils, writing paper, a mirror, a comb, socks, and so on.

[6] A snipe is a long-billed game bird, the centerpiece of a practical joke long known to American hunters. The victim of the joke held a bag into which hunters supposedly would chase the bird. After a sufficient commotion, they would abandon the bag-holder, usually in a dark or unpleasant place.

[7] A "perchman" apparently operated a vehicle of some sort used in a railroad yard. The Marmon was an automobile manufactured in the United States.

[8] "Poor Butterfly" was a song from the musical *The Big Show*, which opened on Broadway on August 31, 1916. It was one of the hit songs of the period.

[9] P. A. probably stands for Prince Albert smoking tobacco, a popular brand of the period.

[10] M.R.C. stands for Medical Reserve Corps, Q.M.C. for Quartermaster Corps.

[11] Apparently Richardson had in mind the Medical Corps in using the initials M.C.

[12] Althea intended to attend a "girls' school" in Cincinnati run by Helen F. Kendrick.

[13] Bobby was entering the University of Cincinnati and hoped to join Tri Delta, a chapter of Delta Delta Delta, a social sorority.

[14] Richardson was alluding to a subject or parodying an expression that might offend his mother.

[15] The mileage cited by Richardson and his later reference to Orleans suggest that he was going to Orleans and a nearby community.

[16] Joan of Arc was, of course, the "Maid of Orleans."

CHAPTER TWO

[1] In his book, *Flying For France*, McConnell, a member of the Lafayette Escadrille, vividly described the training and flying of his squadron. He was killed in March of 1917 in an engagement with German pilots. For a brief description of his service, see Philip M. Flammer, *The Vivid Air: The Lafayette Escadrille* (Athens, Georgia, 1981), *passim*.

[2] The Cincinnati B.H.U. was the Cincinnati Base Hospital Unit No. 25. Organized in Cincinnati in 1916, it numbered nearly three hundred people, many of them medical specialists. All were members of the Medical Reserve Corps. The unit went to France in July of 1918. Cincinnati newspapers often ran articles on its activities. See, for example, the Cincinnati *Enquirer*, February 25, 1918; March 1, 1918. See also Joseph H. Ford, *The Medical Department of the United States Army in the World War* (Washington, D.C., 1923), 651.

[3] Probably Richardson was using a pre-arranged code, V A C K, as he did on other occasions, to refer to what was happening to him, in this case his transfer to the training program.

[4] Ironically, the son may have encouraged his mother to consider coming to France when in a letter of October 6, 1917, he facetiously wrote that "if you could only come over tomorrow, we would have a blow out and I'd treat you to a good feed."

[5] S.E.P. was, of course, the *Saturday Evening Post*, the popular American weekly magazine.

[6] The historian of the American Red Cross alludes to soldiers' criticism of the Red Cross but does not comment on its relationship with the Young Men's Christian Association. Foster Rhea Dulles, *The American Red Cross: A History* (New York, 1950), 194.

[7] One of the most common of all American acronyms employing an Anglo-Saxon four-letter word, S.O.L. means "shit-out-of-luck."

[8] Richardson was making arrangements to support a French orphan, one Andre Le Gal, probably under the auspices of the American Society for the Relief of French War Orphans, which began its program in 1916. New York *Times*, October 14, 1916; *The Outlook*, October 25, 1916, 402. In 1917 the society merged with The Fatherless Children of France Fund, the resultant organization becoming The Fatherless Children of France Branch of the American Society for the Relief of French War Orphans. New York *Times*, January 14, 1917.

[9] Like the Harley Davidson, the Indian was an American motorcycle.

[10] At completion of their flight training, students received a brevet certificate. R.M. meant Reserve Military Aviator.

CHAPTER THREE

[1] The clipping on quail hunting, appearing in the Cincinnati *Times-Star* on January 3, 1918, quoted Richardson at length on the subject. His mother had made his letter of November 23, 1918 describing such hunting available to the newspaper. Later, in a letter of March 18, 1917, the son admonished his mother not to send his letters to any newspaper.

[2] Richardson was the recipient of a share of stock in Procter and Gamble, the large soap company in Cincinnati.

[3] Richardson was about to fly a Nieuport 24 bis, which was equipped with a 120 horsepower motor.

[4] Lee, of the British Royal Flying Corps, led a British aviation mission to the United States during the war. He told Americans that elimination of stunt flying in training would save a few lives but cost hundreds in combat. He performed stunts over the Capitol, the Immelman turn, for example, and took Congressmen on flights over Washington, D.C., New York *Times*, February 17, 1918; February 24, 1918.

[5] One may clean and preserve saddles and other leather articles with soap, which consists largely of Castile.

[6] Richardson had in mind a German offensive code-named "Georgette"; it began on April 4 on a twelve-mile front between La Bassee and Armentières. Marshall, *World War I*, 358.

[7] We have been unable to locate "Ho to be a Soldier" to determine what kind of "literature" it was.

[8] Apparently the French, who controlled the gunnery school, preempted the use of stands for the viewing of some sort of demonstration or lesson in gunnery.

[9] Obviously Richardson and his friends had been using a poison known as "Rough on Rats" to exterminate rats around the barracks. See Eric Partridge, *A Dictionary of Slang and Unconventional English* (New York, 1984), 990.

[10] *Survey* was a monthly magazine founded in the 1890s titled as *Charities*. Originally publishing articles on charitable activities, later it published articles on a wide variety of social and political subjects, especially on industrial reform, strikes, and child welfare. Such topics evidently did not appeal to Richardson; just after noting that he had received a package of *Surveys*, he requested his mother not to send him any more. Frank Luther Mott, *A History of American Magazines*, 1741-1930 (5 vols., Cambridge, Massachusetts, 1957), IV, 741-756.

[11] Evidently Richardson was writing about "Georgette," the German offensive that had ended late in April. Between then and the date of the letter, neither the Allies nor the Germans had mounted a new drive. Marshall, *World War I*, 362ff.

CHAPTER FOUR

[1] Richardson was putting a dubious foot forward when he declared that "we have the advantage of better pilots." Though writing about the First Pursuit Group, a student who has assessed the quality of German pilots fighting in the summer of 1918 has seen it otherwise. The German aviators, he argues, were skillful; and indeed many had been aces since 1916. They were flying an excellent airplane, the Fokker D VIIS, and had control of the air on their side of the lines. They gave the First a real drubbing in the Château-Thierry sector; through six weeks the Group lost thirty-six pilots. "The Germans," says Thomas Miller, "simply were better pursuit pilots at this stage of the war than the spirited, but unskilled Americans." Thomas G. Miller, Jr. "The Last Knighthood," *Cross and Cockade*, No. 2, 3 (Spring, 1962), 24-33.

[2] Richardson and the "fellows" could have been reading a number of air service journals. Published in the United States, among others, were the *Air Service Journal*, *Aeronautical Engineer*, and *Aerial Age Weekly*. *L'Aerophile* was the official publication of the Aero Club de France, and *Flight* was the journal of the Royal Aero Club of the United Kingdom.

[3] The son was informing his mother that he would use the word "Service" to indicate that he was going to the front. In a letter of August 11, 1918 to her, he said that he would use "SERVICE" in a telegram. He did so in a telegram of August 17, 1918.

[4] Certain magazines included chewing gum in their mailing. Richardson liked gum and may have used the spittle from it for working on his airplanes.

[5] Richardson had witnessed the celebratory commemoration of Bastille Day.

[6] Fearing the consequences of the German offensive early in 1918, Herbert Hoover, head of the Food Administration Board had exercised greater control over the conservation of food in the United States. As it turned out, crops were substantial in the summer of 1918; the problem was finding sufficient shipping for foodstuffs. Herbert Hoover, *The Memoirs of Herbert Hoover: Years of Adventure* (New York, 1952), 256.

[7] Wright was writing a series of articles, "Aces High," for the *Saturday Evening Post*. The first appeared on June 15, 1918.

[8] Richardson referred to an Allied counter-offensive begun on July 18, 1918 at Château-Thierry, which pushed German forces back from the Marne to the Aisne river before concluding early in August. Marshall, *World War I*, 396ff.

CHAPTER FIVE

[1] ". . . one of our group" was Lieutenant Christopher W. Ford. On August 21, he attacked an enemy biplane near Beaumont, scoring a "probable" victory when he fired three hundred rounds into it and saw it descend in a steep side-slip. Ford did not receive confirmation of its destruction because no ground troops witnessed the engagement. Wills, "History of the 213th"; Hudson, *Hostile Skies*, 124.

[2] Evidently Wright exaggerated his exploits. In their account of the Escadrille, James N. Hall and Charles B. Nordhoff subjected him to a satirical attack: "Harold E. Wright's chief claim to distinction as an airman is due to the series of remarkable flights which he made during the summer of 1918, in the *Saturday Evening Post* sector. Flying the *avion* 'Remington Typewriter' he had a long and bitter combat with Baron Richthofen, the greatest of German 'aces.' Richthofen escaped, but Baron Munchausen, the legendary king of ground-flyers, who was hovering at an immense height above the scene of battle, received a mortal *coup* from the Wilson machine gun, and fell upward into the blue serene, host by his own petard, of which ammunition *Sergent Pilote* Wright had a plentiful supply. So far as is known this is Wright's only official victory." James Norman Hall and Charles B. Nordhoff, *The Lafayette Flying Corps* 2 vols., Boston, 1920), I, 509. Nothing in the French record on Wright in the *Bureau de Recrutment D'Seine Bureau Central* bears on the question of his veracity. He was discharged ("resilie") from service with the French on January 21, 1918. Photocopy in editors' possession.

[3] On September 12, 1918, the United States First Army, under Pershing's personal command, launched the first all American offensive of the war, with the intent of lopping off the St. Mihiel salient east of Verdun. The Americans effected the mission in about two days, taking 15,000 prisoners, 257 guns, and two hundred square miles of French territory. American casualties. Corelli Barnett, *The Great War* (New York, 1979), 177; Marshall, *World War I*, 424-425.

[4] Richardson's flight was among the pursuit aircraft attacking retreating Germans on the Vigneulles-St. Benoit Road. According to the report of Major General Mason Patrick, Chief of the Air Service and one of the architects of air strategy for the offensive, the Third Pursuit Group, which was "equipped to carry small bombs, did particularly effective work in destroying a number of motor trucks on this important road." The Group "effectively continued" ground strafing on September 13 and 14 "when good targets presented themselves on the St. Benoit-Chambley and Chambley-Mars-La-Tour Roads." Quoted in Toulmin, *Air Service*, 368. Pursuit groups engaged in two distinctive kinds of missions: protective and offensive. For a detailed definition of such missions, see Maurer, *Air Service*, I, 302. Clearly the Third Pursuit Group was on the offensive.

[5] See above, xxii.

[6] Among Woodrow Wilson's Fourteen Points for ending the war was one calling on Germany to evacuate French territory. At the time Wilson and Prince Maximilian, newly appointed Chancellor of Germany, were exchanging cablegrams discussing terms for an armistice. Marshall, *World War I*, 433-435.

[7] In September of 1918, influenza, apparently brought from Europe, struck the Atlantic coast of North America. Rumor had it that Germans had deliberately spread the germ. Nearly a quarter of the population of the United States contracted the disease, with nearly 500,000 dying. The "flu" struck army camps, killing half as many American soldiers as died in Europe. Mark Sullivan, *Our Times: The United States, 1900-1925* (6 vols., New York, 1935), V, 652-654.

[8] Apparently Richardson referred to communications between Wilson and Maximilian. On October 5, Maximilian had sent a cable to Wilson asking for an armistice. Without discussing the request with the Allies, on October 8 Wilson called on Maximilian to clarify his proposal. Specifically, did he agree to all of Wilson's Fourteen Points and did he speak for the "constituted authorities of Europe"? Wilson then awaited a reply. Marshall, *World War I*, 434.

[9] On October 12, Prince Maximilian replied that Germany accepted the Fourteen Points. But negotiations broke down, in part because of what seemed a dastardly act by German soldiers in the Argonne and the sinking of the British mail boat *Leinster* by a U-boat and in part because German General Erich Ludendorff of the High Command was determined to scuttle the Fourteen Points. Marshall, *World War I*, 435-436.

[10] Richardson attributed cancellation of a contract for production of Spads to American officials' misplaced faith in the D.H.4. It was hardly that simple. In the summer of 1917, the United States had placed an order for three thousand Spads with the Curtiss Aeroplane Company. The French had promised an American mission headed by Colonel Reynal Bolling to send certain parts early in July but did not do so until late in August and did not ship a sample Spad until then. Concerned about "the uncertainty of possible deliveries, the Aircraft Production Board cancelled the order. *History of the Bureau of Aircraft Production*, VI, Historical Office, Air Material Command, 1019-1022; Edgar S. Gorrell, "The Measure of America's World War Aeronautical Effort," A Lecture Delivered by Colonel Edgar S. Gorrell under the James Jackson Cabot Professorship of Air Traffic Regulation and Air Transportation at Norwich University, Publication N. 6, November 26, 1940, 4.

[11] Manfred von Richthofen, the leading ace of the war, shot down eighty Allied aircraft. He was the squadron leader of a combat group known as "Richthofen's Flying Circus." At the time that Richardson referred to the circus, Richthofen had been dead about six months, having been shot down on April 21, 1918, probably by Roy Brown, a Canadian aviator. For an American's perspective of the Flying Circus, see Rickenbacker, *Fighting the Flying Circus*.

[12] Organized by the Committee on Public Information, which received assistance from the Division of Military Aeronautics and the British Air Museum, the tour of the "Wild Cats" was a cross-country flight intended to demonstrate to the Middle West of the United States the progress of American military aviation — to give "towns, villages and hamlets en route a close up view of the modern flying planes." It would also prepare pilots for crossing the Atlantic. Three British pilots joined ten Americans — later the number rose to at least twenty-two — for a trip of three thousand miles beginning in Cincinnati and stopping in fourteen cities — from Ohio on west and north. Earl Carroll, "3000 Miles through the Air," *Flying*, (September, 1918), 718-719. As chronicled by the New York *Times*, the tour was expected to be a triumph of technology in the air. A squadron of twenty-two American and British airplanes was scheduled to depart from Cincinnati on August 14. Americans flying H Curtiss airplanes and the British flying Avros would perform various stunts and maneuvers. It was "expected that the program" would be "carried out without a hitch." New York *Times*, August 8, 1918. But at Cincinnati Captain James Fitzmorris of the British Royal Flying Corps was killed instantly when his engine stalled and his airplane plunged to the ground. New York *Times*, August 15, 1918. Then on August 24, at Effingham, Illinois, Major William Ream, the flight surgeon, was killed when an airplane piloted by Lieutenant Wesley Brenner fell 150 feet. New York *Times*, August 25, 1918.

CHAPTER SIX

[1] Richardson saw *Monna Vanna*. The composer was Henry Fevrier; Maurice Marterlinck wrote the lyrics. *Program*, Opera de Paris, November 26, 1918.

[2] Evidently the mother proposed an unusual plan for circumventing censorship.

[3] Richardson attended a presentation of *General Post*, a comedy by J. E. H. Terry. First performed in 1917, it portrayed social change brought about by the war in Europe. A provincial tailor became a major general, then saw his social status change dramatically. New York *Times*, January 8, 1918; *Cumulative Dramatic Index*, I (Boston, 1965), 529.

[4] Pilots used "Kewie" as a term of derision for officers in the Air Service who did not fly. The word derived from "kiwi," a flightless bird of New Zealand.

[5] Richardson was about to sew on an overseas chevron, a small chevron worn on the sleeve for each full six months of overseas duty in a theater of operations. John Quick, *Dictionary of Weapons and Military Terms* (New York, 1973), 337.

[6] Arriving in Hoboken, Richardson went on to the Air Service Depot at Garden City on Long Island for his discharge.

[7] Written by Anthony Kelly and playing at the Cohan & Harris theater, *Three Faces East* began its run in New York in August of 1918. The title came from the password used by a gang of German spies in England. According to the reviewer for the New York *Times*, it was "void of any really dramatic interest." New York *Times*, August 14, 1918.

APPENDICES

Appendix A

Soldiers and Civilians: A Glossary

Throughout his letters and diaries, Roland Richardson took note of many persons — of relatives and friends in and around Glendale, of hometown friends who came to France as soldiers and civilians, of Air Service men whom he knew well or met in passing, and of a few Europeans. We have attempted in this glossary to identify by full name and other details those whom he mentioned more than once or twice, especially when he did so in more than a casual way.

We have used several sources for construction of our biographical entries. Richardson's letters and oral history provided identifying information on a few persons; and the Richardson family, including Roland Richardson, drew on their memory to recall men and women appearing in the letters. We made some use of directories of Cincinnati, which, however, only occasionally included residents of Glendale. In the original census returns of 1910, we found the complete names and occupations of about ten individuals. The University of Cincinnati *Record* supplied us with useful information on students whom Richardson had met at the university.

No single source was particularly important for identifying Richardson's friends and acquaintances in the Air Service. Richardson, of course, compiled a brief record of the pilots of the 213th, noting whether they had shot down any enemy airplanes, had been wounded or killed, had been taken prisoner, or had come "thru" the war. We examined histories of the Air Service, notably Maurer Maurer's *The U.S. Air Service in World War I*, finding in them some bits and pieces. Also yielding fragmentary details were a few contemporary accounts of American aviators in France. Air Service records did not prove very useful. We have supplied full names wherever possible.

*   *   *

Aiken, John.   Lieutenant John Aiken was a pilot in the Third Flight of the 213th. As Richardson put it, he "came thru" the war.

The Allens.   The Allens were William and Virginia Allen. They lived on Ivy Avenue in Glendale near the Richardsons. William was the president of the Title Guarantee Company.

Althea (see *The Fords*).

Baker Newton.   The Secretary of War, Baker visited Issoudun in March of 1918.

Barnes, Jerry (Gerry).   Formerly a physical education instructor at the University of Cincinnati, Barnes came to France with the American Ambulance Service. Richardson had known him at the university and saw him in France.

Bellows, Clarence M.   Lieutenant Bellows, a pilot with Richardson in the Third Flight of the 213th, was killed in combat on September 30, 1918.

The Benedicts.   Residing near the Richardsons were Charles and Ella Benedict. Charles was an attorney.

Brent, Charles Henry.   Brent, a bishop in the Protestant Episcopal Church, was the Chief Chaplain of the American Expeditionary Force. At the turn of the century, he had become the first bishop of the Episcopal Church in the Philippines.

Bobby   (see *Richardson, Adelaide*).

Brown, Elizabeth.   A friend of the Richardsons, Elizabeth Brown lived on Albion near Ivy. Probably she was a sister of Harry Brown.

Brown, Harry.   Brown was a neighbor of the Richardsons. He served in the infantry and returned to the United States on the *Adriatic* with Richardson.

Brownell, E. Garnsey.   Brownell was a surgeon in the First Reserve Squadron, the first and only reserve squadron to go overseas. He became a Senior Medical Officer in the Air Service. Richardson met him at Issoudun.

Campbell, Douglas.   Campbell became the first American "ace." He shot down six "Boche" planes.

The Carruthers.   The Carruthers, Thomas and Reba, and their son, James, lived near the Richardsons. Reba died during the war in her early forties.

Cauffman, L. E.   On his way home, Richardson met Lt. Cauffman of the Ninety Third Squadron at Angers. Though he did not know him well, Richardson kept in touch with him after the war.

Coombsie (see *Richardson, Annis*).

Christie, A. R.   Major Christie was at Tours when Richardson was in training there. Later he served with the Fifth Observation Group. Richardson told him of his wish to "get up on the line as soon as possible."

Churchill, Lawrence.   Commanding the Twenty-Ninth Provisional Squad, Major Churchill led the first contingent of enlisted men, about two hundred, to Issoudun for construction of the training center.

The Dansons.   Edward and Ann Danson lived in the Richardsons' neighborhood. Edward was the president of an advertising firm.

Dubied, Maurice.   Richardson had met Maurice Dubied in the Swiss school at Neuchâtel before the war. Apparently Richardson spent more time with Dubied's sisters, Margaret and Nellie, than he did with their brother.

Eaton, Warren.   Eaton, who became a member of the Ninety-Third Squadron, engaged Richardson in mock combat at Orly.

Este, Richard.   Richardson became acquainted with Lieutenant Este at Orly. Este nosed a DH-4 into the ground there.

Eustis, Allen [?].   Captain Eustis commanded Richardson's training unit at Issoudun; Richardson, believing that he was arbitrary, disliked him.

Faran, Angeline.   A sister of James Richardson, the father of Roland, "Angeline" was Roland's aunt.

Favier, Maurice.   Favier was a student at Richardson's school in Switzerland; they became friends there. During the war he served with a French antiaircraft artillery battery, the 283rd.

Foch, Ferdinand.   The French general held various commands in the French army before 1918 and became commander-in-chief of all Allied armies in April of 1918.

Ford, Christopher.   Commander of the First Flight of the 213th, Lieutenant Ford received unofficial credit as the first member of the squadron to shoot down a Boche.

The Fords.   The Fords, who lived on Ivy near the Richardsons, were Lewis and Elizabeth Ford. Their daughter was Althea, with whom Richardson corresponded during the war. She was about eighteen years old in 1918. They were married soon after his return to Glendale.

Frank, G. S.   Lieutenant Frank was one of Richardson's fellow officers in the Twenty-Ninth Squadron.

Freeman, "Buck."   Richardson knew Lieutenant Freeman during their training at Issoudun. Freeman went on to the Thirteenth Squadron. He was shot down during the St. Mihiel offensive and taken prisoner.

Gaillard, S. P. (Gilly).   A pilot in Richardson's Third Flight, Lieutenant Gaillard bagged one Boche and "came thru" the war.

Garvin, Hugh.   Garvin, who was from Santiago, Chile, was a student in mechanical engineering at the University of Cincinnati when Richardson was there. When he became engaged to Bobby, Richardson feared that they would marry while Garvin was in war-time military service.

Geohegan Edmund. Richardson met Geohegan at the University of Cincinnati, probably in 1915, when Geohegan was a third year student in chemical engineering. Richardson saw him two or three times in France, where he served in an artillery unit.

Goldthwaite, George. Goldthwaite (Richardson spelled his name as Goldtwaite) was an officer in the Twenty-Ninth. Soon after he arrived in France, he served on a special board that recommended the kind of service and rank Americans in the Lafayette Escadrille should have on entering the Air Service.

Grace. Evidently Grace was a domestic in the Richardson household; probably she was a Black.

Gramps (see *Withenbury, Russell Sr.*)

Grey, Charles. Captain "Charley" Grey was commander of the Third Flight of the 213th. He shot down four Boche.

Hambleton, John A. Commanding the 213th, Captain Hambleton shot down two enemy airplanes.

Hark, "Joe." Hark was a boyhood friend of Richardson in Glendale.

Honneur, "Mr." Honneur was a French photographer who accompanied Richardson on several flights from Orly around Paris.

Huntington, F. Daniel. A member of the Twenty-Ninth, Captain Huntington was one of the officers directing construction at Issoudun.

Innis, Wallace. An acquaintance of Richardson, Innis was a civil engineer from Cincinnati whom he saw in France.

Johnston, Margaret (Mardie or Marty). A sister of Mary Johnston, Margaret Johnston became engaged to Charles Sawyer, later Secretary of Commerce under President Harry Truman, during period when Richardson was escorting Mary around Paris.

Johnston, Mary. Johnston, who had resided near the Richardsons, served as a nurse in a French hospital. Richardson escorted her around Paris while he was at Orly. Probably she was six or seven years older than he. They remained friends after the war.

Kale, May. A nurse and friend of Mary Johnston, she accompanied Mary on a visit to Richardson at Orly.

Kent, Margaret. Margaret Kent was one of the Kents, a family that Richardson met while in Switzerland.

Lamb, L. Lieutenant Lamb was a member of the First Flight of the 213th; he bunked with Richardson one night at Châlons.

Leach (Leech), "Mal." Before becoming a member of the Twentieth Air Squadron, Lieutenant Leach "combatted" with Richardson at Issoudun.

Lee, Charles E. Lieutenant Colonel Lee, heading up a British aviation mission in the United States for the Royal Flying Corps, was a vigorous advocate of stunt flying in training, arguing that it effectively prepared pilots for combat.

Lee, J. C. Lieutenant Jack Lee flew in the First Flight of the 213th.

Le Gal, Andre. Le Gal was a French boy, perhaps an orphan, supported by Richardson under the auspices of the American Society for the Relief of French War Orphans.

Loomis, Henry S. Not to be confused with Lieutenant W. F. Loomis, also of the 213th, Lieutenant Henry "Dick" Loomis commanded the First Flight of the squadron. After leaving the 213th, Richardson spent much of his free time with Loomis.

Lyster, Lua ("Tanta"). The wife of Theodore Lyster, Lua Lyster was a sister of Annis Richardson and an aunt of Roland.

Lyster, Theodore. The husband of Lua and an uncle of Roland Richardson, Brigadier General Lyster was a leading medical officer of the Air Service. He has been called the "original" medical officer of the Air Force. The Lyster Army Hospital at Fort Rucker in Alabama is named for him. Richardson often looked to him for advice on his career in the Air Service.

Lyster, Thomas L. B. A cousin of Theodore Lyster, Captain Thomas Lyster, formerly a contractor, was in charge of construction at Issoudun. Later he directed the Air Service Projects and Designs Committee.

McClure, David. Lieutenant McClure served in the Second Flight of the 213th; the Germans captured him following the crash of Spad in September of 1918.

Mell, P. H. Lieutenant Mell commanded the Second Flight of the 213th.

Meyers, Alonzo. A member of the Medical Reserve Corps, Lieutenant Meyers was one of Richardson's friends at Issoudun during the building of the training fields there.

Mitchell, William ("Billy"). General Mitchell was chief of the Air Service in France. He inspected the 213th at Lisle-en-Barrois.

Morse, Wellslake D. Morse was one of Richardson's classmates in the College of Engineering at the University of Cincinnati. He and another one of Richardson's friends in the college, Ben Schneider, were roommates.

Moss, James ("Jim"). James Moss was a seventeen year old boy whom Richardson knew in Glendale.

Munn, W. A. Lieutenant Munn was a member of the Second Flight of the 213th.

Nash, *"Chick."*   Richardson met Lieutenant Nash at Orly. Nash, along with Eaton, became a member of the Ninety-Third Squadron. He was shot down during the St. Mihiel drive.

Ogden, Jack.   A fellow pilot of Richardson in the Third Flight, Lieutenant Ogden was captured by the Germans in a bizarre incident in September of 1918. He was instrumental in getting Richardson assigned to the 213th.

Osgood, James.   Osgood was a legendary instructor at Issoudun.

Outcalt, Dudley M. (*"Red"*).   Richardson met Outcalt, whom he had known at the University of Cincinnati, at Field 8 at Issoudun.

Patton, I. W.   An officer in the medical service, Patton examined Richardson at his enlistment in Washington, D.C. and at his discharge in New York.

Perrault, Arthur.   One of Richardson's friends, Lieutenant Perrault (Richardson spelled his name "Perronet" years later in an interview published in *Cross and Cockade*) was killed in a training accident at Issoudun in March of 1918.

Pershing, John J.   General John "Black Jack" Pershing was commander of American forces in France. Richardson flew in a review for him at Orly.

Phelan, Richard.   A good friend of Richardson and a pilot in the Third Flight, Lieutenant Phelan was killed in combat on October 31, 1918. His death and A. H. Treadwell's death a few days later considerably dampened Richardson's thirst for combat.

Powers, Walter.   Powers, a civilian, was a friend of Captain Thomas Lyster and came with him to France for construction of the training center at Issoudun.

The Procters.   William and Jean Procter were neighbors and friends of the Richardsons. According to the census of 1910, William Procter was the president of a "soap company." It was Procter and Gamble!

The Resors.   Richardson noted in a letter that "the Resors" had spent a winter near Tours. They could have been one of two families. Charles and Jean Resor of Cincinnati knew the Richardsons. Charles was the president of a manufacturing company. At Neuchâtel Richardson was a friend of a Mr. Resor, a teacher at the school, and his family.

Richardson, Adelaide.   Known as "Bobby," Adelaide was Richardson's oldest sister. She entered the College of Liberal Arts at the University of Cincinnati in 1917. She married Hugh Garvin.

Richardson, Angie.   Another sister of James Richardson, Angie Richardson was one of Roland's aunts.

Richardson, Annis. "Coombsie," as she was called, was the second daughter in the Richardson family.

Richardson, Annis W. Annis Richardson was Roland's mother.

Richardson, Emily. Emily was the third and youngest daughter in the Richardson family. Evidently she had no nickname.

Richardson, Francis. The daughter of Howard and Mabel Richardson, an uncle and an aunt of Roland, Francis was Roland's first cousin.

Richardson, Gertrude. An aunt of Roland, Gertrude was the wife of Charles Richardson.

Richardson, James. The son of Howard and Mabel Richardson, James Richardson was one of Roland Richardson's first cousins.

Richardson, Mabel. Mabel Richardson, the wife of Howard Richardson, a brother of James Richardson, was one of Roland's aunts.

Richardson, Robert. One of Roland's first cousins, Robert was the son of Charles and Gertrude Richardson.

Richthofen, Manfred von. The squadron leader of a German combat group known as the "Richthofen Flying Circus," Richthofen, the leading "ace" of the war, shot down eighty Allied aircraft. He was shot down by Roy Brown, a Canadian, on April 21, 1918, near Amiens.

Roosevelt, Quentin. Richardson met Roosevelt, a son of Theodore Roosevelt, when he first went to Issoudun. Like Richardson, Roosevelt was responsible for procuring building materials. Setting an example for Richardson, he transferred to flight training in the Air Service. Unfortunately, he lost his life in combat at the Château-Thierry sector on July 14, 1918; probably Sergeant Thom of the Richthofen Flying Circus shot him down.

Ruetter, Jean Louis. Richardson and Ruetter, a Swiss boy, were close friends in the school at Neuchâtel; Richardson punctuated his diary of 1913 with references to Ruetter.

Schneider, Ben. Ben Schneider was another one of Richardson's friends at the College of Engineering at the University of Cincinnati. Evidently he became engaged to one "Jean," whom Richardson knew.

The Selsers. The J. M. Selser family were friends of the Fords.

Sutherland, Paul ("Bud"). Richardson had known Sutherland in Glendale and met him while training at Issoudun. Lieutenant Sutherland served in both the 331st Infantry and the 140th Aero Squadron. He was seriously wounded in August of 1918.

Swallom, George. Richardson knew Swallom at Neuchâtel and visited him at his home there.

Symons, Gilbert P.   Symons was the pastor of the Protestant Episcopal Church in Glendale.

Thompson, George.   Thompson, a clerk in Glendale, was a friend of the Richardsons.

Thurlow, "Ish."   Lieutenant Thurlow was Richardson's immediate superior at Orly.

The Titus Family.   Thomas and Margaret Titus were neighborhood friends of the Richardsons. Thomas Titus was a salesman for a coffee firm.

Treadwell, Alvin H.   One of Richardson's best friends and commander of the First Flight of the 213th, Lieutenant Treadwell was killed in action on November 6, 1918, only a few days before the Armistice.

Weirick, Arthur M.   Lieutenant Weirick, a pilot in the First Flight, was wounded and taken prisoner early in October of 1918.

Wilmer, William.   A graduate of the medical school of the University of Virginia, Colonel Wilmer was the commanding officer of the Medical Reserve Board. He was interested in testing pilots returning from active service to ascertain requirements for training of future pilots.

Withenbury, Russell Jr.   "Uncle Russ" Withenbury was a brother of Annis W. Richardson.

Withenbury, Russell Sr.   "Gramps" was Roland's maternal grandfather.

Withenbury, Virginia.   Virginia Withenbury was the wife of Russell Withenbury, Jr.

Wright, Harold.   After leaving the Lafayette Escadrille, evidently under a cloud, Wright greatly magnified his exploits in the air in a series of articles for the *Saturday Evening Post*.

Appendix B

Richardson's Record of Service

Roland Richardson appended to his notebook (see Appendix F) a summary of the types of aircraft that he flew and of the time and, in part, the nature of his service in the air. It appears below.

*   *   *

TYPES OF PLANES FLOWN

1. Caudron-G3 and G4
2. Nieuport-23, 18, 15 Meter
3. Nieuport-Types 17-21-24 bis-27-28
4. Morane-Saulnier Monoplane
5. Sopwith-1A2 and 1B2
6. Avro-D.-K.
7. Spad-180-150-220 H.P.

Total Time in Air — 173.15
Total Time over Lines — 58.50
Total Time at Front — 62.35
No. of Bombs Carried — 28
No. of Bombs Dropped — 12
Maximum Altitude — 5000 m.

Appendix C

Airplanes Flown by Richardson

Roland Richardson flew principally five kinds of airplanes in training, ferrying, and fighting: Caudrons, Nieuports, Sopwiths, Avros, and Spads. Because varying types, evolutionary in nature, comprised a series of each airplane, no one version represented distinctive characteristics common to a series — the structure of wings, for example, could vary considerably. Except for Nieuports, though, Richardson flew only one or two types of airplanes within any one series; and thus they permit at least a loose definition of their peculiar qualities. Readers interested in a single volume detailing characteristics and structure of airplanes of World War I should consult Dale McAdoo, trans., *Color Profiles of World War I Combat Planes* (New York, 1974).

Richardson usually flew a Caudron G-3 in flight training at Tours. Built by Frenchmen Gaston and Rene Caudron, who had been developing a series of Caudrons before the war, the G-3 was a single-engine, two-seater sesquiplane (a wing and a half). Though occasionally used for reconnaissance and light bombing, it was primarily a trainer. Pilots liked its stability and ease of control. Giving it a peculiar dimension was an unusual combination of tail structure and traction propeller. The engines powering it were of the radial type, fixed in the Anzani, rotary in the Le Rhone. At Tours Richardson also flew a Caudron G-4 several times. A twin-engine aircraft, it was capable of an unusual rate of climb and was especially useful in bombing missions in mountainous areas in the Austrian-Italian Alps. It also had occasional use in training; the American Air Service acquired ten in 1918 for that purpose.

At Issoudun, Cazaux, and Orly, Richardson was in the cockpits of various types of Nieuports: the 10, 12, 17, 21, 24, 27, and 28 (often, like other pilots, he identified his airplane by the area of its plane in square meters). Nieuports were manufactured by the Nieuport Company, founded by Edouard de Niéport in 1910. Early on the company earned international repute for its fast monoplanes. In production before the war began, the Nieuport 10 (18 meter) was a two-seat reconnaissance aircraft, its top wing a conventional plane, its bottom wing scarcely more than a support for the "V" interplane struts; this sesquiplane design was used for all the Nieuport series but the Nieuport 28. The Nieuport 12 (23 meter) was nearly identical with the 10 but employed a more powerful engine, a 110 or 130 horsepower Clerget. Combining excellent maneuverability and good speed was the Nieuport 17 (15 meter), a renowned fighter plane. Evolving from it, the Nieuport 21 (15 meter) was a two-seater intended to serve as a training plane. With its rounded fuselage and rounded tailplane, the Nieuport 24 (15 meter) presented a different configuration from earlier Nieuports. Quite similar to it was the Nieuport 27 (15 meter), which the Air Service procured as an advanced training plane. The Nieuport 28 (16 meter) was not a sesquiplane and was more nearly streamlined than its predecessors; but it was not a remarkable combat airplane. Nieuports were notorious for the fragility of their wing structure; Rickenbacker took special note of this defect.

At Orly Richardson usually flew Sopwith Camels, the English-made pursuit plane. Because of the concentration of engine, fuel, armament, and pilot in a small space, the Camel could effect very tight turns. But the torque reaction, forcing the nose upward in left turns and downward in right turns, rendered it an unstable airplane, one that could easily punish careless or unskilled pilots. Richardson also flew at least four AVRO 504 Ks at Orly in July. Very likely they were part of a shipment of fifty-two AVRO Ks from England destined for Issoudun. Manufactured by the A. V. Roe Company in England, the AVRO K derived directly from the AVRO J, which, with its light and powerful controls, was especially suitable for training.

At the front Richardson flew the Spad XIII, probably the best pursuit plane used by the Allies. The Spad XIII was one of a generation of Spads evolving from the original design of Louis Bechereau and bearing the acronym for his company, the *Société Provisoire des Aéroplanes Deperdussin*. Louis Bleriot continued use of the acronym when he reorganized the company in 1912 as the *Société pour l'Aviation et ses Dérivés*. The Spad XIII, using 220 horsepower Hispano-Suiza engine, a stationary engine, replaced the Spad VII beginning in May of 1917 and was in general use in the French and American air forces by the fall of 1918. Excellent in its rate of climb, it necessarily lost some maneuverability; and because of its thin wings, it tended to stall at reduced speeds. But owing to its otherwise rugged character, it was capable of sudden and lengthy dives permitting it to maneuver vertically more effectively than German aircraft.

Appendix D

Aviation Terms

Roland Richardson punctuated his letters and diaries with aviation terms, many of them French in origin. They are briefly defined below.

*   *   *

Cheval de bois: Whirling in a circle on the ground, a so-called "ground loop."

Cross-country triangle: A flight forming a triangle of three towns or air-fields required for pilot certification.

Deflection: Leading the target (purpose of trapshooting).

Loched: Successfully completing one phase of flight training before moving on to the next phase.

Panne: A forced landing caused by engine failure.

Pique: Diving vertically downward.

Renversement: A half roll followed by a half loop.

Side-slip: Sliding sideways in a downward direction.

Tour de Piste: Circling an airfield and landing.

Tour de Porte: Circling an airfield and landing.

Virage: A bank or circle in the air.

Vrille: A tail spin (the airplane falls earthward as tail above swings around nose of machine).

Appendix E

Richardson's Record of the Officers of the 213th Squadron

Soon after the war ended, Roland Richardson constructed a brief record of the officers of the 213th Squadron. It appears below in the format that he employed.

*   *   *

Record of Officers of 213th Aero Squadron

		Boche	Came Thru
1.	Capt. J. A. Hambleton — C. O.	2	x
2.	Capt. C. G. Grey — Commander 3rd Flight	4	x
3.	Lt. C. W. Ford — Commander 1st Flight — Trans. about Oct. 3, 1918	2	
4.	Lt. W. F. Loomis — Commander 2nd Flight — Trans. about Oct. 24, 1918	1	
5.	Lt. J. E. McGehee — Pilot 1st Flight		x
6.	Lt. A. M. Weirick — Pilot 1st Flight — Wounded — Prisoner Oct. 3, 1918		
7.	Lt. K. W. Matheson — Pilot 1st Flight		x
8.	Lt. A. H. Treadwell — Commander 1st Flight — Missing Nov. 6, 1918, Killed	3	
9.	Lt. H. S. Loomis — Commander 1st Flight		x
10.	Lt. P. H. Mell — Commander 2nd Flight	2	x
11.	Lt. J. W. Ogden — Pilot 3rd Flight — Prisoner — Sept. 19, 1918		
12.	Lt. J. W. Aiken — Pilot 3rd Flight		x
13.	Lt. S. P. Gaillard — Pilot 3rd Flight	1	x
14.	Lt. F. Sidler — Pilot 3rd Flight — Killed — Sept. 13, 1918		
15.	Lt. R. Phelan — Pilot 3rd Flight — Killed — Oct.	1	
16.	Lt. R. W. Richardson — Pilot 3rd Flight	1	x
17.	Lt. J. C. Lee — Pilot 1st Flight	1	x
18.	Lt. I. W. Fish — Pilot 1st Flight — Wounded — Sept. 13, 1918		

	Boche	*Came* *Thru*
19. Lt. V. J. Packard — Pilot 1st Flight — Sick, Hosp. — Oct. 31, 1918 (about)		
20. Lt. D. McGlure — Pilot 2nd Flight — Prisoner — Sept. 18, 1918		
21. Lt. M. McAlpan — Pilot 2nd Flight — Died — Hosp. Oct. 17, 1818 (about)		
22. Lt. R. Hoffman — Pilot 2nd Flight — Trans. — Oct. 16, 1918		
23. Lt. W. A. Munn — Pilot 2nd Flight	1	x
24. Lt. H. C. Smith — Pilot 2nd Flight — Wounded — Nov. 3, 1918	1	
25. Lt. G. Deathrage — Pilot 3rd Flight — Trans. — Oct. 19, 1918 (about)		
26. Lt. C. M. Bellows — Pilot 3rd Flight — Killed — Sept. 30, 1918		
27. Lt. J. C. Cone — Pilot 1st Flight — Trans. — Oct. 21, 1918	1	
28. Lt. L. Dudley — Pilot 3rd Flight — Prisoner — Oct. 22, 1918		
29. Lt. R. Aldworth — Pilot 2nd Flight — Prisoner — Nov. 2, 1918		
30. Lt. H. F. Coleman — Pilot 2nd Flight		
31. Lt. L. Lamb — Pilot 1st Flight		x
32. Lt. J. F. Merrick — Pilt 3rd Flight		x
33. Lt. J. Poulton — Pilot 2nd Flight		x
34. Lt. J. A. Steward — Pilot 2nd Flight		
35. Lt. H. Raynolds — Pilot 3rd Flight		
36. Lt. G. M. Long — Pilot 2nd Flight		
37. Capt. R. Austin — Pilot 3rd Flight		
38. Lt. H. B. Hinton — Pilot 3rd Flight		
39. Lt. G. S. Taylor — Pilot 3rd Flight		
40. Lt. C. S. Younger — Pilot 3rd Flight		

Lt. W. P. Norfolk — Adjutant
Lt. W. Shultz — Operations Officer *2
Lt. E. N. Hunt — Operations Officer *1
Lt. J. R. Dille — Armament Officer
Lt. L. V. Doyle — Engineering Officer
Lt. H. D. Roberts — Supply and Trans. Officer

At the signing of the Armistice we had 14 pilots.

Appendix F

Roland Richardson's Notebook

Following is a transcription of Roland Richardson's Notebook on training and combat — his *Carnet d'Emploi du Temps* — running from October 27, 1917 through November 24, 1918. Except for the entries by days, which have been completely excised, the transcription of the original notebook is verbatim.

★   ★   ★

Date	Emploi du Temps	Détail des Services Aériens	Durée	Altitude
10/27/17	P.M. Double Control 10 min. in air 1 Landing		10	200 m.
10/28/17	A.M. Double Control 10 min. in air 1 Landing. P.M. Flying	Lecture on types of motors. 1 Landing, Double Control	10	200 m.
10/29/17	A.M. Double Control. P.M. Double Control	1 Landing, 1 flight 1 landing, 1 flight lecture on cooling	10 10	200 m. 200 m.
10/30/17	A.M. Too windy to fly P.M. Rain	Lecture on Carburation		
10/31/17	Bad weather	Lecture on rotary motor, carburator		
11/1/17	Holliday			
11/2/17	Day of rest after	Lecture on strut, etc. design		
11/3/17	A.M. No mechanics, P.M. 20 min. Double C.	No lecture, 2 landings	20	150
11/4/17	Bad weather	No lecture on flying		
11/5/17	A.M. Bad weather, P.M. Ground School Pilot — De Bellville	No lecture on flying, 6 landings	10	
11/6/17	A.M. Too windy	No flying		
11/7/17	No flying	2 lectures (struts to wings)		
11/8/17	I did not fly	1 lecture (wings)		
11/9/17	No flying	1 lecture (wings)		
11/10/17	No flying — 2	2 lectures (stability)		

Date	Emploi du Temps	Détail des Services Aériens	Durée	Altitude
11/11/17	No flying — 1	lecture — maps and compasses		
11/12/17	2 landings, 2 flights	1 lecture — (hints), etc.	25	200
11/13/17	1 landing, 1 flight A.M.	No lecture	10	200
11/14/17	No flying — me	No lecture		
11/15/17	Flew twice, two landings	" "	25	200
11/16/17	Flew 1 landing	" "		
11/17/17	No flying foggy	" "		
11/18/17	Flying, 1 landing	No lecture	10	200
11/19/17	Flying, 7 landings	" "	55	200
11/20/17	No flying, monitor on leave	" "		
11/21/17	" " "	" "		
11/22/17	Flying, 6 landings	No lecture	30	100
11/23/17	Flying, 4 landings	No lecture	10	100
11/24/17	Flying (me) 3 landings	Lecture, magneto	1 hr.	400
11/25/17	No flying	" " (LOCHED)		
11/26/17	Flying, 6 landings	" "	40	200
11/27/17	No flying	Lecture — (rotary motors)		
11/28/17	Flying, Solo Hop (AM.) Solo	Tour de Piste (P.M.) 2 landings	10	100
11/29/17	Flying Solo, 4 landings	Tour de Piste	40	100
11/30/17	Flying " 5 landings	" " "	50	"
12/1/17		Not me		
12/2/17	Flying Solo, 2 landings	2 Tours de Piste	20	100
12/3/17	Flying, 2 landings	2 Tours de Piste	20	100

Date	Emploi du Temps	Détail des Services Aériens	Durée	Altitude
12/4/17	Flying Gnome, 4 landings	3 trips Anzani, tour de piste graduated to Anzani	40	600
12/5/17	Flying, 3 trips to Anzani	3 landings	45	1200
12/6/17	Flying, 4 trips on Anzani	4 landings	60	1300
12/7/17	Flying, 4 trips " "	4 landings	60	800
12/8/17	Flying, 2 trips " "	2 landings	30	750
12/9/17	NO FLYING — RAIN AND BAD WEATHER			
12/10/17	NO FLYING — ME	SICK		
12/11/17	No flying — bad weather	Me sick		
12/12/17	No flying	Me sick		
12/13/17	Flying One trip from Spiral field to Hangar #10		10	300
12/14/17	NO FLYING	BAD WEATHER		
12/15/17	FLYING, NOT ME			
12/16/17	FLYING, From & to Spiral Field — Hangar #10		20	200
12/17/17	NO FLYING	BAD WEATHER		
12/18/17	NO FLYING	BAD WEATHER		
12/19/17	FLYING, SPIRAL & HAIRPIN, FINISHED.	GOOD & COLD	25	600
12/20/17	No Flying	Bad Weather		
12/21/17	NO FLYING	BAD WEATHER		
12/22/17	FLYING Me tried to make altitude, too cloudy, came down		30	2000
12/23/17	NO FLYING	BAD WEATHER		

Date	Emploi du Temps	Détail des Services Aériens	Durée	Altitude
12/24/17	NO FLYING	BAD WEATHER HOLLIDAYS		
12/25/17	NO FLYING	BAD WEATHER HOLLIDAYS		
12/26/17	Flying Me — Altitude Made ½ of it, Stayed above 2000 for 15 min.	HOLLIDAYS	1 hr. 10 m.	2400
12/27/17	NO FLYING	BAD WEATHER		
12/28/17	NO FLYING	BAD WEATHER		
12/29/17	NO FLYING	BAD WEATHER		
12/30/17	NO FLYING	BAD WEATHER		
12/31/17	NO FLYING	BAD WEATHER		
1/1/18	NO FLYING	HOLLIDAY		
1/2/18	NO FLYING	BAD WEATHER		
1/3/18	Voyage to Pontlevoy & return	tried altitude, bad motor 3 landings	1 hr. 35 m	1250
1/4/18	Triangle, Chateaudun — Pontlevoy — Tours	3 landings	2.50	2500
1/5/18	Triangle, 2nd Altitude, 1 hr above 2000 m.	4 landings	3.25	2800
1/6/18	NO FLYING, BROKE MY COLLARBONE			
1/7/18	"			
1/8/18	"			
1/9/18	"			
1/10/18	"			
1/11/18	"			
1/12/18	"			
1/13/18	"			
1/14/18	"	BAD WEATHER		

Date	Emploi du Temps	Détail des Services Aériens	Durée	Altitude
1/15/18	NO FLYING, BROKE MY COLLARBONE	BAD WEATHER		
1/16/18	NO FLYING	BAD WEATHER		
1/17/18	"	"		
1/18/18	"	"		
1/19/18	"	"		
1/20/18	"	"		
1/21/18	NO FLYING A.M. Some P.M. NOT ME			
1/22/18	Made 2nd Petit Voyage, to Vendome, 2 landings	Vu a Tours le 23 Janvier	1.35	1400
	Brevete Militaire	Le Chef Pilote		

NIEUPORT TRAINING

Date	Emploi du Temps	Détail des Services Aériens	Durée	Altitude
1/31/18	Flew G 4, 5 tours de piste	5 landings D.C.	50	800
2/8/18	Went to Paris			
2/9/18	Came to Issoudun			
2/12/18	Assigned to Sect. 38 machine gun training, motor instruction Rouleurs		40	
	8 round trips			
2/13/18	Trap shooting & theorie [sic] of flight (P.M.)			
2/14/18	Pistol instruction, theorie [sic] of flight			
2/15/18	Pistol instruction, trap shooting			
2/16/18	Machine gun inst. trap shooting, 23 D.C. P.M. (Didn't fly)			
2/18/18	Trap Shooting, machine gun	6 Tour de Piste 6 landings	30	100

Date	Emploi du Temps	Détail des Services Aériens	Durée	Altitude
2/19/18	Trap shooting, machine gun	3 TOURS DE PISTE, 3 landings	15	100
2/20/18	2 TOURS DE PISTE, 2 landings	Theorie of flight, trap shooting	10	100
2/21/18	2 machine gun classes & class in Deflection today. No flying			
2/22/18	2 machine gun classes " " " " "			
2/23/18	" " " " "			
2/24/18	2 machine gun classes & 1 class in Deflection, no flying			
2/25/18	" " " " "	HELL		
2/26/18	Machine gun, etc. Pistol practice, no flying			
2/27/18	Machine gun etc. " " "			
2/28/18	Bombing & pistol practice today			
3/1/18	Bombing, trap shooting & pistol practice today			
3/2/18	On Guard			
3/3/18	Holliday			
3/4/18	Our class excused			
3/5/18	Ground classes today			
3/6/18	Flying A.M. 3 landings 23 D.C. P.M. 4 landings		30	100
3/7/18	Aerial gunnery all day today. Perrault killed on 18 today.			
3/8/18	Flying, 7 landings singles 23 today		35	100
3/9/18	Flying A.M. 4 landings 23 Singles loched, P.M. 13 landings, 18 Singles, ½ hr. in air & 2 Spirals left/right, loched		2.45	1200
3/10/18	NO FLYING DAY OF REST			

Date	Emploi du Temps	Détail des Services Aériens	Durée	Altitude
3/11/18	Flying A.M. 18 landings, P.M. 11 or 12 landings, 15s, loched to Spirals, shot traps		2.30	150
3/12/18	Did 4 good spirals & altitude today, 12000 ft. for 15 min. Shot traps		2.00	3500
3/13/18	Did acrobatics A.M. 2 vrilles, cross country to Vineuil this P.M.		1.10	1200
3/14/18	Went to Romorantin on cross country		1.10	2000
3/15/18	I did not fly today. Waiting for acrobatic class to fill up			
3/16/18	Finished acrobatics today — 2 vrilles 4 rennersements [renversements], 4 vertical virages, 2 wing slips		1.20	1200
3/17/18	Didn't fly today			
3/18/18	Made 3 landings on 120's & flew in a formation of 4		1.30	1300
3/19/18	Flew in one formation of 3 this A.M. No flying this P.M.		1.30	1400
3/20/18	NO FLYING ALL DAY			
3/21/18	Flew in 4 formations of 3 today. Dropped a package of tobacco at Vineuil, went all over today		6.00	2200
3/22/18	Flew in 3 formations on altitude 5000 m.		4.30	5000
3/23/18	Flew in 2 formations one stunt, went to Tours this P.M.		3.30	2100
3/24/18	Came back from Tours this P.M. arrived here at 6.15 P.M.		1.10	2500
3/27/18	Flew machine type N. 27 fom maint. field 8 this A.M.		10	700 m.
4/3/18	Flew my machine, very bumpy, rained so I came down early		30	1200 m.
4/5/18	Flew. Aimed & shot at fixed target, aimed & shot at parachute (camera gun)		3.30	1500 m.
4/10/18	Flew. Tour de Piste at Cazaux		10	250 m.
4/11/18	Flew. Chased parachute around above field & sighted on it.		20	1800 m.
4/12/18	Flew. Chased parachute again, & baloons [sic] but couldn't find the latter		40	2000 m.

Date	Emploi du Temps	Détail des Services Aériens	Durée	Altitude
4/13/18	Flew. Chased parachute again — 1 trip		25	1800 m.
4/16/18	Flew. Chased parachute this A.M. & P.M. today.		40	1800 m.
4/17/18	Flew. Chased parachute again.		20	1800 m.
4/18/18	Flew. Chased parachute again.		20	1800 m.
4/20/18	Flew. Chased parachute again this A.M. Machine wouldn't throttle.		15	1000 m.
4/23/18	Flew. Took a new 27 up & did some acrobatics with it, some class.		20	1800 m.
4/24/18	Flew. Shot at baloon [sic], had 3 jams & shot 188 rounds, 15 hits 8%		1.00	200 m.
4/25/18	Flew. Shot at sleeve — Vickers — 1 trip had 5 jams, came down on last, Lewis — 2 trips, had 4 jams, shot all up 207 rounds		2.50	3000 m.
4/28/18	Flew. Shot at sleeve, Vickers. 1 trip, 1 jam fixed, shot 100 rounds, 7.7%		40	2300 m.
4/30/18	Flew. Shot at sleeve about 40 rounds, came down.		40	2500 m.
5/1/18	Flew. Shot at Sleeve. 100 rounds, finished		1.00	2800 m.
5/2/18	Had our exam and left for Issoudun.			

FINISHED TRAINING AS CHASSE PILOT TOTAL — — 71 hrs. 10 min.

Date	Emploi du Temps	Détail des Services Aériens	Durée	Altitude
5/14/18	Flew D.C. 23. Tryout for monitor Anified [?]		15	200 m.
5/15/18	Flew Type 27, Field 8 Solo did some acrobatics		35	1500 m.
5/16/18	" Aimed at fixed target this P.M.		1.00	1000 m.
5/17/18	" Shot at fixed target with films, did some acrobatics		1.15	1500 m.
5/18/18	" Line of flight with Este & Solo, did some acrobatics and combat.		2.15	2000 m.
5/20/18	" Solo, fixed target, solo, did some combat.		4.00	2000 m.

Date	Emploi du Temps / Détail des Services Aériens	Durée	Altitude
5/21/18	Flew Line of flight both morning & P.M. Took pictures P.M.	3.00	2000 m.
5/22/18	" Line of flight. Big baloon #2. Dual combat this P.M.	4.00	2500 m.
5/23/18	" Group Combat, ½ roll film.	1.30	2000 m.
5/24/18	" Group Combat, ½ roll film. Solo 1, Dual Combat P.M. ½ roll.	4.00	3000 m.
5/25/18	" Solo, Contour ? chasing ceiling 250 m. flew twice	1.10	200 m.

FINISHED FIELD 8
TOTAL HOURS IN AIR — 94.10

AT THIS POINT IN THE GAME I WAS SENT BOMBING. CHASSE PILOTS ARE NOT NEEDED AS BAD AS BOMBING PILOTS. DIDEN'T GO BOMBING AFTER ALL

Date	Emploi du Temps / Détail des Services Aériens	Durée	Altitude
6/13/18	Piloted a Sop 1 A2 around Orly this A.M.	15	200 m.
6/16/18	Flew a Sop 1 B2 around the field.	15	300 m.
6/17/18	Flew Sop 1 A2 to Villacoublay & back with M. Honneur	30	1000 m.
6/20/18	Flew Nieuport Type 28, did a few stunts & came down	15	900 m.
6/24/18	Tested 5 Sops today with passenger. Flew to Villacoublay	1.20	600 m.
6/26/18	Tested 4 Sops today with passenger	60	1000 m.
6/25/18	Flew to Villacoublay & back with passenger	20	600 m.
6/27/18	Tested 1 Sop with passenger.	15	600 m.
6/28/18	Tested 1 Sop with passenger.	10	300 m.
6/29/18	Tested 2 Sops & flew another for Gen. Pershing, 3 trips.	50	1000 m.

Date	Emploi du Temps	Détail des Services Aériens	Durée	Altitude
7/1/18	Tested 1 Sop today with passenger.		15	400 m.
7/2/18	Flew a Spad 180 H.P. today for about 20 min. Tested Sop with photographer, 30		50	800 m.
7/3/18	Tested 1 Sop today.		10	300 m.
7/6/18	Flew a Morane-Saulnier Monoplane to Is, forced landing south of Orleans		1.00	1000 m.
7/8/18	Flew a Type 27 N. today, it was great.		15	800 m.
7/9/18	Flew & tested a Sop		10	500 m.
7/13/18	Tested a Sop & flew a Type 28 N. today.		35	1000 m.
7/15/18	Tested and equipped Sop, got hit with the dynamo prop.		15	500 m.
7/17/18	Flew Spad to Issoudun, had a forced landing at Pandy.		2.20	2700 m.
7/19/18	Flew a Sop & an Avro today.		30	1100 m.
7/20/18	Flew an Avro again. Came down on account of gas pump.		5	200 m.
7/21/18	Flew a Spad 220 H.P. to the front — Saint, all ok.		20	1500 m.
7/22/18	Flew a 27 Nieuport from St. Cyr to Orly, all ok.		15	1500 m.
7/25/18	Flew a Spad 220 to Colombey les Belles, all ok.		1.35	2100 m.
7/27/18	Flew a 28 Nieuport around field, also tested a 24 bis Nieuport		30	1000 m.
7/30/18	Flew an Avro twice and a Sop once today.		25	1000 m.
7/31/18	Flew the Avro this P.M. good ship.		15	1000 m.
8/1/18	Flew the Avro twice and a Sop once today.		40	1000 m.
8/2/18	Tested two Sops for wireless today.		20	800 m.
8/7/18	Combated Eaton with Spad against the 28 N. he beat me.		20	1500 m.
8/9/18	Combated Eaton again with 28 N. against the Spad, I beat.		20	2500 m.

Date	Emploi du Temps	Détail des Services Aériens	Durée	Altitude
	AT THE FRONT. TOUL SECTOR			
8/10/18	Took a passenger up in a Sop today.		10	400 m.
8/11/18	Flew Spad today. Wing heavy		20	1300 m.
8/12/18	Flew Spad again. Still a little wing heavy.		30	2800 m.
8/13/18	Flew 28 N. in combat, Spad to Saint & a N 28 back here again.		60	1300 m.
8/14/18	Flew a N type 21 and combated again in a type 28 N.		20	1200 m.
8/15/18	Flew Sop 3 times today with passengers.		25	700 m.
8/17/18	Took Ed. Geohegan up for a hop in a Sop.		10	700 m.
8/19/18	Took a hop in MY new Spad #15304, little wing heavy.		30	1200 m.
8/21/18	Took a hop in my Spad, all ok. Came down & turned over, wheel collapsed, very bad.		40	1600 m.
8/25/18	Flew a Spad XIII from C. les B. here this A.M.		10	1500 m.
8/29/18	Flew my machine on a test flight & a patrol this P.M. Came down half way throttle.		25	2000 m.
8/30/18	Flew Squadron formation	Didn't get together very well	35	3200 m.
9/2/18	Flew Squadron formation, pretty good	Patrol 3.30 mag broke, came down	1.15	3000 m.
9/4/18	Flew on 8.30 A.M. patrol alone, didn't see anything important		1.20	4800 m.
9/7/18	Flew patrol 6.00 P.M. Went over the lines St. Mihiel-Flirey. A.A. shot at us.		1.15	3600 m.
9/8/18	Flew low patrol & also practiced formation. Tried out new carb. adjusted		1.15	4000 m.

AT THE FRONT TOUL SECTOR — VERDUN-BEY (CHAMPAGNE & ARGONNE SECTORS)

Date	Emploi du Temps / Détail des Services Aériens	Durée	Altitude
9/12/18	Straffed Vigneulles-Chambley road this A.M. Went up this P.M. too	2.30	800 m.
9/13/18	2 patrols, straffed Chambley-Mars le Tour road. I was attacked by two Fokers, narrow escape.	2.50	2000 m.
9/14/18	1 patrol, 2000 m. Fierme-Chambley. Shot down red Foker	1.30	2400 m.
9/16/18	2 patrols, same sector, first patrol I came down, motor trouble. Ok second patrol.	2.20	2800 m.
9/17/18	1 patrol, clouds low, weather bad, got lost coming home, all Ok now.	1.10	1200 m.
9/18/18	Couldn't stay with patrol, new carb. wasn't adjusted. Had a test flight, still not properly adjusted.	30	1200 m.
9/21/18	Flew No. 24 from Vaucouleurs to our new field — Lisle en Barrois	35	700 m.
9/25/18	Flew on patrol. Clouds very low, saw nothing. A.A.A. shot at us.	1.50	800 m.
9/27/19	Flew on 2 patrols, didn't make front, went up to lines anyhow, O.K.	2.00	3500 m.
9/28/18	Flew on 3 patrols, was in a dog fight, dropped some bombs.	4.45	5000 m.
9/29/18	1 patrol, old sector. I led it. Saw some Spads or Boche?	1.45	3500 m.
9/30/18	1 patrol & 1 reconnaisance trip, clouds very low.	2.30	800 m.
10/1/18	1½ patrols, first one didn't pan out. Second one I panned.	45	2700 m.
10/4/18	1½ patrols, protected some bomber pilots. Second pressure line broke.	2.00	2800 m.
10/5/18	1 patrol, dropped some papers to the dough boys.	1.55	2400 m.
10/6/18	Flew new machine from Bar le Duc here.	10	
10/7/18	1 patrol above clouds. Saw nothing important	1.30	1800 m.

Date	Emploi du Temps / Détail des Services Aériens	Durée	Altitude
10/9/18	1 patrol, protecting bombers. Were attacked by 7 fokkers. Blew Dick P. up but he got down OK, sure was lucky, all got back.	1.45	4600 m.
10/11/18	Test flight to test weather, came right down.	10	700 m.
10/12/18	Tried for 2 patrols. 2nd weather very bad foggy & raining. Didn't make either one.	40	1200 m.
10/14/18	Flew a machine here from Bayonne today, very foggy, ceiling 150 ft.	5	50 m.
10/15/18	Test flight 15 min. & Patrol alone this P.M. Lost the formation, weather very bad.	1.05	1100 m.
10/18/18	Flew on a patrol this P.M. Couldn't keep up, bad motor, came home.	45	3200 m.
10/21/18	Flew out to lines & back. Foggy, nothing doing.	40	1000 m.
10/19/18	Flew a patrol. Clouds low, saw no Boche.	1.45	1000 m.
10/22/18	Flew protection patrol for bombers over Buzancy. Lots of Archies and four planes bothered us.	1.45	4500 m.
10/24/18	Tested weather this P.M. Very bad, ceiling low.	5	400 m.
10/26/18	Tried for a patrol this P.M. Got lost, fog very bad.	1.00	2500 m.
10/27/18	Tried for two patrols & made a 3rd, a bombing mission, dropped 4 bombs.	2.00	1600 m.
10/28/18	Flew one patrol & a test flight, had a scrap but my motor was bad.	1.40	3100 m.
10/29/18	Test flight No. 26. Vibrates very badly.	20	1000 m.
10/30/18	Test flight " still "	5	100 m.

2ND DRIVE ON ARGONNE FRONT

Date	Emploi du Temps / Détail des Services Aériens	Durée	Altitude
10/31/18	Flew a bombing mission dropped 4 bombs & 1 test flight.	1.20	1500 m.
11/1/18	Tried for a patrol, landed at 1st Pursuit in fog, flew home at 3.30 P.M.	40	2500 m.
11/3/18	Test flight & bombing mission, didn't catch the other Squadron.	1.00	2500 m.

Date	Emploi du Temps	Détail des Services Aériens	Durée	Altitude
11/4/18	Test flight & tried for a patrol, came down engine trouble.		10	400 m.
11/5/18	Bombing patrol, had to come back again, mags.		45	2500 m.
11/6/18	1 patrol, & two test flights, had a scrap, lost Treadwell.		2.30	3000 m.
11/8/18	1 bombing mission, my bombs didn't drop off.		1.00	500 m.
11/10/18	1 bombing mission, had to come back with motor trouble.		35	2000 m.
11/11/18	Armistice signed with Huns today.			
11/12/18	Flew practice formation. I led the patrol.		1.05	2100 m.
11/14/18	Tried for a practice patrol but had to come down.		15	1300 m.
11/19/18	Flew trial formation this P.M. 3 of them.		45	800 m.
11/20/18	Flew practice formation, came down with loose mag.		10	1000 m.
11/21/18	Flew, mag trouble again, sa,e mag.		20	1200 m.
11/22/18	Two patrol formations, 10.30 came down with mag. trouble.		10	1100 m.
11/23/18	Flew to Moulin & return on a visiting trip.		45	2400 m.
11/24/18	Tried to go to Metz but my pressure wouldn't stay up, came home.		15	1600 m.

173.15 —
TOTAL FLYING
TIME

FINI LA GUERRE — FINI FLYING

Index